Heinrich von Kleist

UNIVERSITY OF NORTII CAROLINA
STUDIES IN THE GERMANIC LANGUAGES
AND LITERATURES

Initiated by RICHARD JENTE (1949–1952), established by F. E. COENEN (1952–1968)

SIEGFRIED MEWS, Editor

Publication Committee: Department of Germanic Languages

For other volumes in the "Studies" see pages 193–194.

Send orders to: (U.S. and Canada)
The University of North Carolina Press, P. O. Box 2288
Chapel Hill, N.C. 27514
(All other countries) Feffer and Simons, Inc., 31 Union Square, New York, N.Y. 10003

NUMBER NINETY-FOUR

UNIVERSITY
OF NORTH CAROLINA
STUDIES IN
THE GERMANIC LANGUAGES
AND LITERATURES

Heinrich von Kleist

Studies in the Character and Meaning
of his Writings

by
JOHN M. ELLIS

CHAPEL HILL
THE UNIVERSITY OF NORTH CAROLINA PRESS
1979

Both the initial research and the publicaton of this work were made possible in part through grants from the National Endowment for the Humanities, a federal agency whose mission is to award grants to support education, scholarship, media programming, libraries, and museums, in order to bring the results of cultural activites to a broad, general public.

© *University of North Carolina*
Studies in the Germanic Languages
and Literatures 1979

Library of Congress Cataloging in Publication Data

Ellis, John Martin.
    Heinrich von Kleist: studies in the character
and meaning of his writings.

    (Studies in the Germanic languages and literatures;
no. 94 ISSN 0081-8593)
    Bibliograhy: p. 183–192
    1. Kleist, Heinrich von, 1777—1811—Criticism
and interpretation. I. Series: Studies in the
Germanic languages and literatures (Chapel Hill,
N.C.); no. 94.
PT2379.Z5E54   838'.6'09   78-12116
ISBN 0-8078-8094-9

Contents

Preface

This study was completed in 1975–76. During that time I held a National Endowment for the Humanities Senior Fellowship, which made it possible for me to take a leave of absence from my teaching duties at the University of California, Santa Cruz. I am grateful to the NEH for its support of my work. Some of the material included in this book has been published before. Chapter Three is a much revised version of my article "Kleist's *Das Erdbeben in Chili*," which first appeared in *Publications of the English Goethe Society*, NS 33 (1963), 10–55, and later as part of my book *Narration in the German Novelle: Theory and Interpretation* (Cambridge: At the University Press, 1974). Chapter Four is a somewhat revised version of "Kleist's 'Der Zweikampf,'" *Monatshefte*, 65 (1973), 48–60. Chapter Six takes a view of the play based on that of my monograph *Kleist's "Prinz Friedrich von Homburg": A Critical Study* (Berkeley and Los Angeles: University of California Press, 1970). (The reader is referred to that source for a much more extensive and detailed study of the play than was possible within the confines of even this kind of consciously selective general account of Kleist.) In each case I have included some second thoughts, however, as well as some consideration of criticism that has appeared since the original dates of these three separate studies. My thanks are due to the English Goethe Society, the University of Wisconsin Press, and the University of California Press for kind permission to include this material in the present volume. I am very much indebted to the painstaking and shrewd scrutiny of my manuscript by the general editor of this series, Professor Siegfried Mews; his helpful suggestions concerning both substance and form of this book have much improved it. That one scholar should give so much of his time, skill, and energy to improving the work of another is an act of selfless generosity that is greatly to be admired.

Introduction

It is important to explain what this book is, and what it is not. It is neither a standard comprehensive survey of Kleist's life and work nor simply a collection of essays on diverse aspects of Kleist. Its focus is on what I take to be the most central issue in criticism of Kleist, the essential character and meaning of his best and most mature work. To put the same point differently, I shall be concerned with what is characteristically and uniquely Kleistian, and with the reasons for his importance as a figure in German literature. For reasons that I shall set out in a moment, I do not think that a comprehensive survey of an author's entire output and life is a form of critical study that is well adapted to this kind of concern; I have chosen instead a form that is conducive to the fundamental critical inquiry that my focus entails.

In this book I have chosen to analyse and interpret in considerable detail six of Kleist's best and most mature works, all taken from the last few years of his life. Following these discussions in the first six chapters, I then consider in Chapter Seven the general picture of Kleist that emerges—his fundamental concerns, the temper and basic strategies of his works, the kinds of human issues upon which he focusses, and how he approaches and develops them. In the final chapter I place my results in the general context of prevailing critical views of Kleist. In the process of doing so, I show how those results differ from prevailing views and why those views are insufficient, but my aim is not simply to carp and criticize. Anyone who puts forward a view that he claims to be new has an obligation to show clearly how it differs from older views, where and how those older conceptions went wrong, and the reason why the new view is to be preferred to prevailing ideas. Original scholarship is always a contribution to an existing field, and the precise character of its contribution to that field can only be judged when it is seen in relation to the existing work that it either supplements or attempts to render obsolete and replace.

It will readily be seen that I am concerned with the general character of Kleist's work rather than selected aspects of it; but had I entitled this book simply *Heinrich von Kleist*, I should have run the risk of misleading and disappointing the reader who expected a complete chronological survey. To obviate that possibility, I have adopted in my subtitle the notation *Studies in*, but I do not believe that the standard complete survey has any more right to a simple and absolute title than my own book does—in fact, rather less. The reason for my choosing the form that I have adopted is in fact not entirely a matter of my having aims which are fundamentally different from those of a comprehensive survey; on the contrary, I share the most important of those aims—to achieve a general characterization of the author's work, for example—but do not believe that they can be or are achieved by studies that profess to pursue them through a standard survey.

The most obvious and serious limitation of the critical survey is superficiality. There is not space in a book of readable length for an adequate treatment of more than half a dozen works. The comprehensive survey appears to avoid the problem of selection, but that is an illusion: a different and more damaging kind of selection is being made. The desire to have "coverage" of all works, important and unimportant, is here given priority over any depth of treatment of the most important works; after the content of everything has been described, together with the circumstances of Kleist's life that surround the composition of each work, there is little time for anything more than some fairly standard, and usually rather familiar, critical comment. That may work moderately well in the cases of some authors, but surely not in the case of so subtle a writer as Kleist. Indeed, if the results of my investigation should prove correct, Kleist's meaning is especially likely to elude the treatment predominating in that kind of critical study. Kleist often presents a plausible first impression that subsequently becomes more and more problematic, and eventually must be abandoned. Survey volumes are inherently likely to miss the whole point of Kleist as a writer by presenting that first impression as *the* meaning of the work.[1] Superficial treatment of an author who specializes in probing beneath the surface of what is going on in the world is especially dangerous.

Another danger of the comprehensive survey is the likelihood of its degeneration into a routine operation, a factor that again reinforces superficiality and reduces the critic's wakefulness and receptivity to the complexity of Kleist's texts. If a critic feels that he needs to say something about everything, including works that he may not find very interesting, an insidious change in his motivation occurs: he begins to say things not because he has something worth saying, but because he feels he ought to say something. It becomes too easy to get by with making a few worthwhile comments on some texts and to revert to well-worn views on everything else. And that is why the majority of the comprehensive treatments of Kleist repeat much the same standard interpretations of his works; in the process they have perpetuated and sanctified many superficial and bad readings, as well as many simpleminded and trivial ideas about the essence of Kleist's work.[2]

The author of a critical survey will commonly try to obviate the problem of superficiality by taking a specific approach to the whole of Kleist's output, usually through tracing a specific theme or attitude through each of his works, one by one. But that only makes matters worse; this exercise too degenerates into a monotonous identification of the binding theme in each case, and so great a degree of prejudgment of each work allows only a very superficial glance at it.

It is to avoid this kind of mistake that I have placed my discussion of the general character and meaning of Kleist's work after the chapters that investigate the individual works, rather than before. Again, this arrangement is unlike that of most general books on literary figures, which normally begin with chapters that serve as an introduction to the discussion of individual works. That is neither the natural order of the critic's thought nor the best order for the reader to follow. To start with a general discussion would be to give the chapters on the individual works a pre-established framework—whether biographical or thematic—which would effectively set limits on their scope. The general discussion too would be limited since it would not grow out of careful scrutiny of the individual works. It is clearly preferable, when dealing with complex entitites such as literary texts, to proceed from the particular to the general rather than vice versa. Accordingly, my general analysis of the significance and character of Kleist's work is placed after, and is the result of, the detailed investigations of the meaning of the individual texts.

Chapter Eight, a discussion of how Kleist criticism has seen his work to date, might too have been expected to precede the others. Again, I think that the order of the chapters here makes more sense; to discuss the way Kleist has been seen after, and therefore always in the context of, the results of the first seven chapters is to add another dimension to those chapters—to see more clearly what is really characteristic of the view I have taken of Kleist. In addition to more general arguments for this procedure, a further reason for it emerges from the view that I take of Kleist's characteristic quality. An examination of how critics have interpreted his work and of how they have responded to its figures and situations has a very special relevance to Kleist because he makes the process of interpreting characters and events an important part of the thematic structure of his writings.

There are some functions of a survey volume that mine cannot serve, but those functions are far more limited than might be supposed. A survey volume can at least make a claim to be a survey: a complete annotated catalog of the facts and circumstances of Kleist's life and works. Such volumes clearly have a usefulness, but many such exist already, and I see no need for another. Another function of a survey may be to study Kleist's development as an author, since that particular aim necessitates a look at everything in chronological sequence—the good and the bad, the important and the trivial. To claim these functions for criticism that is in the form of a comprehensive survey of Kleist's entire body of writing is fair enough; but many other claims for that form seem to me very dubious. For example, it is commonly said that such volumes are designed to introduce Kleist to the beginner, but it appears to me that the reverse ought to be the case. The beginner is best introduced to Kleist through his best and most characteristic work—he should be taken immediately to the heart of what is most intriguing and exciting about Kleist, as I have tried to do. The comprehensive survey belongs to a much later stage in the student's acquaintance with an author, one at which he is prepared to look at the more obscure features of Kleist's work, having already become well acquainted with much of his best and more celebrated texts.

The view that the beginner needs a comprehensive survey of an author is in fact one of the great myths of literary criticism; it is surely a pale introduction to a great writer to give the beginner a volume full of the insignificant detail about the writer's life and work, plot résumés and superficial comment. If instead he is introduced to Kleist through the medium of his most important work, he will quickly want to know more.

An even stranger view is that general surveys serve the interests of those who have not read Kleist. I doubt that those who have not read Kleist can have much interest in knowing about him, or that they can be said to know anything meaningful about Kleist without having read him—whether or not they have read a comprehensive survey of his work. At all events, let me say that this book is very definitely for those who have read Kleist and will go on reading him. It is intended for those readers who like to think about the meaning of Kleist's brilliant work, and who want for a while to do so in the company of another who likes to do just the same. Can criticism of literature make any sense if it is otherwise? If the comprehensive critical survey of an author needs to be justified by reference to a nonreader of Kleist, so much the worse for such an undertaking.

I return, then, to the view that the most important task for Kleist criticism is to focus sharply on the essential character and meaning of Kleist's best, most mature, and most characteristically Kleistian work. This book is dedicated to that aim, and its form is chosen accordingly.

Granted that selection is always inevitable, I must comment on the particular choices that I have made. The six works that I have chosen for detailed discussion include five *Novellen* (*Der Findling*, *Die Marquise von O . . .*, *Das Erdbeben in Chili*, *Der Zweikampf*, and *Michael Kohlhaas*) and one play (*Prinz Friedrich von Homburg*). There are several general factors involved in this choice. One is the question of maturity: all of these works date from the last few years of Kleist's life. Kleist died in 1811; *Prinz Friedrich von Homburg* was written in 1810–11, *Der Zweikampf* and *Der Findling* were published for the first time in 1811, and *Michael Kohlhaas* in 1810, though a fragment of it was published in 1808, in a version which was later considerably changed for the first complete publication of 1810. Only *Die Marquise von O . . .* and *Das Erdbeben in Chili* were completed earlier (1808 and 1807 respectively), but not by much. Another criterion was acclaim: *Michael Kohlhaas* and *Prinz Friedrich von Homburg* deserved inclusion as Kleist's two most celebrated works.

The fact that I have included more *Novellen* than plays in the first six chapters is a more complex matter. It relates first of all to the two criteria that I have mentioned above. Kleist's last three dramas are *Das Kätchen von Heilbronn*, *Die Hermannsschlacht* and *Prinz Friedrich von Homburg*. The first two were finished in 1810. I have not chosen *Kätchen* or the *Hermannsschlacht* for detailed discussion because there is a general consensus that in spite of their late date they are not among Kleist's most important works. I do not quarrel with that consensus: these two plays do not seem to me to match the thematic complexity and interest of his best work. Kleist's best-known drama, apart from *Prinz Friedrich von Homburg*, is *Der zerbrochne Krug*, but it is one of his earliest plays and so does not belong in the category of his most mature works. The one other exclusion I must comment on is that of *Penthesilea*, also among the better-known plays. In this case, a critical judgment of my own comes into play: *Penthesilea* seems to me atypical when set beside Kleist's most characteristic work. The endings of his works are seldom either clearly positive or negative but are most often ambiguous. This can be seen in all of those works discussed in the first six chapters. By contrast, *Penthesilea*'s ending is unambiguously savage and despairing. In this sense, *Penthesilea* is unlike the rest of Kleist's work and so represents a case in which a man who generally expressed a complex attitude to life suddenly, almost primitively, reduced that complexity to a savage destructiveness. The general view of Kleist as a morbid and even pathological writer derives largely from the notorious ending of *Penthesilea*, in which Penthesilea sets her dogs to tear Achilles, the man she loves, to pieces. I think it unfortunate that the brutality of that event is so much part of Kleist's image as a writer, since it is atypical as a *resolution* in his work. To be sure, there are other violent episodes in his work; but, as I shall argue in Chapter Seven, these are part of the development of a particular text rather than a key to the tone and meaning of the whole. My decision not to take *Penthesilea* as one of the six works discussed in detail here is in part due to a wish to change that aspect of the image of Kleist with which it is associated. Kleist's best and most characteristic work is remarkable precisely for a complexity and balance that are not maintained in *Penthesilea*. If it seems unusual not to devote extended treatment to *Penthesilea*, my point in this volume is to argue for a view of Kleist that would make that play much less of an automatic choice than it has been.

It was with these considerations in mind, therefore, that I selected the six works discussed in the first six chapters of this book. Taken together, the reasons for my choices add up to a general comment on Kleist's dramatic work as opposed to his prose fiction. The fact that an early drama (*Der zerbrochne Krug*) and a drama with a rather sensational ending (*Penthesilea*) have been more popular than the later plays *Das Kätchen von Heilbronn* and *Die Hermannsschlacht*, taken together with the fact that the popularity of *Prinz Friedrich von Homburg* so completely eclipses that of *all* his other plays, indicates to me that Kleist's dramatic work is less uniformly successful than his stories. His last play is in a class by itself, but there is no one story which stands so far above the others. My conclusions are that Kleist found his most interesting vein, the writing on which his position in German literature rests, and the style and thematic complexity that are uniquely his, only in the last few years of his life; that this happened first of all in the *Novellen*, all of which appear to be late compositions; and that only the very last of the dramas shows this development completely. To set out these general conclusions is to state in a different way the reasons for the choices I have made. I have, however, made some compromise on the question of the dramatic work by including discussion of *Der zerbrochne Krug*, *Amphitryon*, and *Penthesilea* in the general evaluation of Kleist in Chapter Seven.

I have avoided any concern with Kleist's biography. This decision is in part dictated by a theoretical view on the relevance or irrelevance of biography to criticism, a matter on which critics are still deeply divided, with strong opinion on both sides of the question. Here each critic, since the debate is far from settled, must make his own choice. I have contributed to this debate and set out what seem to me very powerful arguments for my own standpoint in my *Theory of Literary Criticism: A Logical Analysis* (Berkeley and Los Angeles, 1974). And I have attempted to show in Chapter Eight how critics who have adduced such aspects of Kleist's "intellectual" biography as his Kant-crisis have succeeded only in narrowing and simplifying the meaning of his work. But the theoretical question of the relevance of biographical evidence to criticism cannot yet be said to allow of any final judgment; no one is in a position to say that anyone else is simply right or wrong here, and until a consensus begins to emerge, no scholar is in a position to insist that another ought to conform to his own notions as to whether and how biography is relevant. I could not, without such a consensus, impose on others the notion that any book that adopts such a framework is simply in error; likewise, in these circumstances those who disagree with my own position would be foolish to assert that my book lacks a framework that is obligatory.

In any case, I do not think that this issue should divide Kleist critics on theoretical grounds: there are in this instance some additional practical reasons for proceeding as I have done. Biographical information on Kleist is rather sketchy and often ambiguous. As a result, critics who have insisted on a biographical framework have seemed to restrict the terms of the discussion unnecessarily and to hold it at a level of complexity far below that of the works themselves. A rather convincing demonstration of the ambiguity of certain key issues in Kleist's biography is seen in the fact that biographically oriented critics have produced exactly the same range of opinions and disagreements on *Prinz Friedrich von Homburg* as have other critics.

Heinrich von Kleist

I

Der Findling

Some of Kleist's stories have provoked widely differing interpretations, but *Der Findling* is not one of them.[1] Its critics have, with almost no exception,[2] taken the view of the story that would seem to be suggested by the outline of its plot: the kindly old Piachi finds that his generosity to his adopted son Nicolo is rewarded only by ingratitude and treachery, and when the old man finally comes to see that he has nurtured a viper whose evil nature has caused the death of his wife and the loss of all his property, he is driven to the murder of Nicolo. Some critics, while committed to this overall interpretation of the story, have seen only too well that it does present problems, and that the text seems on occasion to be inconsistent with it; but they have blamed the text rather than the interpretation for any discrepancies between the two and so have judged the story to be flawed in certain respects. The Piachi of the ending, for example, may well seem somewhat out of character with the Piachi that we see in the interpretation:[3] can the kindly, generous old man really be the person who at the end is so consumed by the idea of revenge against Nicolo? Piachi's obsession with vengeance is so extreme that, after he has killed Nicolo by crushing his head against the wall, he stuffs the legal decree confirming his adopted son's possession of what the old man had given to him down the dead Nicolo's throat; and not satisfied even with this, he then refuses absolution so that he may go to hell in order to pursue his revenge against his adopted son even further.

If the ending of the story must seem inconsistent with the interpretation given, much of the rest seems completely irrelevant to it. The text of *Der Findling* concerns itself a good deal with the strange history of the disturbed Elvire who still grieves obsessively and unhealthily for the young knight who rescued her from a fire when she was only thirteen years old—some fifteen years ago. Much is also made in the text of the apparent resemblance of Nicolo to the dead man. On the whole, critics have seen the ending as unnecessarily and inconsistently violent, and the strand of the story that concerns Colino and his resemblance to Nicolo as being not integral to the general drift of *Der Findling*.[4]

Now there is no doubt that the interpretation can find no use for

1

the parts of the text in question; but perhaps that should lead us to ask whether the text can find any use for the interpretation. The character of the material that has to be discarded should make us doubly cautious, for Kleist's endings commonly pose enigmas that function to make us think again about whether we had really understood the work properly. It is, furthermore, another common characteristic of his stories to introduce an excursus into its prehistory halfway through the story, so that a situation with which we thought we were familiar then appears in a new light. Both kinds of material serve to introduce new emphases and issues to complicate what had previously seemed a simpler situation.

The ending of the story is indeed a shock. Nevertheless, it is not entirely unprepared, and it is an instructive exercise to separate out those aspects of the story that make us disturbed by Piachi's incredibly savage vengefulness from those other aspects of the text that might, with hindsight at least, have prepared us for this behavior. When we do so, an interesting fact comes immediately to light: what is hard to reconcile with the ending is mainly the narrator's characterizations of Piachi as "der gute Alte," "der redliche Alte," and so on. The frequent occurrences of such phrases lull us into thinking of Piachi as a gentle and relaxed harmless old man, devoid of malice. But they are only characterizations by the narrator, and the actual events described are always at odds with them. Piachi appears to be more determined and self-willed, and not at all relaxed and kindly when, for example, he strictly forbids Nicolo to see Xaviera. And that impression of him as a determined figure is taken one stage further when he finds out that his order has been disobeyed, for his punishment of Nicolo is already then of a needlessly cruel and vengeful character. The entire episode, in fact, stresses the relentlessness of Piachi that is so characteristic of his behavior at the end of the story. When he sees Xaviera's maid coming out of the house and guesses that she has carried a message from Xaviera to Nicolo, he is immediately ruthless in his attempts to get the letter: "Zufällig aber traf es sich, daß Piachi, der in der Stadt gewesen war, beim Eintritt in sein Haus dem Mädchen begegnete, und da er wohl merkte, was sie hier zu schaffen gehabt hatte, sie heftig anging und ihr halb mit List, halb mit Gewalt, den Brief, den sie bei sich trug, abgewann" (205). A genuinely kindly or tolerant old man might have concluded at this point that he had been wrong to compel Nicolo to marry a woman whom he did not love; or, failing this, he might at least have concluded that the now-adult Nicolo's affairs were none of his business, and that intercepting his correspondence was in any case unconscionable. No such thoughts occur to this "guter Alte," however; Piachi is only angry that he has been disobeyed, and he sustains this anger long enough to make the complicated arrangements necessary to stage a deep humiliation for his son, in the process also usurping a husband's right to arrange the burial of his wife. Already, Piachi, when crossed, shows himself to have one thought uppermost in his mind—to attack and wound anyone who has defied him. Why, then, are we surprised that such is Piachi's response at the end of the story? It is surely because the narrator, just a few lines after this episode, still goes on to call Piachi "der redliche Alte" just when "Redlichkeit" would seem to be very remote from the behavior he has displayed. This is evidently another example of what Wolfgang Kayser had observed when he said that the judgments of Kleist's narrator do not give us a secure authoritative standpoint since they are "oft aus der Perspektive einer Gestalt und immer unter dem Eindruck der jeweiligen Situation gesprochen."[5] Not only are the narrator's evaluations limited to the specific situation in which they occur—therefore affording no secure judgment based on the entire text of the story—but they can even be limited to the point of view of one character in that single situation. Evidently, the narrator's terming Piachi "redlich" at this point of the story follows a view of Piachi that is in line with the character's own view of himself, not with the events that the reader witnesses.

Let me take one more example of the discrepancy between the narrator's evaluations and the events he describes, one which, once more, can only be resolved by the assumption that the evaluation involved is a *pro forma* assumption of the view of the situation that Piachi himself would adopt. Early on in the story, as Nicolo grows up, we are told that Piachi is very pleased with him except in one respect: "Nichts hatte der Vater, der ein geschworner Feind aller Bigotterie war, an ihm auszusetzen, als den Umgang mit den Mönchen des Karmeliterklosters, die dem jungen Mann, wegen des beträchtlichen Vermögens das ihm einst, aus der Hinterlassenschaft des Alten, zufallen sollte, mit großer Gunst zugetan waren" (201). The word "Bigotterie" seems to go well beyond the evidence of the rest of the sentence. The most plausible way of relating this value judgment to the facts we are given might be to assume that monks who have their eye on access to Piachi's money are not sincere Christians. But even if we assume that any interest in a source of financial support for the monastery must be synonymous with greed (though it seems a little harsh to rule out any possibility that monks can take a legitimate interest in philanthropic support), that is still not the same thing as bigotry. Bigotry, after all, is intolerance, not greed; but the only issue of intolerance raised by the text is that of Piachi's attitude to the monks.

The next occurrence of the word "Bigotterie," however, makes clear that its reference was in any case not to the monks but to Nicolo (205), for in that context *Nicolo's* bigotry is under discussion. But we never see any evidence of bigotry on Nicolo's part; his friendship with the monks appears to be the only explanation for Piachi's judgment. What this all seems to show is Piachi's intemperate and intolerant attitude, and it indicates that anyone who acts contrary to Piachi's wishes and beliefs can expect not the tolerance of a kindly old man but vigorous and bitter disapproval.

It would seem, then, that the prevailing critical interpretation of *Der Findling* follows too faithfully the image of Piachi provided by the narrator, but that this reading is actually inconsistent with the events of the narrative; and that being the case, it is not surprising that this interpretation also has to reject both the ending of the story and the whole question of Colino. There is in fact a very good reason for the narrator's stance, and I shall return to it at a later stage. For the moment it would appear necessary to approach the more fundamental question of the text's thematic structure: if the view of Piachi as the kindly old man wronged is indeed an insufficient account of the story, what other view will do? Is there a thematic basis of the story which organizes all of its aspects and figures, and is there a thematic unity that is developed throughout its various episodes and to which each episode makes its own necessary contribution?

Our starting point can be a conspicuous fact about relationships in the story that seems strange yet can be observed in the case of every character of importance in it: it is that there is much substitution of one character for another in the lives of the central figures. Everyone loses someone who has a major role in his or her life and makes up for it by substituting another; but the substitute is never really successful. What binds together the stories of Piachi-Nicolo on the one hand and those of Elvire-Colino on the other is precisely the loss of an important relationship and the subsequent attempt to fill the gap by substituting another for it. The title of the story draws our attention mainly to one example of this pattern, the adoption of the foundling Nicolo by Piachi, through which the old man hopes to have Nicolo fill the position and assume the role of his recently dead son Paolo; likewise the young boy Nicolo lets Piachi and Elvire fill the role of his own recently dead parents. But wherever we look, a similar pattern can be found. In the story of Elvire's past, Piachi enters Elvire's life soon after she has lost Colino and adopts Colino's role as her male protector; meanwhile, Elvire is to substitute for Piachi's recently dead wife. From this point of view, the Colino subplot is suddenly far more interesting: Nicolo's attempt to substitute for Colino in Elvire's life is the most drastic and the most problematic substitution of all, but it is also one that concerns the most emotion-charged void of any—the gap in Elvire's emotional life that Piachi has never even begun to fill. Even Constanze, Nicolo's wife, is seen by his adoptive parents as a substitute for Xaviera in his life. This pattern of one character substituting for another, or conversely of calling on another to assume a role in his life by substituting for the one who recently played that role, is clearly the basis of the story's thematic coherence and the thematic strand that perseveres through its diverse episodes. What, then, does Kleist do with this theme? This question can best be pursued by looking at the quality and character of the relationships in the story and how they are affected by the persistent substitution and role-playing.

In the main, relationships in the story seem extraordinarily distant and formal, a fact that is hardly surprising in view of their origin in rather indiscriminate attempts to substitute one person for another; when relationships are hastily replaced in this way, the emphasis is clearly on the need of people to have a certain spot in their lives filled by someone—perhaps anyone—rather than on their having a relationship that arises from the affinity of the two people. It is already possible to see how this may relate to the old man's inappropriate attitude to his adopted son and his continued generosity long after warning signs have appeared; Piachi acts toward Nicolo as father to son in almost mechanical fashion, and regardless of the real person he is dealing with. His judgment of Nicolo is not just poor, for it scarcely operates at all; what motivates him here is simply a notion of a father's role.

Nothing stresses the predominant quality of relationships as much as the opening of the story, where we see the way in which Piachi takes Nicolo into his life. After his son's death, Piachi sets out to return home: "Er bestieg eben, sehr von Schmerz bewegt, den Wagen und nahm, bei dem Anblick des Platzes, der neben ihm leer blieb, sein Schnupftuch heraus, um seine Tränen fließen zu lassen" (200). It is then that Nicolo appears and Piachi decides to take him "an seines Sohnes Statt, mit sich nach Rom" (200). The emphasis is clear: it is the sight of the empty place beside him that makes Piachi weep, and it is to fill that empty place that Nicolo is taken back home by Piachi. The text might have stressed that this was a kindly old man taking pity on an orphan, but instead it stresses Piachi's own need for a replacement for his son. And the relationship, as it develops, stays

very much within the mold established by this initial textual emphasis. Throughout, Piachi has a rigid set of expectations of Nicolo, and
Nicolo is expected to conform to them; he must play the prescribed
role or face considerable anger.

The relationship between Piachi and Elvire is substantially similar
in all important respects. She too is a kind of foundling. Just as in the
case of Nicolo, Piachi finds a defenseless young person in great distress while on one of his business journeys. She also has just lost an
important figure in her life (Colino) and is taken home by Piachi not
because he takes pity on her but in order to fill the gap in *his* life that
has recently been created by the death of his wife. Once again, there
is a relationship based not on two individuals but on formal substitutions. It is, of course, painfully obvious that Nicolo is inappropriate to
the role offered him, because he repeatedly transgresses against it.
Less obvious, but equally true, is the fact that the role Elvire is given
in Piachi's life is no less inappropriate. She is in her twenties and he
in his sixties when they both die; there are never any signs of love
between them throughout,[6] and it is her emotional distress while in
that role that is the most prominent cause of the final disaster.

The substituting of Nicolo for Colino requires a careful consideration all of its own. It is evidently more enigmatic than any other
substitution and even on the surface involves on both sides a more
serious need for human contact than is displayed in any other relationship in Piachi's household. Elvire's need for Colino or a substitute
for him is a human, emotional need, not a formal or social one, as
Piachi's need for wife and son turns out to be. But for the rest, relationships are sad things indeed in this family. The individuals all live
in their own private worlds and play only a *pro forma* role in the lives
of the others. The history of their substituting for their predecessors
in those roles points to the fact that those who now are to each other
husband and wife, or father and son, were arbitrarily pushed into
those positions to fill a vacuum that had occurred after more natural
and more appropriate choices had been removed; and it is mainly
Piachi who seems both to have been the original moving force in
setting up a household of this kind and to have a continuing attitude
to Elvire and Nicolo that prevents any development beyond mere
formal role-filling. It was he who found two young people to sit in the
empty seats beside him, and in both cases these young people were
in such a desperate condition that they had little freedom to refuse
the role Piachi offered them.

It is of course true that from one point of view they are protected by
Piachi when in a vulnerable state. But that does not exclude the
possibility of a quite different view of the situation: there is a sense in

which he exploits this vulnerability to satisfy his own needs. He does give them shelter but otherwise wants little from them, and has little to give them. To Elvire he cannot be a real husband, and we are told that she cannot expect children from him; but she is required to occupy the formal position of wife nonetheless. Piachi's demands of Nicolo are similarly restrictive. He is to behave as Piachi expects him to, and he is forbidden to do whatever does not fall within Piachi's notion of what a son should be. Nothing shows more clearly the extent to which the members of Piachi's household must conform to his image of them than Nicolo's marriage to Constanze. This marriage, too, is evidently formal only, and Nicolo, not surprisingly, treats it as a formal obligation rather than an emotional commitment, another distant and detached relationship in a household that, having no room for real human attachments, remains a loveless and oppressive place. Even Piachi's apparent acts of generosity towards Nicolo, when examined closely, have a formal aspect and even an ungenerous side. He gives Nicolo a position in the office of his business—but he has had to dismiss another clerk in order to substitute Nicolo in that position. On his retirement he makes a formal (!) gift to Nicolo of his entire fortune "mit Ausnahme eines kleinen Kapitals" (202), which all sounds very fine until we realize that he has actually disinherited Elvire, who is still in her twenties. If at first sight these appeared generous actions, on closer inspection they appear more as gestures dominated by Piachi's formal sense of having a son and heir that are inappropriate to his real relationship with Nicolo and brush aside any more genuine ideas of generosity or considerateness to the other people involved in the situations.

Even so, it might seem that this household, cold as it is, is still to be preferred to the immoral world of Nicolo,[7] with shady characters such as Xaviera and unsavory episodes such as Nicolo's carrying on his illicit liaison even as his wife lies dead in his house. Yet once again, if we look more closely, things are not quite as they appear to be. The text, to be sure, speaks of Nicolo's general proclivity for "das weibliche Geschlecht" (200) and somewhat later of his "Hang zu den Weibern" (205). But this is a judgment that, as in the case of his alleged "Bigotterie," begins as a view of one parent (this time Elvire) and only then passes into general use by the narrator; and it is once more not justified by the facts as we see them presented to us in the narrative. Apart from the later episode involving Elvire herself, to which I shall return, Nicolo is seen to be involved with only one woman, Xaviera Tartini. We are told that Nicolo is seduced by her when he is only fourteen, but when he is twenty he is still seeing her. If we only put aside the judgment of the narrator, it might be possible to call this a relationship to which both sides are remarkably faithful, and which appears to have considerable human importance for both, they show evidence of an attachment to each other that in its character completely transcends the *pro forma* relationships of the Piachi household. During the entire six years in which complaints about Nicolo's sexual behavior occur in the story, voiced either by his parents or by the narrator as if on their behalf, what we see is only a doggedly persistent relationship with this one person. There is no hint of promiscuity, no hint that any other woman is involved with Nicolo. It is not difficult to see the point of the relationship: Xaviera's youth is exploited in one way by the Bishop, while Nicolo's youth is exploited in another way by Piachi. Each has a role dictated by an older figure of authority that is not humanly satisfying, and it seems natural enough that the two should want and be able to find with the other a warmer and more personal relationship, one in which the partner is chosen rather than imposed. The paradox here is that the relationship between Nicolo and Xaviera seems immoral and unwholesome because of Xaviera's being mistress to a bishop, on the one hand, and because of Piachi's strong disapproval on the other —yet the basis and value of the relationship for the two are surely in their reacting against the influence of the Bishop and Piachi in their lives. If the narrator's conventional judgments are set aside and we take note of the inappropriate and exploitative character of both Piachi's marriage and the Bishop's liaison with a young girl, the relationship between Xaviera and Nicolo looks by contrast natural and human—and a source of real emotional support to both. Even the apparent scandal of Nicolo's going to see Xaviera when his wife lies awaiting burial in his house does not seem so scandalous after all if we remember that Constanze was Elvire's niece. It would be consistent with everything else that happens to Nicolo in Piachi's household if he had not been entirely a free agent in making the marriage, which was from the beginning irrelevant to the relationsip that persisted both before and after it—that with Xaviera. If his wife had been virtually imposed on him, that would put his faithlessness to her in a different light.

What little we see of the two together only confirms the importance of the relationship. Xaviera, far from being promiscuous and indiscriminate, shows feelings about Nicolo that suggest a unique relationship with him: she is very jealous of Nicolo's developing feelings for Elvire, which she correctly judges to be the growing threat to their relationship. When Nicolo manages to smuggle her into the house during Elvire's absence so that she might see and possibly identify the picture of the Genoese knight, Xaviera registers alarm as she sees how like Nicolo himself the picture is: "Xaviera verstummte" (208). Xaviera's child and Nicolo then carry on with their ambiguous conversation about the picture, but as for Xaviera: "Doch Xaviera, in deren Brust das bittere Gefühl der Eifersucht rege geworden war, warf einen Blick auf ihn; sie sagte, indem sie vor den Spiegel trat, zuletzt sei es gleichgültig, wer die Person sei; empfahl sich ihm ziemlich kalt und verließ das Zimmer." Xaviera knows immediately what the point of the whole situation is, and her stepping towards the mirror is an instinctive reaction of looking to the weapons she still possesses—her own femininity—in the struggle over Nicolo that she now knows herself to be in. When Xaviera finds the truth about the picture—that Elvire's knight died twelve years ago—she immediately and triumphantly summons Nicolo to tell him about it, appearing "schalkhaft" and "schelmisch" (211–12) as she does so: she is clearly delighted. None of this is consistent with the possibility that Nicolo promiscuously forms sexual liaisons with anyone and everyone, or that Xaviera is an immoral woman; it indicates instead a degree of closeness and uniqueness of the relationship that is not found elsewhere in the story—at least not until the strange situation between Nicolo and Elvire begins to take shape.

The superficially odious relationship of Xaviera and Nicolo is, then, in reality the only one in the story that actually works in a humanly valuable way, on more than a formal basis; yet the relationship between Nicolo and Elvire seems potentially the most powerful and necessary relationship of all. It is no accident that the positive relationships in the story involve the three exploited foundlings Nicolo, Elvire, and Xaviera. On the surface, the narrator evaluates the Elvire-Nicolo situation in a consistently negative way, but the text gives us good reason not to follow him. Take, for example, the judgment of the narrator that Nicolo's emotions concerning Elvire are "unnatürlich" (211); here he is evidently thinking of the fact that Elvire is technically Nicolo's mother—though she is actually only so by adoption. The problem with using the word "unnatural" here is that it is almost a provocation to the reader to think about the natural as opposed to the formal situation—and if we do that, it will reverse the judgment as to what is unnatural. Elvire's age is not directly stated, but as so often, Kleist gives us all the details we need to work it out for ourselves—once we see that we need to do so. During most of the story we know only that Elvire was thirteen when saved from the fire by her Genoese knight, sixteen when he died, and eighteen when married to Piachi. But when Xaviera tells us that Colino had been dead twelve years, we can conclude that Elvire must be twenty-eight, which means that if Nicolo entered the Piachi household as a child of eleven, Elvire herself was still little more than a child, only nineteen. At the end of the story, then, the household consists of Piachi, aged sixty, Nicolo, aged twenty or twenty-one, and the twenty-eight year-old Elvire. The unnaturalness of the marriage[8] of the old man with a very young girl is underlined by the news that she could not hope to have children by him. There is, then, no natural husband-wife relationship here, and by contrast, if we focus on what seems natural, a relationship between the two people in the household who are in their twenties would appear more natural than that of the married couple. Indeed, the whole history of the relationship between the two shows just how natural it is that *both* should be and are attracted to each other.

It would be a very superficial reading of the text to conclude that only Nicolo is attracted to Elvire, while she is exclusively concerned with the memory of her dead knight and thus with Nicolo only in that he resembles Colino. There is, on the contrary, much direct evidence that Elvire gravitates just as strongly towards Nicolo as he towards her, and towards Nicolo not merely as the double of the dead man. From the beginning, Elvire shows an interest and involvement in Nicolo that is strong, instinctive, and not well controlled. As he grows up, Piachi is the one, we are told, who disapproves of Nicolo's "Umgang mit den Mönchen," but it is already Elvire who takes an interest in his relations with women, one that looks surprisingly aggressive for so withdrawn a woman. She disapproves of the "früh, wie es ihr schien, in der Brust desselben sich regenden Hang für das weibliche Geschlecht" (201). And Elvire continues to hover around all of Nicolo's activities in this direction, with what would otherwise be a quite uncharacteristic degree of energy and outward-directedness. In general, the picture that we have of Elvire is a passive one, while Piachi is the strong-willed father who forbids Nicolo to do whatever Piachi does not wish him to do; and so it is all the more interesting to note that Elvire is assertive only in one area in the household—namely, that of Nicolo's relations with the opposite sex, or rather with Xaviera. When Elvire sees Nicolo returning home from a masked ball where he had been with Xaviera, the narrator tells us that she has arisen by chance in order to get something for Piachi, who was unwell, "in Ermangelung der Mägde" (204); but that explanation is undercut by the curious phenomenon of the door to Nicolo's room being locked. More suggestive yet, Nicolo finds the key in the bundle carried by Elvire after she faints at the sight of him dressed as a Genoese knight. Had she locked his door and deliberately found reason to be up to catch him coming back? And did she faint not because she thought she saw Colino, but because she now saw the resemblance between

Nicolo and Colino? Kleist leaves the situation open to either interpretation by avoiding any explicit statement of what is going on in her
mind. A further sign of Elvire's excessive interest in Nicolo's seeing
Xaviera is Elvire's discovery of Xaviera's maid with Nicolo, which
occurs in a way that is more than mildly surprising: she walks into
Nicolo's room without knocking, finds the maid, and walks out without a word. She then weeps by the body of the dead Constanze, but
we surely must suspect that, after she had shown so much attention
to this aspect of Nicolo's life, she weeps not only on the dead Constanze's account but also on her own. Meanwhile, Nicolo and Xaviera
both believe that "alle Schwierigkeiten, die sie [Nicolo und Xaviera]
in ihrem Umgang fanden, von ihr herrührten" (208). This is, again,
not seemingly consistent with the shy Elvire.

Even when Elvire does nothing in relation to Nicolo for some weeks
after this, there are hints that she is still in the grip of a growing
emotional involvement with him. The mere fact that she goes off to
the country shortly after discovering Xaviera's maid with Nicolo might
not by itself be significant. If that were all that we saw happening,
one might still speculate that this absence represents retreat from a
developing situation that frightened her, but there would be little to
put the speculation on more solid ground. When she returns, Nicolo
greets her warmly but she gives him only "einen flüchtigen nichtsbe-
deutenden Blick" (209), which begins to suggest that she is indeed
seeking to avoid a growing emotional problem. But when we learn
that she has brought back with her a young relative and that the next
several weeks were "aufgeopfert" to the business of taking the young
girl on visits to any place that would amuse her, the pattern of es-
capism becomes unavoidably obvious. Elvire is evidently using the
presence of the young girl to protect herself from her emotions concerning Nicolo. The narrator diagnoses that something is wrong,
without putting his finger on what it is, when he says that these
weeks "vergingen in einer dem Hause ungewöhnlichen Unruhe."
The household, and Elvire most conspicuously so, is indeed uneasy.
But it requires little interpretation to see that the basis of that uneasy
quality in the household is that two of its members are falling in love
and are in a confused way struggling with that frightening fact—
frightening because while they are naturally suited to each other in
being unrelated and of comparable age, they are also in a socially
unnatural situation through being technically mother and son. That
Elvire's reaction is to withdraw and retreat from her emotions should
be no surprise, for that pattern is well established by all that is said
about her in the story. At emotional crises in her life the withdrawal is
often accompanied by illness, and the end of her life is an extreme

version of that pattern, for she dies of a fever induced by emotional shock.

The household's unusual unrest, then, is an ominous sign of Nicolo and Elvire's growing involvement; and since the unrest is the result of Elvire's actions, it is clear that she is aware of the danger that her own emotions present. Could we still possibly think of this involvement only in terms of Nicolo's resembling Colino? It is surely implausible to think of a mere similarity causing so much real unrest. Nicolo's resemblance to Colino is of course one factor in the situation; but it is only one among others, and even that factor must not be taken too lightly. When Elvire became the substitute for Piachi's first wife, or Piachi for Colino, there were no resemblances between the two successive occupants of the role, and that had much to do with the inappropriateness of the substitution. There is no resemblance possible between the old man Piachi and the young knight Colino, nor between the presumably mature woman who was Piachi's wife and the sixteen-year-old Elvire. The attempts to make one stand in for the other do not work precisely because the two are so unalike. Nicolo's looking like Colino may in one sense be incidental, but in another sense it stresses that they are comparable, and a substitution of one for the other in Elvire's emotional life is indeed a possibility. Paradoxically, then, Nicolo's accidental resemblance to Colino indicates in part a real, not merely a superficial, appropriateness in his assuming Colino's role. And it must be noted that this is the one substitution that is *not* imposed formally but is actually desired by both sides because it is the only substitution based on the realities of the personal situation. To criticize the resemblance as an artificial element in the story is therefore to miss the importance of the resemblance as the symbol of a real potential for Nicolo's becoming to Elvire what Colino had been.

The real disaster in Elvire's life is in fact her marriage to Piachi, an impossible substitute for Colino. After her marriage she falls into a fever, an act which for Elvire always indicates withdrawal, here from Piachi and the marriage. In truth, while Piachi offers her a kind of protection, he can also be seen as her oppressor rather than her protector. Yet one more ironic feature of Nicolo's role in the story is that he very nearly does liberate her from the trauma of her childhood. Piachi, on the other hand, perpetuates that trauma by continuing to offer her protection from it far longer than the issue should have remained dominant in her life. In so doing he of course precludes any possibility that she might solve her problem, because his presence keeps away the most obvious source of such a solution. A new relationship with a suitable figure like Nicolo, rather than an inappropriate substitute, like Piachi, would have been the surest exit from her depressed condition. Yet she is locked into that condition by the almost symbolic return of Piachi in the nick of time, which seems to emphasize the inescapability of the framework that once protected her but now perpetuates the problem she was initially protected from.

Yet even if it is clear by now that Elvire is attracted to Nicolo, and that the character of that attraction is a natural and even a valuable force in her life when compared with her sterile relationship with Piachi, it might still seem that Nicolo's side of the situation was reprehensible and his motivation questionable and even vicious. But this impression, too, is based on the narrator's *pro forma* evaluations. The events of the story, when viewed in themselves, create a quite different impression.

The clues to Elvire's emotional responses to Nicolo can be seen largely in uncharacteristic assertiveness and curiousity about his activities, as well as in her fear and withdrawal from growing awareness. Nicolo's growing attraction to Elvire, on the other hand, is indicated in different ways; he is confused by it, and his attitude to Elvire undergoes violent changes, even from love to hate. But what appears on the surface as hate is easily enough seen in context as an expression of the sense of vulnerability and fear that a powerful new emotional attraction can cause, and therefore as a sudden reaction of self-defense rather than hate. It is true that Nicolo, believing (as it happens, wrongly) that it was Elvire who must have told Piachi about his secret meeting with Xaviera, and hence that she was ultimately responsible for the humiliation he suffers at Piachi's hand, is said as a result to feel "einen brennenden Haß gegen Elviren" (206). Taken only by itself, this might be interpreted quite simply as unambiguous hatred, though the formulation seems a strangely emotional one, and it is odd to think that this hatred is aimed not at the person who has in fact humiliated him but instead at Elvire for her having told Piachi of the visit from Xaviera's maid. But only a few lines later, this interpretation becomes clearly untenable: "Zugleich war ihm Elvire niemals schöner vorgekommen, als in dem Augenblick, da sie, zu seiner Vernichtung, das Zimmer, in welchem sich das Mädchen befand, öffnete und wieder schloß. Der Unwille, der sich mit sanfter Glut auf ihren Wangen entzündete, goß einen unendlichen Reiz über ihr mildes, von Affekten nur selten bewegtes Antlitz" (206). This description of Elvire from the point of view of Nicolo leaves no doubt that Nicolo is indeed falling in love with Elvire, and that his talk of hate is only a measure of the strength and obsessiveness of his emotions with regard to her but does not show their real direction; nor could the language of the passage be interpreted as mere surface sexual attraction, for on the contrary, it is the emotional situation between the two that dominates the description. Nicolo is enchanted by the subtle beauty that arises in Elvire's face precisely when she loses her normally passive look and allows her expression to show her emotions about him. To that extent the description is also another pointer to Elvire's own growing invovlement, and Nicolo is very probably responding to her expressing that emotion in finding her face so beautiful at that moment.

Nicolo's train of thought following this passage is again ambiguous. He wonders why Elvire herself has never transgressed, and he thinks of getting his own back by betraying her secret to the old man, if ever she did, as he imagines she had done with him. But the language of his longing for such a revenge is strangely out of place: "Er glühte vor Begierde, ihr, falls dies der Fall sein sollte, bei dem Alten denselben Dienst zu erweisen, als sie ihm" (206). An anticipation of revenge is not normally linked with the phrase "glühte vor Begierde," and the mismatch shows how a strange new emotion, too frightening to face, is channeled into an aggression that makes it less difficult to handle. The very position of the phrase confirms the point; the jumbled word order of the sentence splits "glühte vor Begierde" from its logical reference (revenge against Elvire) and sets it instead in the middle of Nicolo's thoughts about Elvire's imagined sexual activities. When Nicolo discovers Elvire's secret portrait of Colino, the narrator's formulations of Nicolo's thoughts leave all their ambiguity full play, this time giving them no precise shape. Nicolo is said to leave the room with "eine Menge von Gedanken" and "in nicht geringer Verwirrung" (207). And when Xaviera's small daughter notices the resemblance between the portrait and Nicolo, the range of his emotions is once more not limited by the narrator's comment on his response; there is note only of "ein plötzliches Erröten" (208). Yet this noncommittal observation does, on closer inspection, rule out some possibilities. Nicolo would not have blushed on being faced with the possibility that Elvire loves him if revenge were uppermost in his mind; the most likely reason for that reaction is surely that Nicolo is embarrassed to have Xaviera gain access to a secret emotion that he feels. What could be more embarrassing than Xaviera's seeing that he is loved by and loves another woman? Xaviera certainly sees the point of the situation and Nicolo's blush: she immediately leaves the room coldly, evidently a jealous response to the emotions she has seen revealed. Nonetheless, the narrator continues with commentary as if only revenge were involved for Nicolo, in spite of its growing implausibility: "Der Gedanke, die Leidenschaft dieser, als ein Muster der Tugend umwandelnden Frau erweckt zu haben, schmeichelte ihn fast eben so sehr, als die Begierde, sich an ihr zu rächen" (209). According to the narrator's view, then, he is flattered and looks forward to revenge; but in this instance it is more than usually clear that the narrator here is mainly giving us Nicolo's own conscious attitude—one that serves a self-protective function for Nicolo.

What we see him doing next, however, is quite inconsistent with this view; he waits for Elvire's return from the country "mit vieler Ungeduld"; he is described as being "in dem Taumel, der ihn ergriffen hatte"; he is in a state of "Begierde"; and even in the sound of the name Colino "lag mancherlei, das sein Herz, er wußte nicht warum, in süße Träume wiegte" (209). Again, sweet dreams, desire, dizziness—this is the language of love, not of revenge. But it is a love that Nicolo is afraid even to admit to himself; and so he hides from himself the terrible truth—that he is in love with his father's wife—by seeing his obsession with Elvire as a wish to get even with her. In Piachi's household, to believe that he has a petty and spiteful motive is much less of a threat to him than the more natural emotion, and so the former is used as a defense against any awareness of the latter.

When Elvire avoids returning Nicolo's warm greeting on her return from the countryside and then does her best to avoid him completely in the next few weeks, Nicolo does not see the point of this behavior, as a more detached observer would; only a would-be lover who thinks himself spurned would fail to see the promising side of this situation and fall "in die übelste Laune zurück." Nicolo suffers "mit den bittersten und quälendsten Gedanken"; there is reference to his "verwildertes Herz"; somewhat later he has "trübe Gedanken"; and when he thinks he discovers that the secret of the name Colino lies in its being an anagram of his own, his state is one of "unterdrückter Freude" (210). All this is unmistakably the uncontrollable swings of emotion of an insecure lover, unsure whether his feelings are reciprocated; it is in no way characteristic of one who plots revenge.

The more orthodox, negative narrator-judgments now return with references to his "schändliche Freude" and "unnatürliche Hoffnungen" (211), though even these negative judgments now seem irrelevant to revenge; the last phrase clearly must relate to his unfilial attitude to Elvire and his *attraction* to her. The narrator seems at last to have accepted the fact that revenge is not the issue, and his judgments now shift to the right area, only negatively evaluated. When Xaviera tells Nicolo of her discovery that the name Colino is that of a man who has been dead for twelve years, he shows rapid changes of "Blässe und Röte auf seinem Gesicht," and he leaves Xaviera taking his hat "unter einem häßlichen Zucken seiner Oberlippe" (212). This is evidently a much deeper disturbance than frustrated revenge.

The final scene is introduced with a strong evaluation by the narrator: "Beschämung, Wollust und Rache vereinigten sich jetzt, um die abscheulichste Tat, die je verübt worden ist, auszubrüten" (212). But even if we were to ignore the other evidence we have seen that would indicate a different judgment of Nicolo's emotional state and the fact that making love is an odd act of revenge indeed, the tenor of the description of what then happens is still much at variance with the general judgment. Nicolo does not take advantage of Elvire's swoon and instead is "bemüht, sie mit heißen Küssen auf Brust und Lippen aufzuwecken" (213). The narrator was clearly speaking from Piachi's perspective, the only one which could ignore the obvious naturalness of these two gravitating towards each other in this otherwise loveless household. The emotions of Nicolo that have led up to this scene— his despairs and elations—have not been the reactions of a villain whose infernal plotting is now successful, now frustrated, but signs of a growing love for Elvire. And if Nicolo himself seems to prefer revenge as an explanation, that is because he too finds this a less frightening way to look at the situation.

Critics have on occasion claimed that the first appearance of Nicolo foreshadows the evil in him that is later to come to the surface;[9] he has a face that, "ernst und klug, seine Miene niemals veränderte" (200). But this description, viewed without preconceptions, shows only a certain passivity—the same passivity that Elvire shows, and that Piachi's household requires of them both. Nevertheless, the early part of the story does contain sinister undertones, but they all concern Piachi's behavior. Early in the story he has already twice taken a pliant child home to fill gaps in his life in a way that stresses their fitting the mold he gives them, rather than his giving anything emotionally to them. Elvire must function as wife, though Piachi cannot be a husband. Nicolo is to be a dutiful and obedient son and is punished when he does what the old man sees as being inconsistent with that role. Piachi's giving his fortune to Nicolo might seem to be unambiguously "good" but really is part of the same pattern of behavior that is the root of the trouble. This, too, is all part of Piachi's rigid and indiscriminate pursuit of a set of stereotypes (the devoted wife, the loyal son) without regard to the actual people who fill the roles; after so much friction between Piachi and Nicolo, Piachi's "generous" acts show that he is not thinking of Nicolo but only of a stereotyped image he has of a loyal son.

It is the ending of the story that really shows what was beneath the surface that Piachi had cultivated, and its importance is not limited to a demonstration of the rage and hatred of which the old man is capable. Piachi returns unexpectedly to the house just as Nicolo is about to make love to Elvire, a "chance" event that suggests rather strongly that the old man too has not remained untouched by the powerful new currents in the household and is at best uneasy at being away, at worst downright suspicious and watchful. After his discovery of Nicolo with Elvire, an interesting scene takes place. Nicolo begs for forgiveness, and "in der Tat war der Alte auch geneigt, die Sache still abzumachen; sprachlos, wie ihn einige Worte Elvirens gemacht hatten . . . nahm er bloß, indem er die Vorhänge des Bettes, auf welchem sie ruhte, zuzog, die Peitsche von der Wand, öffnete ihm die Tür und zeigte ihm den Weg, den er unmittelbar wandern sollte" (213). Here is one of those occasions, common in Kleist's work, where the narrator suddenly stops telling us what was said and what was thought, and makes neither comment on motivation nor any evaluative judgment, in spite of the fact that this is a critical juncture in the story. As a result the reader is compelled to ask himself what really is happening here. What does Elvire say? How much of Elvire's emotional life and her secret adoration of Colino does Piachi know? How much of her feelings towards Nicolo does Elvire understand, and how much of that has she told Piachi, either now or previously? How does Elvire view Nicolo's attitude to her? These questions are of course unanswerable, and it is important only that they be raised in connection with the impact of Elvire's words on Piachi's behavior: he is made speechless and turns to get his whip. Might he without those words simply have forgiven Nicolo and continued in the same old way? Or might he have been even more violent? Whatever it is that Elvire said, its immediate and visible effect is Piachi's expelling Nicolo from his household. The old man might have gone back to the same empty, formal relationships that existed before, but what Elvire said seems to have contributed to the destruction of that possibility once and for all. The most likely explanation is that she made some admission to Piachi that precluded Nicolo's continued presence. And what would most certainly have done that would be her having spoken of her own part in the emotional problems of the household.

The conventional interpretation of the story—that of its narrator and of its critics—has it that Nicolo shows his true colors at last when he attempts to throw Piachi out of the house rather than be thrown out by him; but it is also possible to see what happens as a sudden rebellion against the assertive and repressive old man, the culmination of years in which Nicolo was compelled to do as Piachi wished. The very presence of a whip on the wall of his wife's bedroom is an unnatural and sinister sign of Piachi's menacing attitude to everyone in the household, including even her; and his quietly seizing it as he opens the door for Nicolo is a picture of barely suppressed violence.

The first open rebellion instantly brings on the frightening level of violence that had always been lurking in the strong-willed Piachi; when his orderly world dissolves, one in which others were compelled to play the role he gave them and no other, his anger is total. This violent anger is a key to the force that had held everyone to their assigned position for so long, but that finally is unable to prevent the suppressed personalities of Nicolo and Elvire from expressing themselves. Piachi's fury is evidently disproportionate to Nicolo's mere assertion of his legal right to the house, and that fact has always been obvious to interpreters of the story. But, far from the disproportion being a blemish on the story or out of character with Piachi,[10] it has an important function; it points to the fact that something is occurring which is more fundamental than Nicolo's clinging to his legal possessions, namely a challenge to Piachi's whole exploitative way of life and his right to prescribe to others their roles. The violence of the ending, then, is an indicator of the more subtle but no less determined violence that was always present in Piachi's iron grip on his household.

There is irony in the fact that revenge possesses Piachi at the end of the story, for revenge was the unreal cloak in which Nicolo concealed even from himself his emotions about Elvire, and as if to point to the unreality of Nicolo's "revenge," Kleist shows us in Piachi's acts just what sort of thing revenge really is and what kind of blind destruction it can lead to.

Der Findling is, then, narrated from a distinct point of view that embodies a moral judgment of the events, but the events themselves at critical points do not fit the viewpoint taken. The limitation on the narrator's perspective is in effect a limitation to the perspective largely of one character, Piachi. Only from this perspective does the whole ending emerge as something shattering and incomprehensible, and its point is precisely that it is a challenge to the narrator's framework of interpretation. Throughout, the conventional judgments of the narrator[11] have seen the story as one of a kindly old man who offers refuge to an orphaned child and to a desperately disturbed young girl, and whose reward for his kindness is evil. But in the process of telling the story Kleist lets another image of it appear from time to time, one in which Piachi is repressive and exploitative, and his foundlings are rigidly forced into emotionally unsatisfying lives in order that gaps in his own can be filled, at least formally. It is the jarring note of the ending that suddenly forces the reader to ask whether the narrator's conventional judgments were ever adequate to the situation. And it can then be seen that the hints that prepare and justify the ending supply the alternative explanation of what really has been happening.

But why, we might ask, does Kleist choose to tell the story in this oblique and confusing way? The answer surely lies in the fact that a moral paradox is involved in the relation of the two views of it. The point of the partly hidden real explanation emerging clearly only after the superficial one has ground to a halt is that the story is about the way in which kindness can have a dark and sinister side. The effects of Piachi's good-hearted offer of protection to his foundlings is to restrict considerably their ability to be themselves and live their own lives. Looked at more closely, his generosity to them involves an exploitation and repression of them, even a crushing of their individuality. Conversely, the most valuable relationship in the story appears superficially the most unnatural and destructive. The tension between the narrator's judgments and the events of the story is the same as that between the discrepant aspects of the moral paradox that is the basis of the story; the paradox is therefore embodied in the entire strategy that Kleist employs in having his narrator take a superficial view, while the events themselves push us towards a deeper view of what is occurring. *Der Findling* is a pessimistic story, but it is not merely or even primarily the violence of its ending that is pessimistic; it is most deeply pessimistic in showing how conventional kindness can do covert violence to its recipients, and how that covert violence is always ready to erupt into overt violence if it is ever challenged.

Der Findling is a study in the character of relationships, where the repeated substitution of one character for another serves to place the emphasis on how the needs of one person in a relationship dictate the role of the second, regardless of the appropriateness of the second to that role. Nothing in the story so bares this theme of substitutions and of people projecting onto others their own notions of what they should be as the episode in which Xaviera and her little daughter are with Nicolo in Elvire's room looking at the portrait of Colino. The little girl sees the resemblance and cries out "Signor Nicolo, wer ist das anders, als Sie?" Nicolo, embarrassed, replies: "Wahrhaftig, liebste Klara, das Bild gleicht mir, wie du demjenigen, der sich deinen Vater glaubt!" (208). The ambiguity of the reply is almost inexhaustible. The surface meaning, which Nicolo may well intend for Klara's understanding, must be: "I look as little like that man as you look like the Cardinal—not at all." But Kleist's text carefully avoids meaning only that, first, by omitting the negative, and second, by inserting the word "glaubt." We have been told that Klara is Xaviera's daughter by the Cardinal, but even if we take this as a given, the reference to him who *believes* himself Klara's father is not solved. Nicolo, the Bishop, and the Cardinal are three possibilities. At least one other possible interpretation of what Nicolo says, then, is: "Yes, I do resemble this man just as you, my daughter, resemble me."

But the point is just that that interpretation is speculative too. Kleist leaves Nicolo's utterance ambiguous, and it would be hard, from the point of view of the plot, to see why. From a thematic point of view, however, this ambiguity is central to the meaning of the story. Here we have the possibility of many candidates for a role in Klara's life, the uncertainty as to who appropriately fills the role, and resemblances as a key, albeit also an uncertain one, to the possibility of substituting one for another. And the resulting meaning of the sentence, as far as its key issues are concerned—who is like whom, and who appropriately relates to whom—is as ambiguous as is the story itself with regard to those issues.

Die Marquise von O . . .

Die Marquise von O . . . is evidently one of Kleist's most bizarre and intriguing stories; and yet in spite of its strangeness, it has produced remarkably little critical discussion and even less controversy.[1] Of the nine separate studies of the story, three treat it in conjunction with other works of literature (a procedure that always results in a partial view of the work that is mainly relevant to the others selected for discussion with it), two concern its sources, and one is a brief comment on its sentence structure. Only three are serious interpretative essays. Yet even in these the reader finds little that is not obvious on first glance. The best known and most often cited of them is by Walter Müller-Seidel, whose title announces a focus on "die Struktur des Widerspruchs." But while this imposing title may seem to indicate a thematic interpretation, all that actually follows are some remarks on the contradiction between the fact of the Marquise's pregnancy and her sense of her own innocence of any illicit sexual behavior. Far from being genuinely interpretative, this is only an elementary description of one aspect of the plot that any reader can see easily enough for himself. Most other critics have spoken of the Marquise's strength of mind or her struggle to retain her own sense of purity and equilibrium;[2] but again, this is superficial description rather than interpretation, adhering to what is obvious while avoiding the text's real puzzles.

Some critical disagreements have been generated by the figure of the Count. Reusner,[3] for example, disliked the ending of the text because of the Marquise's acceptance of the Count after his earlier behavior towards her, which he considers unthinkable—how can she possibly marry such a man? But even here the overwhelming consensus has been the bland view that the Count is acceptable as a man who is neither angel nor devil, but simply a human being, as Klein puts it.[4] The Count, then, is an ordinary man, guilty of a momentary lapse but still much like anybody else. Perhaps it is symptomatic of the apparent lack of controversial issues that Müller-Seidel[5] tries to produce an artificial controversy by taking a fellow critic to task for his carelessly paraphrasing the Marquise's final comment in a way that makes the Count seem to her devil and angel at the same time,

21

instead of first angel, then later devil. Müller-Seidel goes on to insist that only the second formulation makes sense of the Marquise's rejection of the Count when she learns the truth. But the real puzzle over the Count's actions and the Marquise's reactions is scarcely affected by this distinction; whether revealed in sequence or simultaneously, it is evident that the existence in the same man of the capacity for both modes of behavior is what troubles the Marquise, and the reader.

That so bizarre a text can have aroused so little interpretative comment and almost no critical controversy is exceedingly strange; a reader new to the story and to the critical literature would surely be surprised to find such an unusual work responded to with so little sense of its oddness. One of the problems may well be that the central event so arrests our attention that we tend to lose sight of the other features of the text that are almost equally strange. For there is much else here that is extraordinary and striking and that does not seem necessarily relevant to a story of a woman faced with a bizarre situation that brings out her courage and strength of character. There are the violent changes of mind of the Marquise at the end of the story; there is the managerial and sometimes devious role of the Marquise's mother and her virtual punishment of her husband; there is the oddness of the obsessively courtly and polite behavior on the part of all the story's characters and the contrast of this civilized surface with the very uncivilized event that is central to its plot; there is the odd way in which the narrator broadly hints at what has happened during the blank in his text yet at the same time refuses to be explicit, treating the event as an unmentionable subject that we are nonetheless allowed and even encouraged to guess at; and finally there is the person of the Commandant, and especially the grotesque scene of his

reconciliation with his daughter. I have left mention of that scene until last because immediately upon contemplation, it becomes the most arresting element in the entire text; there is surely nothing quite so bizarre in all of Kleist's stories. Some critics pass over it in silence; some judge it as what they would perhaps like it to be: "rührende Versöhnungsszenen voll Süßigkeit";[6] and some criticize it as being in bad taste. But whether we instinctively like it or are repelled by it, this is a startling scene and must provoke some thought about why Kleist includes it and what light it sheds on the story's thematic structure. Let us look at the details.

The Marquise's mother has insisted that the Commandant come to his daughter, not she to him, as a sign of his contrition. As he enters the room, "Der Kommandant beugte sich ganz krumm, und heulte, daß die Wände erschallten" (137). His wife finds it hard to carry through with the scene, "da er sich ganz konvulsivisch gebärdete"

(138), but leaves the two together for them to make peace after their quarrel. She returns after a time: "Und, wie sie durchs Schlüsselloch bemerkte, saß sie auch auf des Kommandanten Schoß, was er sonst in seinem Leben nicht zugegeben hatte" (138). She opens the door, and the full description of an extraordinary scene follows:

> . . . die Tochter still, mit zurückgebeugtem Nacken, die Augen fest geschlossen, in des Vaters Armen liegen; indessen dieser, auf dem Lehnstuhl sitzend, lange, heiße und lechzende Küsse, das große Auge voll glänzender Tränen, auf ihren Mund drückte: gerade wie ein Verliebter! Die Tochter sprach nicht, er sprach nicht; mit über sie gebeugtem Antlitz saß er, wie über das Mädchen seiner ersten Liebe, und legte ihr den Mund zurecht, und küßte sie. . . . Sie nahte sich dem Vater endlich, und sah ihn, da er eben wieder mit Fingern und Lippen in unsäglicher Lust über den Mund seiner Tochter beschäftigt war, sich um den Stuhl herumbeugend, von der Seite an. . . . Sie lud und führte beide, die wie Brautleute gingen, zur Abendtafel. (138–39)

In a story that often seems bizarre, this stands out as the strangest passage of all. But more than that, it is actually bizarre within the established terms of the story itself, for it breaks down several of the conventions which had been established in the text up to this point. To begin with, there is the general convention of economy in Kleist's narratives; to judge from the rest of the work, we might have expected him to get all of this over with in half a sentence: "Der Kommandant, als er diese Nachricht erfuhr, versöhnte sich bald mit seiner Tochter." Then there is the related convention of a bare style, without a great deal of emotive language; we should not have thought that he would introduce phrases like "wie über das Mädchen seiner ersten Liebe, und legte ihr den Mund zurecht, und küßte sie." But the most important convention of the story that this passage violates is that of tact and a civilized surface, both in the manner in which the episode is narrated and in the substance of the events described. Coming from the general background of these formal, elegant people and of Kleist's reserved, tactful narrative that is in its way an expression of their civilized ethos, we are shocked to read that the father plants "heiße und lechzende Küsse" on his daughter's mouth, and later that "er eben wieder mit Fingern und Lippen in unsäglicher Lust über den Mund seiner Tochter beschäftigt war."

Quite how far this passage is removed from the convention of the story will become apparent if we compare it to the tact and decorum of the description of that other act that might much more deservedly have been described in a grotesque and repelling fashion but is not: "Hier—traf er, da bald darauf ihre erschrockenen Frauen erschienen . . . " (106). Here, a dash glosses over the scene of the rape whereas the scene between father and daughter is treated in the opposite way.

We are left with a puzzling contrast between the tactful cover up of a potentially repelling scene that was necessary to and indeed the most central part of the plot, on the one hand, and on the other hand a gratuitously explicit description of an event that apparently lacks the same value in the plot of the story, and in which the descriptive language is in gross violation of the tactfulness that had prevailed in the former case. The contrast is one that must be taken very seriously indeed in interpreting the story; when here Kleist's explicit display of a socially unacceptable and even offensive scene reminds us of his conspicuous avoidance of *any* description of a previous event that was even more offensive and socially unacceptable in character, we may be certain that this is a clue to the point of the second scene, for the contrast invites a look at the parallelism.

One feature of the parallel has obvious thematic importance; here we find suggestions of a second socially forbidden act and transgression against accepted mores to follow the first (the rape of the Marquise): incest between father and daughter. In a story that centers on one illicit act, the powerful suggestions of another, equally illicit act must be well considered.[7] This second transgression throws a completely new light on the first and on the responses to it of all the characters in the story throughout. At the very least, it must raise the question of the Commandant's earlier motivation. Does his own repressed desire for his daughter play any part in his becoming uncontrollably furious with her presumed sexual adventure? Is his own latent wish to commit a socially unacceptable act part of the emotional basis for his horror at her presumed immorality? And is the basis for his final ability to accept the Count as husband to the Marquise this partial acting out of his wishes, or at least his facing the reality of what his feelings about his daughter had been? Perhaps a more important question is how we should judge the Count now that his transgression is not unique in the story. We may need to rethink the entire question of illicit desires, and their occurrence in this particular social setting, among these particular people. And further, how shall we view and understand the Marquise's outrage at the Count after her own participation in this suggestive scene?

For the moment, it is best to leave these questions and to look again at the story from the beginning, armed with our new awareness of this fundamental complication that has affected all the judgments we can make about the story. Once again, Kleist has introduced, nearly at the end of the text, a scene that has the effect of making us unsure of our understanding of what has preceded it and calling into question the attitude to the whole that we had been inclined to take until that point. And, once more, it becomes necessary to go back over the whole text to make sure that we have seen all that was there.

From the very first, the story works with a strikingly clear notion of civilized behavior, which even includes civilized violence, as opposed to uncivilized behavior and unacceptable violence. Though the attack by the Russian troops on the Commandant's citadel involves death and destruction and is a violent act by any natural standards, it still counts as socially acceptable and even as perfectly understandable, civilized behavior. Militarily, the Russians may be enemies, but there is no notion that they are personally enemies, or that they are guilty of reprehensible behavior. The Count F. can socialize with the Commandant's family, and while the immediate cause of that may be the gratitude of the family for his gallantry in protecting the Marquise, it is also true that his behavior is expected, and that it does not surprise the reader; how else should an officer and a gentleman behave? The family displays neither bitterness towards the Count as a conqueror nor hostility to him as one who has waged war and killed men on their side. The reader seems easily to accept the strange double standard in their expressing no feelings of outrage at the brutality of acts of war such as storming and bombing the citadel yet being shocked that the Count might be court-martialed for refusing to carry dispatches as his orders dictate. The rules of the game allow the former but not the latter; war is a civilized game that permits violation of persons and property within its artificial limits and conventions but not the violation of those conventions. The family's concern for the Count shows that while within the game he is their enemy, he is more fundamentally one of their own kind.

Had the Marquise been killed through military action, that would have been according to the rules; but there is another kind of violence that is unacceptable and uncivilized. The contrast is strongly emphasized in the text. The Russian soldiers make "abscheuliche Gebärden," they are an "entsetzliche, sich unter einander selbst bekämpfende, Rotte," and they treat the Marquise to "den schändlichsten Mißhandlungen." The narrator calls them "Hunde," and as such they are routed by the Count. Where civilized violence ends and uncivilized violence begins is clear in what he does: "Er stieß noch dem letzten viehischen Mordknecht, der ihren schlanken Leib umfaßt hielt, mit dem Griff des Degens ins Gesicht, daß er, mit aus dem Mund vorquellendem Blut, zurücktaumelte; bot dann der Dame, unter einer verbindlichen, französischen Anrede den Arm, und führte sie . . ." (105). Thus the convention of the story is established: bombing, shooting, burning is acceptable, so gross an act as smashing a soldier in the face may even be gallant, but acts not covered by this agreement as to what will count as civilized violence are unacceptable and "viehisch."

The Count underlines the contrast by taking the gentleman's role in relation to the lady as if they were on a ballroom floor instead of in the middle of a battle and the two on opposing sides; he addresses her in French, showing himself to be a civilized man who speaks the most civilized of tongues. Though he is a Russian and in Italy, his choice of language reassures her that he knows how to behave. The reader gets the strong impression that the fact of the Count and Marquise being on opposite sides is quite artificial, and that in a deeper sense the division is between them and the uncivilized, lower-class soldiers.

From this point on, civilized behavior, politeness and formality prevail—with the one exception of the scene between father and daughter; and in view of the contrast established at this early stage, it is all the more worrying that in the later scene the Commandant's kisses are "lechzend"—a curious reminiscence of the language that referred to the soldiers ("viehisch," "Hunde") earlier. The absoluteness of the distinction between acceptable and unacceptable violence is driven home by the fate of the soldiers; they are shot because they seemed intent on rape, though they did not accomplish it, and the Russian commander gives the Commandant an apology, all of which confirms that the Count's gallant behavior was wholly expected and in accordance with the rules. And yet, having set up these clear notions of what the rules are, the story first has the Count break them and then later has the Commandant at least looking as if he is longing to break them and is partially doing so, with those "lechzende Küsse." The Count is linked to the bestiality of the soldiers by his doing what they seemed intent on doing, and the Commandant by the linguistic reminiscence of that bestiality. The odd fact is that both the Count and Commandant fight an exemplary civilized war over the citadel, but that both transgress against the norms of civilized behavior when the Marquise is the prize.

That the two men take part in two different struggles over two different prizes involving two different codes of behavior is of course more than hinted at in the text. There are frequent analogies between the conduct of war and that of love, as for example when it is said that the family thinks that the Count "Damenherzen durch Anlauf, wie Festungen, zu erobern gewohnt scheine" (114). But the entangling of the different areas of love and war seems all the more appropriate when we notice that the Marquise's position is indeed like that of an overprotected "Festung." She lives under the care of her parents, "in der größten Eingezogenheit" (104). In this withdrawn condition she is protected not merely by her father and mother, her immaculate reputation, and her living in the citadel of which her father is commander. To complete the ring of protection and inaccessibility around her, she is widowed and has sworn not to marry again. An unmarried daughter would normally be subject to the attention of young men; a young widow with small children, on the other hand, can decide not to marry and thus to perpetuate her protected state in a way that an as yet unmarried young woman could not hope to. The Marquise can make this decision and not risk the appearance of strangeness that a single woman would certainly have under identical circumstances.

When the Count wishes to ask for her hand in marriage, he approaches her directly but very soon finds that he has to negotiate not with her, since she falls silent, but with her father; the Commandant speaks for her without any apparent fear of contradiction and without waiting to ask what she thinks, though later on it becomes obvious that she does not agree with what her father has said on her behalf. It is the Commandant who announces to the Count his daughter's basic position: that she has decided not to marry again, that his great service to her may cause her to reconsider, but that she will need some time to think things over. And it is he, not she, who shows signs of irritation when the Count persists. The Marquise seems to be entirely in the protective custody of her father, guarded and defended by him. The story proceeds as a struggle over her between him and the Count, parallel to the military struggle between them over the citadel. When reference is made to the Count's attempting to take the Marquise's heart by storm, there is irony in the fact that, unknown to the family, he has already taken her by storm in a different sense. But whichever sense of "taking by storm" we think of—the superficial or the ironic meaning—there is a curious symmetry between that notion and the notion that the Marquise was previously in an overprotected, defensive position. Can so securely defended a position be taken in any way other than by storm? The story is in the main a realistic one; but this parallelism of the Count's storming the citadel to wrest it from its previous defender and his equally wresting the well-defended Marquise[8] from her current protector looks more like symbolic fantasy, an arrangement of plot elements not merely for overt realistic motivation but at the same time to cast the Count's action in a different light, one in which his kind of approach to her seems curiously appropriate, in its force and intensity, to the degree of her withdrawn, overprotected state of mind.

The text underlines the parallelism by many further details. For example, the Count's strictly military approach is an attack on the peace of the household, and it interrupts the quiet withdrawn life of the Marquise as well; it then subsides, and "alles kehrte nun in die alte Ordnung der Dinge zurück" (109). His second arrival, this time

with intent to take the Marquise instead of the citadel, has a similar
effect of disturbing the calm of the household; once more it is thrown
into a state of being "in der lebhaftesten Unruhe" (115). As before, a
battle of wills between Count and Commandant ensues, the Commandant defending against renewed thrusts from the Count. And,
again as before, the Count is willing to break the rules; he will dis-
obey orders from his superior in order to stay at the home of the
Marquise until she knows him well enough to make a decision. The
Commandant is displeased and remarks, "daß es ihm äußerst leid
tun würde, wenn die Leidenschaft, die er zu seiner Tochter gefaßt zu
haben scheine, ihm Unannehmlichkeiten von der ernsthaftesten Art
zuzöge" (113). Here there is an ironic double meaning since, unknown
to the Commandant, there has already been a different violation of
the rules, also caused by the Count's strong response to the Marquise,
and it too will cause great unpleasantness. The Commandant's re-
minding him of the consequences also has several levels of meaning,
for the Count's military transgression will bring upon him the anger
of those of the Commandant's rank on the Russian side; the Commandant's warning is in one sense an admonition to the Count—as
from a senior to a junior officer. But another part of the meaning of
the Commandant's words that derives from his own identification
with senior officers generally is a threat from the older to the younger
man of retribution for the latter's competing unfairly for the woman
currently in the former's possession.

The language of the family's discussion of the proposal by the
Count to stay at the citadel and neglect his orders continues to make
the analogy between love and war, and particularly to stress the fact
that this is a kind of battle between the Count and the Commandant
for possession of the Marquise. The Commandant thinks the Count's
announced course of action is only a "Schreckschuß beim Sturm"
(114), just a shot to frighten them all into surrender, and his son takes
up the metaphor, calling it a "Kriegslist." The Commandant would
like to stand firm, and not to allow the Count's questionable tactics to
succeed, but he has a shock in store for him. He has lost the citadel in
a fair fight according to the rules of war but is now to find that, to his
disgust and disappointment, he will not be able to make a firm stand
in his defense of his daughter and her heart because the rest of the
garrison suddenly seems to be intent on conniving with the enemy to
surrender without a fight; his family seems eager to arrange it, with
or without his blessing.

When the Count decided to violate his orders, the Commandant
realized that he would win merely by standing pat; and so he demands that no one in the family speak of this matter any further in his

presence. But his wife has an entirely different interest in the outcome of the battle, and she now works to arrange her husband's defeat, as she continues to do throughout the story. While her husband has, holds, and defends his daughter, his wife clearly wishes her daughter were married once more and out of the house, for reasons that become obvious when the basic character of the Commandant's attachment to his daughter appears in their final scene together. Without subversion from within his own household, the Commandant's position can be simple: all he needs to do is wait for the inevitable court-martial of the Count, who would then automatically be no fit husband for the Marquise. Still, something about the young Russian's determination must be worrying to the Commandant, for he paces up and down, betraying his unease and his concern about a situation in which his main antagonist does not play by the rules as he understands them. His wife then asks her daughter what she thinks of the situation, and the Marquise replies: "Wenn der Vater bewirkt hätte, daß er nach Neapel gereist wäre, so wäre alles gut" (116). The reply is short and somewhat oblique—but shattering. It contains several implications, the most obvious being that in criticizing her father's actions on her behalf she already gives us a sign that she does not accept his total control and possession of her. Another implication is that the Commandant is guilty himself of unfair play: as the older, more experienced man, he has stood by and watched while the younger man has made a mistake that must disqualify him. The Marquise is pointing to the fact that her father must bear part of the blame for the Count's fate—he could have saved him from this obvious and unnecessary error.

But something even more important is revealed in the Marquise's quiet, short remark. She has by implication made it clear that the Commandant has already *lost* the struggle: the Marquise is saying that she wants the Count as her husband! She is telling everyone what, after all the maneuvering, she wants the outcome to be, for what else can the oblique phrase "so wäre alles gut" refer to? She says, in effect, that if her father only managed things properly, she could (and would want to) marry the young man. The Count evidently *has* taken this lady's heart "durch Anlauf, wie eine Festung." From this point on, all that the family talks about is the details of the capitulation, and the poor Commandant is actually criticized by his daughter for not having taken a more active part in it. And so, despite all the shaking of heads over the Count's unreasonable tactics and about needed patience and deference, these tactics have in fact succeeded brilliantly! In this case, at least, an unacceptable breach of social norms does win the lady by storm, and that makes us wonder

again about the earlier, more extreme case. The Commandant pro-
tests in reply that he could have done nothing to change what the
young man wishes to do, but now the Marquise reproves him directly
by saying "lebhafte und eindringliche Vorstellungen tun ihre Wir-
kung" (116). She then returns to her work "ein wenig unwillig,"
which, within the context of her normally silent and deferential bearing towards her father, is a distinct sign of her annoyance with him.

There is a curious irony in what occurs next, for now the theme of
the polite observance of the social conventions and rules as opposed
to taking what one wants directly by storm is reversed. Now it is the
family who wants, when the Count appears, to get over with the
necessary "Höflichkeitsbezeugungen" quickly, "um ihn mit vereinter
Kraft zu bestürmen" (116); they want to make him go to Naples. But
they cannot break through; *he* now turns the tables by using the
forms of polite conversation deftly to avoid the issue being raised. He
defeats them again, using their weapons, so that they are not even
able to mention what they want. When the Count has finally left the
room at the end of the evening, the Commandant is all for leaving
things as they are; but his wife now gives the conversation a decisive
turn by asking directly if the Marquise would accept the Count, given
some time, some inquiries about him, and provided no untoward
revelations result. She replies: "In diesem Fall, versetzte die Marquise, würd ich—da in der Tat seine Wünsche so lebhaft scheinen,
diese Wünsche—sie stockte, und ihre Augen glänzten, indem sie
dies sagte—um der Verbindlichkeit willen, die ich ihm schuldig bin,
erfüllen" (117). This confirms our earlier understanding: she is impressed by him and will accept him, and her eyes shine not from
gratitude but from excitement. Her mother is delighted since she has
always wished to have her daughter marry again.

The details, once this is clear, are quickly worked out: the Count
will go to Naples, inquiries will meanwhile be made about him, and
all will be well on his return. All present seem pleased—but for the
Commandant: "Der Kommandant, der alles gehört hatte, stand am
Fenster, sah auf die Straße hinaus, und sagte nichts. . . . Nun so
macht! macht! macht! rief der Vater, indem er sich umkehrte: ich muß
mich diesem Russen schon zum zweitenmal ergeben!" (118). The
only surface reason for this grumpy reaction is his annoyance over
the active support of the family for a course of action opposed to that
which he suggested; but a stronger and deeper emotional force is
implied by his linking the two defeats, a parallel which stresses once
more that it is the loss of the Marquise (the clear parallel to the loss of
the citadel), not just a disagreement with his family, that upsets him.
The real content and shape of that emotional force only becomes

completely apparent in that strange scene of reconciliation between himself and his daughter.

After the family has learned that the Marquise is pregnant, the confusing of love and war becomes more than metaphor; in his interview with his daughter, the Commandant actually seizes a pistol and fires a shot. The situation between father and daughter receives new emphasis and force here; after this there can scarcely be any doubt about the depth of emotion involved in the Commandant's attitude to his daughter, or that the relationship has major importance for the thematic structure of the whole story. He is first intensely affected by the news of her pregnancy and wants nothing more to do with his daughter. When she tries nonetheless to see him against his express wish, he behaves in a way that displays barely controlled violence, and she leaves immediately. The scene is striking in many ways. An added dimension to the confusion of the military and family situation lies in the Commandant's grasping his pistol almost in self-defense against the Marquise's breaking into his sanctuary and taking his room by storm against his command. But this quasi-military act of naked force is also another of those primitive acts in the story that break in gross fashion the civilized convention of the social relations among these normally elegant people. The civilized facade crumbles and something deeper reaches the surface, as usual something with distinct sexual overtones, for the strange act of firing a pistol into the ceiling looks like a displaced and only barely averted act of male aggression. Once more, what we see here is uncomfortably close in spirit to the Count's original misdeed. The interpretation of the Commandant's state of mind is not difficult, given all that we have seen of him in the story. He feels again betrayed, but this time more deeply. He lost the military battle to the Count, then the battle for his daughter's heart; but now he finds that he has lost even more completely to some unknown male. The Marquise has been guilty of immorality, it seems, from the point of view of the social conventions—but that cannot be what moves the Commandant to such violence. His reaction is surely provoked by the fact that she is, from his point of view, guilty of extreme unfaithfulness to him. The Marquise's state indicates to him that she has been involved in a forbidden relationship; but his response has surely more to do with his own repressed feelings for his daughter, which are also of a socially forbidden nature, a fact which emerges even more clearly later on when, at last, those feelings are acknowledged and expressed.

In characteristic fashion, the Marquise withdraws after this latest familial disaster and goes off to her country estate: "Sie beschloß, sich ganz in ihr Innerstes zurückzuziehen" (126). This is part of her con-

stant pattern of withdrawal from the world and its challenges. But the
language of the text, in equally characteristic fashion, sees her departure in military terms; she seizes her "Beute" (her children) and decides "sich mit Stolz gegen die Anfälle der Welt zu rüsten" (126). It is
not, as most critics have seen the matter, strength of character that is
most conspicuous in her settling down "in ewig klösterlicher Eingezogenheit zu leben" (126); what becomes most obvious is that this
constitutes yet another setting up of a protective fortress around her.
Appropriately enough, the next event in the story is yet another
storming of the fortress by the Count, who, having been refused
civilized entry by the front gate, once again defies convention, scales
the wall, and takes the Marquise by surprise. But her reaction is still
one of withdrawal. On hearing that he still intends to marry her, she
orders him away and rushes off herself when he will not leave; he
tries to tell her something (presumably the truth about the origin of
her condition), but she will not let him, insisting as she goes: "Ich *will
nichts* wissen" (129). This must raise the question whether at some
level of her mind she knows what he wants to tell her. To be sure, her
fury later, when she finds out, is sudden and extreme, but the fact
that she is so insistent on not knowing here must indicate that there is
some notion in her mind that the Count is somehow connected with
what has happened to her. A strange proposal of marriage and a
strange pregnancy are two mysteries that her mind may well begin to
link.

    Kleist now begins what for him is a remarkably slow-moving sec-
tion of the story that leads up to the final discovery of the truth and to
the ending of the story. The Commandant's wife has a large role in
this ending, for it is she who in a sense must tidy up and resolve the
strange state that the relationship between father and daughter has
reached. It is at her instigation that the reconciliation between the two
takes place; and it is part of the paradox of this scene that it is in her
interest to instigate it, for the reconciliation involves both a drawing
together of father and daughter and a disengagement of them in a
more fundamental sense, as an essential prelude to the Marquise
marrying again and leaving her father. It is as if the tension in the
relationship between father and daughter must be resolved before
she can be effectively removed from his circle to marry again. After an
explicit display of the Commandant's strong feelings about his
daughter, the relationship no longer seems so threatening and intense. Here, then, is one important reason for the grotesque scene
between the two: for a brief moment, the Commandant can step
outside the conventions that have limited him and act out what is
forbidden; following that, he is resigned to what has happened and

what will happen. The scene between father and daughter is a kind of granting to the father of a repressed wish, as a prelude to his relinquishing control over his daughter. But this function of the scene as part of the sequence of happenings between the characters has far less importance than its thematic function, which is of course to make us rethink in radical fashion all of the story's moral assumptions, conventions of civilized behavior, and distinctions between what is permissible and what is not.

Until now, the story has viewed as entirely separate the uncivilized, socially and morally unacceptable act of the Count, on the one hand, and on the other hand the elegant, civilized behavior that predominates in the story. There have been only occasional hints, such as the Commandant's pistol shot, of any more complexity in the moral issues of the story than just this simple division. What the scene between father and daughter accomplishes thematically is to question that whole distinction, and with it what had seemed to be the moral values of the story. The single gross transgression suddenly no longer appears to be a mere isolated, freakish act but a possibility that is always present, in one form or another, and waiting to break through the civilized surface. When the Commandant embraces his daughter in a manner that is so clearly sexual, the narrator allows himself only a mild expression of surprise at her sitting on his lap, "was er sonst in seinem Leben nicht zugegeben hatte" (138). But even this characteristically muted comment adds important new information: the Commandant had evidently hidden all his life from his wish to embrace his daughter and even during her childhood had been afraid of her femininity. Now he embraces her in almost explicitly forbidden and incestuous fashion, and this sudden breakthrough from severe inhibition to a forbidden act is structurally so similar to the Count's lapse that it calls into question the whole assumption of the uniqueness of his deplorable act that had up to this point prevailed. If one simply views the acts themselves, the Count's transgression is still very much greater than the Commandant's; the degree of offense, and even offensiveness, makes for a considerable difference between the Count's action and the scene between father and daughter, despite the incestuous nature of that scene. But there are other factors that complicate this judgment. First, what the Commandant actually does is certainly less, but the desires that are thereby revealed are in their nature much more socially unacceptable than the Count's. And second, the entire set of circumstances of the Count's action must be considered. It is by no means an adequate version of that situation to think of it as a forcible, violent rape. If we look at what happens on a level that is admittedly primitive, but that is certainly a real part of the situation, the Count first wins her by fighting off the soldiers; he then offers her his protection and is accepted in that role so totally that she faints when she knows she is safe with him. There is no brutal overcoming of resistance, and again at a primitive emotional level he has taken her only after first defending her as his own and after having her accept his possession of her by her fainting and thus acknowledging the sufficiency of his protection. Of course this is only one way of seeing things, and it does not remove the possibility of more orthodox moral judgments, which indeed are also required. My point in comparing the actions of the two men is not, however, to assess blame. It is merely to show that the Commandant's behavior towards his daughter functions to remove the sense we have had of the uniqueness of the Count's act and to reveal the tension beneath the civilized elegance of the whole world in which these people live. The Count's rehabilitation follows only after the truth emerges that all those who live in this splendidly elegant world are vulnerable to a sudden capitulation to the demands of those more primitive emotions that that world attempts to ignore and repress.

The story's final mixing of the conventions of warfare and courtship (a confusion that, as we can now see, has always been designed to draw attention to the arbitrariness of the rules in both spheres having to do with direct, forceful behavior) appears in the Count's coming to claim the Marquise in the very military uniform that he had worn when he first stormed the citadel. The analogy between Marquise and citadel continues to the last; it is as if the Count still insists on his tactics of taking by storm, which have indeed been successful. The disturbing question arises: could a woman so well defended, so withdrawn, and so wanting to be overprotected have been taken any other way? Once more the Marquise's reaction is one of withdrawal, but now her father is supportive of the Count: "Der Kommandant legte seine Hand auf ihn; seine Augenwimpern zuckten, seine Lippen waren weiß, wie Kreide. Möge der Fluch des Himmels von diesen Scheiteln weichen! rief er: wann gedenken Sie zu heiraten?" (141). The description of the Commandant's exterior contains no very precise guide to his emotions, but his shaky condition is surely not due alone to his learning simply the truth of what has happened; it must also have partly to do with his having faced his own illicit desires and seen their continuity with the actions of the Count.

There remains the slow process by which the Marquise comes to accept the Count; she is cautious, as always, but after a very short time she makes a definite move in his direction. The reason for her initial refusal to accept him when the truth has finally emerged is given in her own words in the much quoted final lines of the story: "Er würde ihr damals nicht wie ein Teufel erschienen sein, wenn er ihr nicht, bei seiner ersten Erscheinung, wie ein Engel vorgekommen wäre" (143). But, if we take this in the context of the whole story and the thematic reversal near the end, there is much more to this remark than simply her having formed an image of the Count that resulted in the maximum disappointment. (She says she would have been prepared instead "auf jeden Lasterhaften.") What is really involved is a whole way of thinking about herself and the social group whose standards of behavior she accepts. She was prepared to meet a man comparable to the animals who originally attacked her because they apparently made no pretense to civilized behavior and so were irrelevant to her and her family's way of life. The only person the Marquise has suspected of being the guilty party is the employee of the family, Leopardo, a lower-class creature who presumably does not know any better. But the fact that the Count was guilty of the act calls in question this whole way of thinking and the basis of the inhibited, civilized world in which she lives. The way in which the story ends does not, as is often said, indicate that it is about the single mistake of a basically good man.[9] On the contrary, it stresses the thinness of the veneer of civilization and the fragility of civilized conventions, both military and social, which are designed to contain aggression, desire, and violence. Nowhere does this thematic basis of the story become more apparent than in the grotesque and seemingly unnecessary scene between father and daughter; and when we consider how the Marquise seemed initially to have chosen a way of life that protected her against her own emotions, and how her father too had never in his life allowed his affection for his daughter to find expression, it almost seems that the Count, in taking them all by storm, has finally had the effect of liberating them from the inhibited condition in which he found them. In a curious way, the degree of his unacceptable directness matched the degree of their having withdrawn behind the walls of a defensive emotional fortress. Could the Marquise otherwise have reached the happy and relaxed state, as she finally does, of having "eine ganze Reihe von jungen Russen" (143)?

Das Erdbeben in Chili

Das Erdbeben in Chili[1] has attracted more critical attention than any other of Kleist's stories, with the exception of the much longer Michael Kohlhaas, and has even been considered by many critics to be a more accomplished work of art. Bonafous thought that "cette nouvelle, par sa composition, ses nuances, son énergie et sa concision nous parait la meilleure que Kleist ait écrit"; Herzog maintained that it was Kleist's "stärkste und elementarste Novelle"; and Korff considered it to be the thematic basis of all the other stories, "denn in allen diesen Novellen bebt die Erde."[2] But it is an intriguing fact about Das Erdbeben in Chili that one critical opinion immediately seems to provoke another that contradicts it. Gundolf, for example, thought the Erdbeben a meaningless story in which Kleist introduced one disaster after another solely to maintain the tension; this judgment is opposed by Bonafous, who said that it was constructed very strictly according to a philosophical idea.[3] There is in fact an astonishing lack of agreement among its critics on every aspect of Das Erdbeben in Chili—its tone and style, its value, its theme and meaning, and even on the judgment of its characters.

Opinion is evenly divided as to whether the story is optimistic or pessimistic. Herzog, Witkop, Wolff, and Silz[4] take the pessimistic view, but each stresses different aspects of the story that lead him to this conclusion, while Pongs, Blöcker, Brahm, and Bonafous[5] believe it to be optimistic, though once more none gives the same reason. There have been many statements of the theme of the story: Wolff thought that it was Rousseauism, the corruption of society as against the inherent goodness of nature; Blöcker, that the world is "ein Rätsel"; Bonafous, that the story shows the goodness of God to man; Bennett, that the incomprehensible and irresponsible forces of the universe break into the ordered life of man; Conrady, that "das Widerspiel zwischen den Wirkungen der Naturkräfte und den Folgen der Menschengewalt . . . bleibt ein wesentliches Thema dieser Novelle"; Klein, that man can begin again by an act of "geistige Neuschöpfung"; Staiger,[6] that it is about the conflict between "Geist" and "Gefühl"; and there are many others. Even the question as to who is the hero or central figure of the story is disputed. The candidates for

36

the position are the two lovers, Don Fernando, and the child Philipp. Faced with this series of disagreements about the story, it is not surprising that some commentators have thought the story obscure; but even here there is still dispute, for others insist on its lack of ambiguity.[7]

I have not introduced this welter of contradictory opinions in order to show that it gets us nowhere, and that a fresh start is needed; on the contrary, this confusion shows one very important fact about the story: that it provokes a great variety of different interpretations and ideas. Any interpretation of the story must certainly come to terms with this fact and explain why it should be so; and indeed on closer inspection we can see that many of these conflicting ideas are relevant to the story, and that it is precisely as *conflicting* ideas that they are relevant, though not as the competing complete explanations offered by its critics. They are, rather, thematic material that Kleist includes in his story, carefully structured and controlled by his overall design. In the *Erdbeben* there is a constant struggle by the narrator, and also by the characters, to interpret the events of the story; and so previous interpretations achieve a special interest for a story whose very theme is interpretation. This is because the point of the story lies not in the meaning of the events themselves but in the attempts made by the narrator and the characters to give them meaning.

The setting of the story itself gives a clue to Kleist's thematic concerns, for earthquakes traditionally have been occasions on which men have been moved to think and even quarrel about the structure and the precariousness of their existence. The most famous earthquake of modern times, the Lisbon earthquake of 1755,[8] had a profound influence on European thought; it was the occasion of a considerable sharpening of the dispute between differing theologies and theories of the universe. The most notable clash was that between the popular optimism of Leibniz's theory of the preestablished harmony (i.e., that this was the best of all possible worlds), a special case of the rationalist, optimistic thinking of the eighteenth century, and the pessimistic strain of thought represented by Voltaire's poem on the Lisbon earthquake and his *Candide*. No other natural event has ever provoked such intense philosophical and theological activity; this disaster made it pressing to think about how the universe worked, and whether everything that happened in it was ultimately an act of God. Kleist's choice of the earthquake in Chile as his subject in 1810 was bound then to evoke memories of the Lisbon earthquake and to have overtones of the debate which followed it; but even for the twentieth-century reader, this choice of subject matter still in itself raises the question of what attitude we can take to suffering on such a scale or

to a disaster that is so uncontrollable and unpredictable, and before
which human beings are so defenseless. Throughout his story, Kleist
alludes to and plays on various kinds of attitudes to the earthquake;
as the narrator describes the events of the story, his formulations
suggest a series of such attitudes and thus the ways in which he is
inclined to construe what he sees at any given time. The role of the
narrator in creating the story is therefore crucial; and it is a role whose
point can only be understood through close attention to the way in
which the narrator's attitudes to the events of the story develop and
change.

The narrator begins on firm ground with the indisputable facts of
the situation: the place and year of the earthquake. But when he
comes to the description of how the love affair between Josephe and
Jeronimo began, he cannot avoid interpreting the situation. He remains at first fairly distant from the emotional tenor of the relationship, describing it cautiously as a "zärtliches Einverständnis" (144).
Yet when he relates how Jeronimo managed to see Josephe even after
her father had placed her in a convent, he says that this happened
"durch einen glücklichen Zufall." It is not clear here whether the
narrator is reading Jeronimo's reactions or giving his own, so that he
is not yet committed to sympathizing with the lovers; but the formulation is bound to arouse in us the suspicion that fortune may be on
the side of the lovers, and that we can side with them too. The story
at this point looks like a conventional romance, with young love
opposed by the world; and with this would go the usual value judgments in favor of the lovers and against those who oppose them. The
narrator is noncommittal when he says that the "junge Sünderin"
(the pregnant Josephe) was thrown into prison, for this is little more
than a conventional phrase. Neither we nor he need feel yet that she
is a sinner, or that she is not. But the description of the meeting in the
garden, on the other hand, was oriented towards a picture of Jeronimo
as a triumphant seducer; *he* had "in einer verschwiegenen Nacht den
Klostergarten zum Schauplatze seines vollen Glückes gemacht."[9] This
is not the usual kind of language we should expect in a description of
young love thwarted by wicked authorities. Already, then, there are
two distinct images of the relationship emerging: young and innocent
love thwarted on the one hand (and this is the dominant image), but
on the other hand seduction through exploitation of the privileged
position of teacher and subsequent defilement of the sacred ground
on which the nunnery stands. The fact that it is on the "Fronleich-
namsfest" that Josephe "in Mutterwehen auf den Stufen der Kathe-
drale niedersank" tends to strengthen the latter image; the injury to
the church is the greater for this. Evidently in some doubt as to how

he should view this matter of the guilt or innocence of the lovers, the narrator nevertheless is more certain when he describes the feelings of the women of the city. A clear evaluation is implied as the narrator describes their *disappointment* that the decision of the Viceroy is to change the planned death by fire of Josephe to a mere beheading. They are described with obvious irony as the "fromme Töchter der Stadt" (145), when those whose houses command a view of the place of execution invite their neighbors to come to see it. The narrator seems almost pleased to be able, at last, to give at least one clear judgment after his uncertainty as to how to judge the conduct of Jeronimo and Josephe, and of the Archbishop and the other authorities responsible for their condemnation.

The next sequence of events begins with Jeronimo in prison. He prays to the mother of God for help, but without results, and decides to hang himself with a rope that "der Zufall" (145) had left for him. This is not the first mention of the role of chance in the story,[10] and we must by now begin to ponder its significance. Could it mean that Providence offers him a fortunate release from a hopeless position? But at this point the earthquake occurs and alters our problem for interpretation. For Jeronimo at the time of the earthquake was trying to fix his rope to an iron hook let into one of the "Wandpfeiler." When the shock came, he clutched at the pillar, which prevented him from falling over and possibly being crushed under falling masonry.[11] All of this seems to hint at an interpretation of the chance by which Jeronimo got the rope. Providence seems to be at work in the lucky "chance" of Jeronimo's finding the rope with which he intends to hang himself, for only that lucky find ensured that, at the moment of the earthquake, he was in the one position in his cell that was safe. When formulated explicitly, this interpretation is implausible; but the point is that it is *not* so formulated, remaining instead as the implied conclusion towards which we feel almost instinctively directed as soon as we start to discern how the various aspects of the situation hang together. And this interpretation suggests an evaluation of Jeronimo: would a man who was to be regarded as guilty of moral crimes be favored in this way?

The narrator's attitude to the earthquake is seen in the simile he uses to describe it: it happens "als ob das Firmament einstürzte." This is one of a number of similar striking similes in the story. But these similes do more than just add power to the description; they show the narrator's construction on the events at this particular moment, his attempts to understand and construe his own story.[12] For the moment it almost seems that the earthquake is a product of divine intervention, for the word "Firmament" suggests cosmic significance.

There follows, to strengthen this suggestion, a seemingly miraculous series of events; the prison building starts to fall but is met by the fall of the building opposite so that an arch is formed. The prison collapsing by itself would have killed Jeronimo, but the arch allows him to crawl out through it and escape. As soon as he is outside, no sooner and no later, the whole street collapses with a second tremor. After this he hurries along to get out of the city, for there is still danger on all sides. But the narrator describes the scene as if some unseen hand were guiding Jeronimo through this maze of destruction so that he finds the right path: "Hier stürzte noch ein Haus zusammen, und jagte ihn, die Trümmer weit umherschleudernd, in eine Nebenstraße; hier leckte die Flamme schon, in Dampfwolken blitzend, aus allen Giebeln, und trieb ihn schreckenvoll in eine andere; hier wälzte sich, aus seinem Gestade gehoben, der Mapochofluß auf ihn heran, und riß ihn brüllend in eine dritte" (146). In this description, Jeronimo seems to have all his choices made for him, as events around him force him to go first in one direction and then in another.

So far, then, there is one issue that has been present in the earthquake and the preceding events: whether the lovers are morally guilty or not, and hence how and why Jeronimo has been allowed to escape. The suggestion that seems to be contained in the way the narrator describes the situation is that the earthquake announces Jeronimo's innocence and frees him. But immediately another issue arises: "Hier lag ein Haufen Erschlagener, hier ächzte noch eine Stimme unter dem Schutte, hier schrieen Leute von brennenden Dächern herab, hier kämpften Menschen und Tiere mit den Wellen, hier war ein mutiger Retter bemüht, zu helfen; hier stand ein anderer, bleich wie der Tod, und streckte sprachlos zitternde Hände zum Himmel" (146).

It may be all very well to think of the earthquake as a kind of divine intervention on Jeronimo's behalf, but now we are made to face the fact that more people are involved than just one. To free an innocent man at the expense of the lives of so many others makes no sense. Certainly Jeronimo can make no sense of it. He oscillates between the good and the bad faces of the situation three times.[13] First, he is seized by a feeling of delight that he is still alive, but then, seeing the others around him, "er begriff nicht, was ihn und sie hierher geführt haben konnte" (146). Next he thanks God for his rescue (for to whom else can he attribute it?) but immediately remembers Josephe and changes his mind: "Fürchterlich schien ihm das Wesen, das über den Wolken waltet" (147). Thus the concept of God has disappeared to be replaced by the vaguer concept of the Being, whoever he might be, and whether good or evil, who controls life. When he hears the erroneous report that Josephe is dead, he goes further in this direc-

tion and now attributes the whole sequence of events to "die zer-
störende Gewalt der Natur"; this is as if to say that he was entirely
mistaken to see any design or intelligence in the recent events, and
certainly that he was mistaken to think of them as in his favor. (For
events to favor him seems in fact to be the same thing as their having
an intelligent design.) His last turn to an optimistic interpretation of
what has happened is hope, and he looks again for Josephe; but his
hope dies as he cannot find her. When at last he does find her, the
concept of divine intervention appears again: "Mit welcher Seligkeit
umarmten sie sich, die Unglücklichen, die ein Wunder des Himmels
gerettet hatte!" (148). The favorable conclusion allows the return to
the most optimistic of the attitudes that had passed through Jeronimo's mind and even permits the feeling that only our ignorance of
the full story has made any other attitude possible. Yet we must
remember that this has disposed of only one of the facts that did not
seem to permit the idea of divine intervention, namely Josephe's
having perished. There remains the stumbling block to that view of
what has happened that so many others have died, all presumably as
innocent as the couple were. But Josephe's story now follows and
seems almost to provide an answer to this, for in the telling of it a
new attitude to the earthquake seems to emerge.

The procession to the execution had been broken up by the earthquake. Josephe then hurried to the nunnery to save her child, found
the building in flames, and saw the Abbess die before her eyes; she
also saw the cathedral in ruins and the shattered body of the Archbishop. Meanwhile the Viceroy's palace was in flames, the court
where she had been tried was demolished, and her father's house
had completely disappeared. In the place of the house "war ein See
getreten, und kochte rötliche Dämpfe aus" (149). This seemed to Silz
a Danteesque picture, [14] and it evidently functions to give the building
the appearance of having been consumed by hellfire. In like manner
the demolition of the seats of all those agencies that had condemned
the pair—church, state, family—seems like a series of exemplary
punishments, pointing to the cruelty and corruption of them all. And
that would give the impression that the earthquake has not merely
saved the lovers but had attacked a corrupt society, in which their fate
was only an isolated example of that corruption. So Josephe's story
suggests a reinterpretation of the entire text on the following lines:
The Archbishop prosecuted Josephe and is now dead; the laws of the
nunnery condemned her, and now it stands in flames; her family
obstructed her love, and they have been destroyed. Many of the
townspeople were delighted at the prospect of an execution, and they
too have suffered. It begins to look fairly safe for the reader to brush

aside doubts about Jeronimo and Josephe, especially since the child
that has resulted from their love is miraculously saved. Josephe rushes
into the nunnery to collect it, and the building collapses as soon as
she comes out, killing all inside. That kind of remarkable luck reminds us of Jeronimo's escape, and the tendency to view such luck as
deserved is irresistible. The narrator produces another of his very
strong similes: Josephe escapes "als ob alle Engel des Himmels sie
umschirmten" (148). At this point, then, the narrator's formulations
seem to explain the earthquake as the destruction of an evil city
(rather like the biblical Sodom and Gomorrah) through the wrath of
God; this is a broader view than the former one that concerned only
the safety of the couple, and it seems a fairly comfortable judgment of
the situation.

But there are still one or two puzzling facts that do not allow us to
be entirely content with this attitude. The Abbess had attempted to
intercede for Josephe when she was being tried, and later she had
promised to look after Josephe's child. When Josephe arrives at the
nunnery, the Abbess stands at the door crying for help to save the
child instead of getting clear of the building and to safety. She ought
not to deserve to die, but does. The obvious conclusion to which we
jump is that she dies as the symbolic head of a corrupt institution; this
would be more or less consistent with the view that has been developing in the narrator's descriptions. Nevertheless, the narrator is
clearly distressed by her death: while the body of the Archbishop is
"zerschmettert," a word that implies no sympathy for him, the Abbess is described as being "auf eine schmähliche Art erschlagen"
(148).[15] And if such an attitude is taken to the Abbess, the Viceroy
becomes an embarrassment, for if anyone should suffer an exemplary
symbolic death, it is he who should do so, as the symbolic head of the
whole society. But these are only disturbing details that are passed by
without explicit comment, and meanwhile the predominantly optimistic interpretation of the situation continues and even strengthens.
Outside the city it is "als ob es das Tal von Eden gewesen wäre" (149),
and the whole tone of the story tends to make us take the view that
what was corrupt in the society has been destroyed and left behind in
the city while only people of good will have been saved.

The first section of the story[16] ends with an idyllic passage showing
the happiness of the lovers after their troubles seem to be as good as
over. A new and perfect existence appears to be beginning; but the
description of the idyll makes us uneasy:

Indessen war die schönste Nacht herabgestiegen, voll wundermilden Duftes,
so silberglänzend und still, wie nur ein Dichter davon träumen mag. Überall,
längs der Talquelle, hatten sich, im Schimmer des Mondscheins, Menschen

niedergelassen, und bereiteten sich sanfte Lager von Moos und Laub, um von einem so qualvollen Tage auszuruhen. Und weil die Armen immer noch jammerten; dieser, daß er sein Haus, jener, daß er Weib und Kind, und der dritte, daß er alles verloren habe: so schlichen Jeronimo und Josephe in ein dichteres Gebüsch, um durch das heimliche Gejauchz ihrer Seelen niemand zu betrüben. Sie fanden einen prachtvollen Granatapfelbaum, der seine Zweige, voll duftender Früchte, weit ausbreitete; und die Nachtigall flötete im Wipfel ihr wollüstiges Lied. (149–50)

Kayser noted that this was the one piece of its kind in all of Kleist's stories, and that it had the effect of a "glatter Stilbruch."[17] The language here does indeed seem far removed from the rest of the narrative, and the idyllic quality thus appears strained. The whole scene appears consequently unreal and too good to be true. The narrator is consistent in the view of the situation that he has adopted, but this very consistency exposes the weaknesses of that view.

There are many other ways in which Kleist makes the calm of the middle section of his story an uneasy one. Consider, for example, the fact that the lovers try to get away from the laments of those who have lost possessions and family in the disaster, "um durch das heimliche Gejauchz ihrer Seelen niemand zu betrüben"; and the further report that "sie dachten, wie viel Elend über die Welt kommen mußte, damit sie glücklich würden" (150). Both passages emphasize the great discrepancy between the good fortune of the couple and the misery of many of those around them. But this discrepancy seems not to worry them at all; their sense of well-being so overshadows their compassion that they can even think in terms of this widespread suffering existing in order that they should be happy. Their moving out of the sight of the suffering in order not to disturb them does show some consideration, but it also makes clear that the misery surrounding them does not inhibit the happiness of Jeronimo and Josephe.[18]

A sense of unease continues to build up, and the entry of Don Fernando and his family into the story is a particularly tense moment, for here the past seems to catch up with Josephe. For a moment, it is not clear what his role is to be; the "Verwirrung" experienced by Josephe may well be felt too by the reader, for here a new character is introduced when the story seemed already to have run through a complete cycle of events. Josephe is confused because she recognizes him as someone she knows, but Don Fernando does not understand this: "Doch da er, indem er ihre Verwirrung falsch deutete, fortfuhr: es ist nur auf wenige Augenblicke, Donna Josephe, und dieses Kind hat, seit jener Stunde, die uns alle unglücklich gemacht hat, nichts genossen" (150). Now we are left to interpret this scene for ourselves,

and it is not the only one of its kind where the narrator's comment is
conspicuously incomplete. We naturally assume that Don Fernando
thinks Josephe's hesitation is due to her uncertainty as to whether
she will be able to feed both children, but that Josephe is in fact
worried because Don Fernando knows she is under sentence of death.
This little episode touches on the theme of the story in its compelling
us to supply an explanation of what we see and in Don Fernando's
jumping to the wrong conclusion. We are also reminded by Don
Fernando that the earthquake has made everyone "unglücklich,"
which emphasizes once more the uniqueness of Jeronimo and Josephe's position.

One last disturbing point concerning the "wrath of God" interpretation of the earthquake is the introduction of Don Fernando's two
sisters as people whom Josephe knew to be "sehr würdige junge
Damen" (151). This sounds very reminiscent of the "fromme Töchter
der Stadt." Could it be that worthy people, in the sense in which the
term would have been employed in Santiago before the earthquake,
have been saved? The feeling that they may constitute a danger subsides slowly. Donna Elisabeth seems from time to time to be looking
at Josephe, but only with a dreamy gaze (151), and we are also told in
the same sentence that she had been invited by a friend to see the
execution but had refused. She seems after all not to be a threat to the
safety of Jeronimo and Josephe or—more importantly—to the interpretation of the events that the narrator has made the basis of his
descriptions. But now, having alluded to this series of mildly disturbing events during his generally optimistic account, the narrator at last
introduces further reports that make nonsense of the view of the story
that had until recently seemed to prevail. The reports are introduced,
characteristically, in midsentence and seem relevant only to a very
minor consideration: Donna Elisabeth's dreamy gazing at Josephe is
diverted by "der Bericht, der über irgend ein neues gräßliches Unglück erstattet ward." But we are then told "wie der Vizekönig in den
schrecklichsten Augenblicken hätte müssen Galgen aufrichten lassen,
um der Dieberei Einhalt zu tun; und wie ein Unschuldiger, der sich
von hinten durch ein brennendes Haus gerettet, von dem Besitzer
aus Übereilung ergriffen, und sogleich auch aufgeknüpft worden
wäre" (151–52). This alarming report puts the whole situation in a
new light. Before this, the reports of the earthquake had tended to
suggest that the guilty had been punished, the corruption of the city
destroyed, and the innocent saved. Yet now it seems that the earthquake has provided new and better opportunities for thieves to flourish; an innocent man has been unjustly executed; and the symbolic
head of the state is indeed alive, exercising authority just as he did

before the disaster. The idyll of the Garden of Eden seems shattered, and with it the model of the earthquake as the destruction of a Sodom and Gomorrah. To make matters worse, Josephe is still untouched by this account: "Josephe dünkte sich unter den Seligen. Ein Gefühl, das sie nicht unterdrücken konnte, nannte den verfloßnen Tag, so viel Elend er auch über die Welt gebracht hatte, eine Wohltat, wie der Himmel noch keine über sie verhängt hatte" (152).[19] This is a disturbing piece of self-centeredness on her part; fully conscious of the sufferings of the rest of the world, she still calls "den verfloßnen Tag" (*all* of it) "eine Wohltat." It is important to note that any optimistic attitude to the earthquake depends heavily on the lovers' having been worth saving; this devaluation of Josephe is thus something of a blow to such an attitude.

The distinction between author and narrator is very important here. While the author in his selection of material is alienating our sympathy from Josephe, the narrator seems not to want to abandon her. He now has one last attempt to produce a favorable interpretation of the story—favorable both to Josephe and to a belief that the world is rationally designed:

Und in der Tat schien, mitten in diesen gräßlichen Augenblicken, in welchen alle irdischen Güter der Menschen zu Grunde gingen, und die ganze Natur verschüttet zu werden drohte, der menschliche Geist selbst, wie eine schöne Blume, aufzugehn. Auf den Feldern, so weit das Auge reichte, sah man Menschen von allen Ständen durcheinander liegen, Fürsten und Bettler, Matronen und Bäuerinnen, Staatsbeamte und Tagelöhner, Klosterherren und Klosterfrauen: einander bemitleiden, sich wechselseitig Hülfe reichen, von dem, was sie zur Erhaltung ihres Lebens gerettet haben mochten, freudig mitteilen, als ob das allgemeine Unglück alles, was ihm entronnen war, zu *einer* Familie gemacht hätte. (152)

This passage no longer formulates in terms of miracles or direct action by God to correct the human situation but refers in broader terms to the beneficial effects of the earthquake. Men rediscover their common humanity and can now bridge what had before seemed important differences of class and status. The brotherhood of man is reestablished. Society's trivial conversations have been replaced by "Beispiele von ungeheuern Taten" carried out by people who had shown "Römergröße" in self-sacrifice and courage. The important things in life have been rediscovered. All this results in the summing up, "daß sich, wie sie meinte, gar nicht angeben ließ, ob die Summe des allgemeinen Wohlseins nicht von der einen Seite um ebensoviel gewachsen war, als sie von der anderen abgenommen hatte" (152–53). After so much confidence in the past, the formulation is now very cautious indeed, preceded as it is by "daß sich, wie sie meinte, gar nicht

angeben ließ . . . " Kleist's narrator is evidently becoming more careful in the way in which he suggests general attitudes to the story.
Nonetheless, there emerges here a recognizably different attitude to
the events so far. A moderately optimistic attitude is now maintained
by weighing the good and bad effects of the earthquake and taking
the sum of the whole; this new way of seeing things does not ignore
the indubitable evil that has been caused by the earthquake but can
find that it is made up for by the impressive reawakening of the better
side of human nature. The earthquake can still seem to be part of a
world that is on the whole rational and benevolent instead of cruel
and chaotic. This is reminiscent of Leibniz's theory of the preestablished harmony, popularized as the view that this is the best of all
possible worlds; for there, too, the problem of evil is dealt with by
putting it in the scale and weighing it against all that is good in the
world. And Kleist's text also allows here the impression of a slow
progress towards a better state in which evil is a necessary mecha-
nism, which further allows us some confidence in the continuation of
the moral progress of the community and in the future safety of
Jeronimo and Josephe. Another of the basically optimistic group of
ideas that appear in this central section is the Rousseauistic notion
that man in nature is innately good and innocent while only his
institutions corrupt him.

The last section of the story now begins after this new attitude has
reoriented our view of all that has happened so far. The news is heard
that there is to be a solemn mass "in der Dominikanerkirche, der
einzigen, welche das Erdbeben verschont hatte" (153). The inference
from this is clear enough; indeed the narrator has drawn it for us in
his formulation. The church is not just the only one left standing; it
has actually been "verschont." The narrator fits the bare event into
his adopted framework and attributes purpose to the fact that this
church and no other was left standing. When, therefore, there is the
suggestion that Don Fernando's party should take part in this mass, it
seems natural that they should do so. This church seems to have been
singled out as the only religious institution worthy of remaining as a
place of worship; it surely cannot be, as the others were, a place of
bigotry. We are not surprised that the party, including Jeronimo and
Josephe, decide to attend the church. Critics often have said that the
lovers act unwisely,[20] but this is only true in the sense that they do
something that eventually turns out badly; at this moment they seem
to be justified in doing what they do, and the narrator shares their
conviction.

Yet as before, the narrator, having once made up his mind, begins
to have doubts. He gives considerable space to the description of

Donna Elisabeth's anxiety before the party sets off—approximately one-twelfth of the story, an unusual amount of space for Kleist to dwell on such a trivial incident. Usually Kleist's narrator describes action rather than reactions. On this occasion, there are no further reports of the earthquake to make us rethink our view of it; there is simply an uneasy atmosphere. Donna Elisabeth's misgivings are expressed three times: first, when she reminds the company of the dangers of going back to the church; second, when she gets ready to go "mit heftig arbeitender Brust" and says that she has "eine unglückliche Ahndung" (154); and third, after she has decided to stay, when she calls to Don Fernando and whispers to him something that neither Josephe nor the reader is allowed to hear. All of this recalls a number of previous incidents in the story: for example, Jeronimo's three times turning from hope to despair and the exchange between Don Fernando and Josephe in which the reader had to interpret for himself what the real content of the conversation was. Both previous incidents occurred as the narrator's interpretation of his story was about to change, a factor which must be borne in mind here too.

This all seems to weigh on the narrator, and accordingly his description of the entry into the church is full of foreboding: "Die Pfeiler warfen, bei der einbrechenden Dämmerung, geheimnisvolle Schatten" (155). We may well remember here the ambiguity of the "Pfeiler" in Jeronimo's prison cell.[21] But the narrator puts his doubt aside firmly: "Niemals schlug aus einem christlichen Dom eine solche Flamme der Inbrunst gen Himmel, wie heute aus dem Dominikanerdom zu St. Jago; und keine menschliche Brust gab wärmere Glut dazu her, als Jeronimos und Josephens!" (155). The genuineness of that religious fervor strikes a safer note, but immediately the sermon begins, and it sets in motion the final sequence of events that ends in the disaster. The real catastrophe is not just the death of Jeronimo and Josephe, together with Donna Constanze and little Juan, the son of Don Fernando; this is its smallest part. The larger issue is that there remains no way to see any coherence in all that has happened.

The most shocking thing about the disaster is that it is set in motion by nothing more than the priest's letting his tongue run away with him: "Hierauf kam er, im Flusse priesterlicher Beredsamkeit, auf das Sittenverderbnis der Stadt" (155). The phrase "im Flusse priesterlicher Beredsamkeit" is among the most important in the whole story. For after the narrator's many attempts to see some kind of shape in what has happened, it is eventually nothing more important than this on which the outcome turns. How much more trivial could the trigger event have been? How can reason deal with it? The only explanation now left is that the whole story has been a series of coincidences, sometimes looking as if they had a purpose but being in reality blind chance. By letting everything turn on a preacher's loquacity, Kleist makes the disillusion as extreme as it could possibly be.

To make matters worse, there is a final sequence of events that several times raises our hopes for the escape of the party and then dashes them again in the next line. After the preacher has condemned Jeronimo and Josephe in his sermon, Don Fernando takes command of the situation and tells Donna Constanze to pretend to faint so that they can all leave. But after this moment of hope, the situation immediately deteriorates again as a voice cries out, "Hier stehen diese gottlosen Menschen!" (156), and Josephe is seized. Don Fernando is at Josephe's side and holds up any action by claiming, rightly, that he is not Jeronimo, allowing thereby the implication that the woman at his side is not Josephe. Again there seems to be hope, but now Master Pedrillo appears, a cobbler who knows Josephe because he has worked for her. He asks who the father of her child is, but since she can say that it is not her child that she carries in her arms, another moment of confusion ensues, and again there are chances of an escape. Another reversal occurs as the child suddenly reaches for his father, which is immediately seen as confirmation that Don Fernando is Jeronimo. Don Fernando is seized, whereupon Jeronimo cries that he is the man they all want. But just as quickly hope appears again, as a "Marine-Offizier von bedeutendem Rang" (157) appears who knows Don Fernando and addresses him as such. All these turns of fortune seem to have eventually resulted in the party's escape, for they are now able to get out of the church unharmed. If the reader were not by now fearful of making any more predictions, he might think that they could not possibly survive all this only to be killed outside the church; but that is just what happens. Jeronimo is struck down by a man who says that he is Jeronimo's own father; characteristically, it is never shown whether he really is or not. There now follow in quick succession the deaths of Donna Constanze, Josephe, and Don Fernando's child. The reader is almost dizzy after this succession of changes of fortune; they are so many, seem so fortuitous, but are so serious in their eventual consequences, that he can make no sense of this bewildering sequence.

Once again the question of interpretation appears in the series of misinterpretations made by the bystanders concerning the identities of the members of Don Fernando's party: a series of misleading images, such as Josephe's walking with Don Fernando and carrying his child, instead of walking with Jeronimo and carrying her own, leads to these misinterpretations. Could it be that we have been similarly misled all the way through the story by images that are equally deceptive? It is as natural for the crowd to reach its conclusions as it seemed for the narrator to suggest his, but both were equally wrong. There now seems to be no design in this confused and contradictory series of happenings where innocent and guilty suffer alike and miraculous escape is followed by brutal murder. Finally the naval officer appears again, to say, "daß seine Untätigkeit bei diesem Unglück, obschon durch mehrere Umstände gerechtfertigt, ihn reue" (158). By now Don Fernando is too tired to ask why this was so; even to ask for the "Umstände" would be to maintain a faith in the rationality of events that neither he nor the reader still has.

But Kleist will not let us rest here, for the story closes with an account of the way in which Don Fernando adopts Philipp, the child of Jeronimo and Josephe. At the beginning of this epilogue, there is yet one more chance event. Don Fernando wishes to conceal the death of their son from his wife until she is well, and he is in any case worried about what she will say of his conduct: "Doch kurze Zeit nachher, durch einen Besuch zufällig von allem, was geschehen war, benachrichtigt, weinte diese treffliche Dame im Stillen ihren mütterlichen Schmerz aus, und fiel ihm mit dem Rest einer erglänzenden Träne eines Morgens um den Hals und küßte ihn" (159). The story then ends with the words: "Und wenn Don Fernando Philippen mit Juan verglich, und wie er beide erworben hatte, so war es ihm fast, als müßt er sich freuen." Kleist does not even leave us the belief that we can believe nothing, for the story seems to end on a note that at least raises the possibility of optimism again. The ending with the words "es war ihm fast, als müßt er sich freuen" is, when compared to the narrator's previous formulations involving "als ob," very cautious indeed.[22] And it is still not entirely clear how much of Don Fernando's reaction is due to a resigned acceptance of what he cannot change, and how much is because there is really something to be glad about, taking events as a whole. Perhaps it is just that to remain alive we must structure the events of our lives and thus act as if they had an overall design; as we look back, for example, we are often aware of the fact that an earlier disaster had the effect of pushing us in a direction which had some satisfactory results, and it even seems that the disaster was a necessary part of the fundamental shape of our lives.

It is, however, the fact that the story ends with a child whose life is still to come that makes it so open, and gives the greatest impression of questions still to be answered, events still unseen that will also need interpretation. What will the child become? Will he be worth his survival, whether or not this was accidental? What will be his effect on Don Fernando's life? Hindsight brings with it the familiar illusion that everything has conspired to secure the child's existence and to keep him alive. He owes his existence to the coincidences through which Jeronimo and Josephe met and were able to continue meeting. The earthquake allowed Josephe to take him from the nunnery only a moment before the building collapsed. He had been saved in the final scene by a number of accidents, beginning with the fact that Juan cried when given to Donna Elisabeth and so was taken to the church and ending with Master Pedrillo's killing the wrong child and not making sure that he had the right one by killing both. And the effect of all this has been to give the child as foster parents the admirable Don Fernando and Donna Elvire. What is his destiny to be? The question is posed but not answered. By now it must be obvious that every new event will raise new questions, however many existing questions it may answer. We shall never be in any better position than we are in now, because to interpret the present we must know the future, which we never do. In a sense the story could now begin all over again, and this is why it comes to an end.

What, then, are we left with at the end of the *Erdbeben*? Is any notion of the world adequate, is there any attitude to it that is appropriate, or is there any character in the story whose behavior is wisest or most admirable? Great care must be taken in answering these questions since we have seen the narrator suggest a series of different answers to them throughout the story, each one being rejected as events have moved on and made nonsense of it. All of the critical disagreements over the themes, values, and characters of the story result, in fact, from a particular critic seizing on something that is strongly suggested on one page of the text and thinking that it is valid for the whole text, not realizing that the text and its narrator move on to different attitudes. Bonafous's benevolent God of the story seems indeed to be there on one page, Braig's Rousseauism on another, and Gundolf's meaninglessness of the world on still another; but all are equally wrong about the meaning of the story. Similarly, the story seems sometimes to approve of the relationship of Jeronimo and Josephe and sometimes to be uncertain of their value. The narrator's attitudes are always tentative and easily abandoned under the pressure of new events that render them obsolete.

But still, we are left at the end of the story with Don Fernando and the child, and our impressions of them and what they represent are the final ones of the text, beyond which there is nothing else to consider or reconsider. Most critics have seen the ending in a positive light, stressing the magnificence of Fernando, and seeing in the innocence and purity of the child an opportunity for a new beginning;[23] but that is to miss the subtlety of the story's final sentences. So unambiguous a conclusion is of course impossible in a story that has treated all attitudes to the world and expectations of it so roughly; and it misses entirely the tone of the much hedged and exceedingly cautious final phrase "so war es ihm fast, als müßt er sich freuen," in which no less than four qualifiers ("es war ihm," "fast," "als ob," and "müßen") distance us from the simple "er freute sich." Don Fernando's instinctive flicker of hope cannot be made into a full-fledged gesture of confidence in the future or a guarantee of the success of the child's life to come. The point of the ending is that even after so many attempts to construe the world in a positive way have failed, despair is impossible too; the instinct to begin again, to construct a new shape for one's life, is too strong for it to be destroyed. Throughout, the story has moved us from one view of the world to the next; its ending serves not as a turn towards hope but as a reminder that the continual process of coming to terms with the world cannot ever stop, however futile it may on occasion have seemed to be.

The value of Don Fernando himself is another matter. Even if we do not know what to make of the world as the story ends, it has seemed to many critics that our attitude to Don Fernando can be one of unambiguous admiration. And this is an important point for the interpretation of the story because he contributes a new idea to the series of possible attitudes to the design of the world and to the behavior appropriate to that design: the stoic ideal. Implicit in his behavior is the feeling that the structure of the world is unknowable, and that its blessings and disasters are equally unpredictable. The stoic learns to bear the latter with fortitude and to accept the former without forming any unreal commitment to them, but he seeks above all to preserve something that has a unique value and does not depend on the unpredictability of fate: dignity and self-respect. Don Fernando is indeed an impressive embodiment of the stoic ideal, and it is significant that he comes to the fore at the very point in the story when all other possible attitudes to the world have been destroyed by the sequence of events. When no other value remains, and when nothing else seems enduring or reliable, his character gives to the scene the only stability it has and the only thing that can still be relied upon. He defends himself and the children with courage and skill, always behaves with impeccable tact, courtesy, and even chivalry, and accepts what fate offers without complaint. On the death of his child he is silent, only raising his eyes, "voll namenlosen Schmerzes" (158) to heaven. Several meaningful contrasts are established between Don Fernando and the couple, Jeronimo and Josephe.[24] Compare with Don Fernando's calm acceptance of disaster, for example, Jeronimo's instability and despair as he escapes from the earthquake, unable to control his thoughts or attitudes; compare, too, Josephe's enthusiasm and unreal optimism with Don Fernando's cautious search for the positive side of what remains in the story's last line. The couple seems completely overshadowed by this powerful, attractive figure. The narrator finds him so impressive that during the struggle outside the church he calls Fernando "dieser göttliche Held" (158); at no other point does the story seem to give so unambiguous a judgment in favor of one of its characters. Gunter Blöcker draws from this what he thinks to be the moral of the whole story: "Nur wer bereit ist weiterzuleben mit dem, was das alles verzehrende Schicksal übrigließ, und noch das Fremde als das Seine anzuerkennen, ja dessen Wert vermehrt zu sehen um das Gewicht des eignen Leides—nur der besteht die schwere Prüfung des Lebens." [25] Yet again, the point must be remembered that no single comment of the narrator is authoritative in this story; and a closer look at the text shows how Kleist has undermined the stoic answer to its world too.

Near the end of the text, we are told that Don Fernando was uneasy about seeing his wife and finding out "wie sie sein Verhalten bei dieser Begebenheit beurteilen würde" (159). The worry turns out to be groundless in the sense that "diese treffliche Dame" does not criticize him, and we may even wonder why it was mentioned at all. The answer must surely be found in the earlier passage in which Donna Elisabeth whispered to Don Fernando as the party set off to go to the Church: "Donna Elisabeth näherte sich ihm hierauf, obschon, wie es schien, mit Widerwillen, und raunte ihm, doch so, daß Josephe es nicht hören konnte, einige Worte ins Ohr. Nun? fragte Don Fernando: und das Unglück, das daraus entstehen kann? Donna Elisabeth fuhr fort, ihm mit verstörtem Gesicht ins Ohr zu zischeln. Don Fernando stieg eine Röte des Unwillens ins Gesicht; er antwortete: es wäre gut! Donna Elvire möchte sich beruhigen; und führte seine Dame weiter" (154–55). The clues to the meaning of this enigmatic passage are in the two mentions of Josephe: Elisabeth says something that Josephe is not to hear, and Fernando's response is to lead Josephe forward with a flourish, to which the narrator gives a particular character by using "seine Dame." Evidently, these words reassert the dignity of Josephe so that what was said was felt by Fernando to call it in question; and we can conclude that Elisabeth's worry is about Don Fernando's going into the town with Josephe at his side. His asking what harm can come of this is answered by the later events of the story. Don Fernando is here confronted with exactly those dangers in the situation that later prove disastrous, and the important thing is that he does not weigh them at all; he simply refuses to think in any way that will dishonor Josephe, even by implication. Many critics have said that he makes an error of judgment here, but it is important to see that this is not the case: he makes no judgment at all.[26] He relies on the stoic ideal: disaster can come at any time and is not predictable, but dignity and chivalry can be preserved. In this veiled way—a suggestion from a whispered exchange and a brief allusion on the last page—the story makes that same complex of behavior that is so impressive at the end also lead directly to the final disaster. Don Fernando was put in a position where the future disaster confronted him, and he was the one man who might have averted it; but that very ethic that we later admire prevents him from doing so. Small wonder, then, that he becomes aware that his behavior can be questioned. And thus the story's last possible answer to the question how the world should be faced is itself called into question: attempts to think about the structure of events can lead to disaster— but failing to think can just as easily have the same result.

Kleist's *Erdbeben* is, then, one of those works that, like Voltaire's poem, though in a very different way, reflect on the structure of the world and the possibility of the existence of providence. Throughout the story the characters and the narrator struggle to understand the earthquake in these terms; the reader too is led to find an explanation of what is happening, and the excitement of the story lies to a large extent in his constantly having his explanations overturned, some- times quite gradually and almost unobtrusively, sometimes with a violent shock. At the end we have almost given up trying to see coherence when a new possibility emerges, and so we are left skepti- cal but still wondering whether the world is patterned or chaotic. Finally, we are skeptical even of skepticism as a reaction to the world. In a way the *Erdbeben* is like a detective story on a cosmic scale. Always facing us are the questions "Who (or what) did it?" and "What was his motive?" There are many suspects and many false trails. The act being investigated is not an ordinary crime but the whole shaping of human existence, so that the identity of the culprit involves not only the characters in the story but all of those who read it too.

IV

Der Zweikampf

Kleist's *Der Zweikampf*[1] might appear to be a uniquely optimistic work and to be quite unlike any of the other *Erzählungen* in that respect. The hero and heroine of the story both survive, are married, and seem set to live happily ever after while the villain is punished by a particularly unpleasant death. Truth and justice may seem in danger for a while, but perhaps the suspense only makes their eventual triumph the more satisfying. Faith and virtue are rewarded while sin is punished. The framework of the story assumes a simple faith in an omnipotent and benevolent God, and if He seems to be obscured for a time, that may only be because He is preparing what turns out to be a remarkably accurate resolution of the duel. From a narrow, technical point of view, the duel concerns Friedrich's accusation that Count Jakob lied when he said Littegarde had been with him on the night of the Duke's murder. But the broader issues that eventually lead up to the duel are the murder itself and the question of Littegarde's virtue. It is clear that Littegarde *is* innocent, and that the Count *is* guilty of arranging his brother's murder, but he happens not in fact to be guilty of telling a lie when he says that he spent the night with Littegarde—he believes that he did. Technically, therefore, the Count must win, but morally he ought to lose. The solution to the problem is very precise: the Count wins the duel only to die of an infection resulting from a superficial wound received during it. This is just the technical victory and moral defeat needed to meet the situation.

To be sure, the hero and heroine have suffered cruelly. But we can, with apparent justice, look on this as the essential prelude to the greater awareness of God's goodness and so think of the ending in terms used by Heinrich Meyer: "die Vereinigung des schwergeprüften Paares."[2] This account of the story sounds very attractive yet somehow unlike Kleist. Unhappily, this clear and sunny outline begins to break down as soon as the text is examined more closely; it turns out to be utterly deceptive. As we shall see, in *Der Zweikampf* Kleist uses even the familiar suspense-and-happy-ending melodrama and the medieval framework of a naive belief in God as an ironic vehicle for his skepticism.

The story obviously invokes a stereotyped situation: the good, chivalrous, gallant, courageous (etc.) knight confronting his treacherous, wicked adversary. In the stereotype, we admire and identify with the knight as he struggles against his evil opponent. But though the story invokes this stereotype, it does not seem to respect it, for we very soon find elements in the text that undermine it. These are the first disturbing signs that all is not as it might seem to be in this story.

Friedrich often does not seem to be well suited to his role as male romantic hero, for example. Our first impression of the contact between Littegarde and Friedrich scarcely suggests that he is a very attractive figure; Littegarde apparently likes him but decides not to marry him "aus Besorgnis, ihren beiden, auf die Hinterlassenschaft ihres Vermögens rechnenden Brüdern dadurch zu mißfallen" (235). The narrator here deals something of a blow to Friedrich's masculinity: he reveals that the impression made upon Littegarde by her brothers' displeasure is greater than that made by Friedrich. There does not even seem to be much of a conflict; the word "Besorgnis" is distinctly low-key for the situation. And when after the birth of her brother's son she decides to make the matter more definite, the narrator once again adds details which are mildly insulting to Friedrich: "So nahm sie, durch manche deutliche und undeutliche Erklärung bewogen, von Herrn Friedrich, ihrem Freunde, in einem unter vielen Tränen abgefaßten Schreiben, förmlich Abschied" (235–36). Even unclear factors had helped to outweigh any feeling she might have for Friedrich, the reference to him as her "Freund" is less than it might have been, and the phrase "förmlich Abschied" is strangely bloodless. Friedrich apparently did not have the resourcefulness to fight the influence of the grasping brothers and seems to have accepted the situation, which in turn may imply something about how it arose in the first place; a certain lack of impressiveness on his part seems common to all phases of this sequence of events. All of this leads us to a fact that, given the prominence of the relationship between the two in the story's plot, is surely very strange: at no time, not even towards the end, are we told that Littegarde loves Friedrich, and it would even be hard to abstract that fact from any event that is reported. The only reference to her emotions regarding Friedrich is the statement that he was, *among her other suitors,* "der Teuerste und Liebste" (235).

The first occasion on which we see the two together gives us some further impressions of Friedrich that help to explain the absence of any strong feelings for him on Littegarde's part. After being thrown out of her home by her brothers, Littegarde is led to Friedrich, "der in Akten, womit ihn ein Prozeß überschüttete, versenkt, an einem Tische saß" (239), by his sisters (he seems always to be surrounded by his female relatives). The narrator conveys the impression that Friedrich belongs at a desk, buried in papers; he looks more like a clerk than a knight. As Littegarde had set out to go to him, she had thought of him once more as her "Freund" (239), and Friedrich himself uses the word in his offer to help her. Rather than offer himself as her champion, protector, or even possessor, he describes his help in terms that are consistent with our view of their relationship so far; he will be to her as brother to sister: "Nehmt mich, weil Eure ungerechten und ungroßmütigen Brüder Euch verlassen, als Euren Freund und Bruder an, und gönnt mir den Ruhm, Euer Anwalt in dieser Sache zu sein" (240). If her brothers had been available, they would have sufficed, apparently. This pointed avoidance of the fact that a woman might, in the circumstances, want somthing beyond a brother's support is emphasized by the almost comic juxtaposition of "Ruhm" and "Anwalt": to be her "Anwalt," we feel, is not quite what is needed to earn "Ruhm" here and simply calls to mind Friedrich's being buried in a different set of "Akten," still at his desk.

There is no development of the relationship beyond the terms used for it here; even at the end of the story, just before the two are married, the word "Freund" occurs again, as Littegarde appears "an der Hand Herrn Friedrichs, ihres Freundes, dessen Kniee selbst, unter dem Gefühl dieser wunderbaren Rettung, wankten" (259–60). Thus Littegarde, our heroine, ends the story at her valiant knight's side; the trouble is that *he* seems to be the one whose knees sag, and *she* to be holding him up, a comic reversal of the convention in which the strong knight supports the swooning girl. But the story does have an attractive male figure whom we are tempted to admire, a dashing romantic figure, who might even seem more suited to the hero's role than Friedrich if he did not occupy the position that, in the stereotype, belongs to the villain. Count Jakob the Redbeard is a "großer Liebhaber von der Jagd" (231), not a man who sits buried under papers at a desk; his red beard suggests a flamboyant and exciting character, and even when acting badly he seems altogether to be on a grander scale than Friedrich. He may arouse revulsion in Littegarde (but that may reflect on her too, and I shall return to this point), but at least he arouses strong feelings. To be sure, no one could feel revulsion for Friedrich, but on the other hand we cannot imagine even a "Kammerzofe" expending the ingenuity to get Friedrich to spend the night with her that Rosalie must employ for the Count.

Once we have begun to notice Friedrich's inadequacy for the role in which he is cast by the plot outline, additional evidence piles up. His performance in the duel is conspicuously unheroic, and he defends until the spectators are so bored that they complain:

Schon hatte der Kampf, die Augenblicke der Ruhe, zu welcher Entatmung beide Parteien zwang, mitgerechnet, fast eine Stunde gedauert: als sich von neuem ein Murren unter den auf dem Gerüst befindlichen Zuschauern erhob. Es schien, es galt diesmal nicht den Grafen Jakob, der es an Eifer, den Kampf zu Ende zu bringen, nicht fehlen ließ, sondern Herrn Friedrichs Einpfählung auf einem und demselben Fleck, und seine seltsame, dem Anschein nach fast eingeschüchterte, wenigstens starrsinnige Enthaltung alles eignen Angriffs. Herr Friedrich, obschon sein Verfahren auf guten Gründen beruhen mochte, fühlte dennoch zu leise, als daß er es nicht sogleich gegen die Forderung derer, die in diesem Augenblick über seine Ehre entschieden, hätte aufopfern sollen. (246)

The narrator shows puzzlement here,[3] as if he cannot understand why Friedrich is not attacking; he feels bound to suggest that there may have been "gute Gründe." But the fact reported next (his fall) and Friedrich's prior defensive reaction to the groans answer the question of his motivation in a perfectly adequate way: he is a poor swordsman. He is not the proverbial knight in shining armor, and he knows it. Throughout this passage the discrepancy between Friedrich's stereotype role and his actual performance is underlined by the narrator's giving us the stock value judgments of the former and the facts of the latter, with the contrast then causing him embarrassment. The Count's blows, for example, are described as "tückisch," since the stereotype demands that the villain fight treacherously, but the facts reported show the Count conducting a spirited attack, an attractive, aggressive fight, while Friedrich is passive and dull. The best example of this, however, comes with Friedrich's fall; having justly been criticized for his poor performance and having bored all the spectators, he now tries an aggressive move at last and immediately makes a fool of himself by tripping over his own spurs and falling! The narrator ignores the ludicrousness of Friedrich's performance and still speaks from his official stance, but his preserving that stance so rigidly only widens the gap between it and the events he talks about; when we visualize the situation for ourselves and compare it to the narrator's commentary, the discrepancy becomes comic. He seeks an explanation in the absence of the "higher powers" that should have been watching over the contest, not in Friedrich's lamentable incompetence, and he supplements this with the notion that the villain was treacherous once more, as villains always are:

Aber schon in den ersten Momenten dieses dergestalt veränderten Kampfs, hatte Herr Friedrich ein Unglück, das die Anwesenheit höherer, über den Kampf waltender Mächte nicht eben anzudeuten schien; er stürzte, den Fußtritt in seinen Sporen verwickelnd, stolpernd abwärts, und während er, unter der Last des Helms und des Harnisches, die seine oberen Teile beschwerten, mit in dem Staub vorgestützter Hand, in die Kniee sank, stieß ihm Graf Jakob der Rotbart, nicht eben auf die edelmütigste und ritterlichste Weise, das Schwert in die dadurch bloßgegebene Seite. (246)

As the gap between the situtation reported and the narrator's stereotyped commentary becomes more apparent, we cannot avoid wondering whether it is really so ignoble of the Count to act on the assumption that the will of God is revealed in Friedrich's fall. By now, Kleist's design for the narration of the story is becoming clear; the narrator in telling the story adopts a rather simple, optimistic view of its events, but the events themselves are such as to make it more and more difficult to retain the narrator's view of them.

One feature of the text might appear to save Friedrich's heroic stature: did he not save Littegarde from a wild boar? Unhappily (but characteristically) the relevant passage serves only to remove heroic overtones from the event and even to detract further from Friedrich's stature generally. For the phrase used to qualify Friedrich's feat in saving Littegarde from the charge of a wild boar is, in the context, strange: "tüchtiger Weise" (235). He apparently did a neat and competent job, but there is no mention of danger or of a show of courage, so that the text seems to preclude admiration of him.[4] Worse, the event supplies a basis for Littegarde's regard for him that detracts even more from his personal attractiveness—mere gratitude.

In the light of his weakness as a heroic figure, our attitudes to his faith in Littegarde must be, at best, ambiguous.[5] It is true that his faith is vindicated. But the reader must at least on occasion wonder whether this is not the good luck of the simpleton rather than the sound intuition of a strong character. Is his constancy to be regarded as saintliness—or just foolishness? Friedrich's general ineffectualness does not allow us to ignore the latter possibility.

Some events that suggest Friedrich's imagination is very limited must be taken into account in evaluating his unshakeable faith since it cannot be regarded in a completely positive way if he appears only to understand events and people in very simple and limited terms. For example, he is surprised that Littegarde does not want to see him in her dungeon. Consider the position: she knows she is innocent, and she has been assured by Friedrich that he will protect her. His performance in the duel was very weak. Before his offer of help, she had merely been slandered; as a result of that help, she is condemned to death, and the slander seems proven. Friedrich has in effect made things much worse for her, and she has good reason not to be well disposed toward him. To approach the matter from the other side: Friedrich is now condemned to death, and Littegarde's innocence has not protected him. She might well feel guilty about her part in his downfall. Yet, in spite of all this, he cannot imagine why she should not wish to see him!

Another significant means of undermining Friedrich's expressions of faith in Littegarde can be seen in the entire set of circumstances surrounding the most important occasion of those expressions, the scene in the dungeon. Here, the details of Kleist's description constantly harp on Friedrich's mental and physical weakness, just as his declaration of faith in Littegarde is at its most ardent. Friedrich is here in the middle of a group of women—his mother, sisters, and Littegarde—and is somewhat bullied by all of them, even abused by Littegarde. He is held up by his mother (250), who also fusses over him and plants a kiss on his forehead as if he were still a little boy (252); and he allows his mother to insult Littegarde without protesting, faints, and finally allows himself to be taken back to his cell when his family becomes anxious about his condition. Even though Friedrich turns out to be right, we are still left with the impression that his faith was based on weakness rather than strength,[6] that his simplemindedness is what makes it easy for him to continue believing in what he does, and that this is not to be regarded as a display of the kind of courage that would be needed to stand by a conviction derived from a less feeble imagination.

At this point it becomes interesting to consider some common criticisms of the story, in particular of its thematic structure and language. Erich Schmidt speaks of its "wohlfeile Abrechnung zwischen Tugend und Laster,"[7] while Crosby maintains that there are flaws in the language of *Der Zweikampf*: "Striking, however, is the too-frequent repetition of certain phrases, a symptom of haste, one suspects, and a flaw which could easily have been corrected if Kleist had lived to revise the work."[8] The observations involved here are at least in part accurate; but the features observed, far from being weaknesses of the story, are crucial aspects of its design, used by Kleist for his thematic purposes. The point becomes clearer when we see that both features— the too-easy separation of vice and virtue, and the repetition of stock phrases—are almost exclusively associated with our supposed hero and heroine; these two facts of the story are related, and one explains the other. Friedrich is thematically a cliché, and thus the language used to describe him is full of clichés too. He is a cardboard "good" character with all the standard good responses but no depth. Yet he is also too weak to be adequate to his cliché role, a fact that the language brings out by the repetition of certain phrases that sound forced and unreal. Two common ingredients of the stock phrases used in connection with Friedrich are "äußerst" and "trefflich." For example, he is termed "äußerst betroffen" (229) and "der treffliche Kämmerer"

(239), suffers "äußerste Besorgnis" (249), and is Littegarde's "edler und vortrefflicher Freund" (250); and at the end the two become "die beiden trefflichen Brautleute" (261). Littegarde is "äußerst ermüdet" (239) after her journey, and her being found by the villagers had made them "äußerst bestürzt" (238). This is only a sample of the stereo-typed verbal characterization of the two; an example of a complete situational cliché occurs when Littegarde arrives at Friedrich's castle. She is received by Friedrich with the words "Meine teuerste Litte-garde! . . . was ist Euch widerfahren?" (239) and then tells her story. The key to Friedrich's long response is provided by the way in which repetitions of stock phrases function in the story's language, for Friedrich begins with a phrase identical to the one he first used:

"Genug, meine teuerste Littegarde!" rief Herr Friedrich, indem er mit edlem Eifer ihre Hand nahm, und an seine Lippen drückte: "verliert kein Wort zur Verteidigung und Rechtfertigung Eurer Unschuld! In meiner Brust spricht eine Stimme für Euch, weit lebhafter und überzeugender, als alle Versiche-rungen, ja selbst als alle Rechtsgründe und Beweise, die Ihr vielleicht aus der Verbindung der Umstände und Begebenheiten, vor dem Gericht zu Basel für Euch aufzubringen vermögt." (240)

Littegarde responds, appropriately, with "Tränen vor Dankbarkeit und Rührung" at such "edelmütigen Äußerungen." But these noble expressions are too obviously standardized and contrast too plainly with the signs both of Friedrich's weakness and of the bloodless character of their relationship; and, in view of later events, the re-mark that Friedrich's faith is stronger than any proof she may be able to bring before the courts at Basel must even count as heavily ironic.

By contrast, the Count is more individual, more credible and un-derstandable, and more likeable; we are always in danger of admiring the wrong man. His red beard contrasts with Friedrich's colorless-ness, his love of hunting with Friedrich's life at a desk, and his attrac-tiveness to women with Friedrich's conspicuous lack of success in impressing Littegarde. The text contrasts every aspect of the perfor-mance of the two men, and the results are always the same: the Count is always more impressive. Unlike Friedrich, the Count is quick-thinking and resourceful. He weighs the circumstances of his brother's death and the succession of his nephew carefully, shrewdly deciding not to pursue the matter of the legality of that succession; and when the letter from the duchess arrives he thinks only for a moment before he seizes accurately and firmly on his best course of action. Judging that he will not be able to ignore the matter of the arrow and the news of his absence from the castle, he decides to face the issue squarely and thereby to choose the most favorable conditions under which to do so. In both these cases, he has made a quick and accurate appraisal of the realities of the situation and subordinated what he might wish to be the case to those realities; this is most unlike Friedrich. The Count is as resolute and courageous in battle against Friedrich as he is in facing his own death. He faces a just punishment calmly whereas there seems to be something abject about Friedrich's acceptance of an unjust fate. The Count is admired by the people, and when the messenger arrives at his castle, the atmosphere is pleasant and convivial: "Der Graf der eben mit einer Gesellschaft von Freunden bei der Tafel saß, stand, als der Ritter mit der Botschaft der Herzogin, zu ihm eintrat, verbindlich von seinem Sessel auf; aber kaum, während die Freunde den feierlichen Mann, der sich nicht niederlassen wollte, betrachteten, hatte er in der Wölbung des Fensters den Brief überlesen: als er die Farbe wechselte" (232). This is a relaxed Count, courteous to his visitor, described in terms that demand a positive response. On the other hand, when we first meet Friedrich, he seems lonely and joyless. The same suggestion of the Count's being in the good company of those whom he likes and who like him is contained in the description of his arrival at Basel "mit einem glänzenden Gefolge von Rittern" (234). Friedrich's gathering seems more prosaic; he sets out "mit einem zahlreichen Gefolge von Reisigen und Knappen" (241). Where the Count has companions, Friedrich has only retainers. Nor is the authority of the Count matched by Friedrich; when the Count's sons express their greed and resentment at having been cheated of the succession to the Dukedom, he simply silences them "mit kurzen und spöttischen Machtsprüchen" (230). For purposes of symmetry, and therefore juxtaposition and comparison, the story gives a pair of unpleasant young relatives to the hero and heroine too, but their unpleasantnesses are not checked in this authoritative way. Littegarde is weak in dealing with her brothers and does not check their greed. Friedrich seems not to be able to control the expressions of doubt and fear on the part of his female relatives, although they are by implication insulting to Littegarde.

That the "wohlfeile Abrechnung zwischen Tugend und Laster" does not apply to the Count emerges clearly at the end of the story when he tries to save Littegarde and Friedrich from execution: "Ich will nicht, ohne eine Tat der Gerechtigkeit verübt zu haben, sterben!" (258). The Count's candid admission that his sins are growing with his age (230) makes them sound less dangerous, and pride (257) at his having made an important conquest (of Littegarde) at his age seems more like a human failing than wickedness. The Count's demise is, however, announced with a ringing phrase, "Er . . . hauchte seine schwarze Seele aus" (260), and the description of his funeral pyre is the most vivid part of the story's end—not the marriage, which is quickly dismissed, nor the happiness of the couple, which is not even mentioned. The result of this series of contrasts between the two men is that the Count, in spite of his misdeeds, appears human, colorful, attractive, forceful, resourceful, and thoroughly impressive, while Friedrich, for all his "noble" sentiments and faith, strikes us as a weak and irresolute simpleton. Here Kleist is invoking a situation not uncommon in literature, one which seems to imply considerable skepticism about morality; it can be seen in the many versions of the Don Juan theme and in more modern times in film roles typically played by Errol Flynn. In Mozart's *Don Giovanni*, for example, we grudgingly acknowledge that Don Ottavio is a "better" man than Don Giovanni but find him (and his music) shallow and uninteresting in comparison with the villain.

Littegarde, too, is an uninteresting paragon of virtue, described in the same stock language as Friedrich. She is weak and unintelligent in dealing with her brothers; how could she have failed to recognize their real motives in opposing her possible remarriage? She never displays a romantic attachment to Friedrich at any point in the story, and it is almost a surprise that they are married at the end, for never do they express any intent to do so. The text studiously avoids any scene after their ordeal in which declarations of love might occur.

In some ways Littegarde and Friedrich are differentiated, but hardly to her advantage or to the advantage of the conventional framework of the narrator. Her being a widow makes her rather less appropriate to the role of the helpless princess in need of a champion and tends to make Friedrich look more inexperienced and ineffectual than he otherwise might. Her greater experience even takes on an unpleasant aspect when she turns to Friedrich for help; the phrase "immer noch ergeben" discreetly underlines her previous refusal of the man whose devotion to her she will nevertheless now rely upon and use: "Und niemand schien ihr des Vertrauens, zur Verteidigung ihrer Ehre aufgerufen zu werden, würdiger, als ihr wackerer, ihr in Liebe, wie sie wohl wußte, immer noch ergebener Freund, der treffliche Kämmerer Herr Friedrich von Trota" (239). It never occurs to her to ask whether her previous refusal has placed in question her ability to call on Friedrich, and far from being hesitant on that account she seems almost arrogant in thinking only of the honor she bestows on him by thinking him worthy to defend her honor.

In general, then, the story offers a stereotyped situation of hero, heroine, and villain, and at the same time raises the question of the real human worth of the three in such a way as to reverse our normal attitudes to them and to allow the morally skeptical possibility of the "good" people being dull, the "sinner" more interesting and humanly valuable, a possibility that would effectively devalue the "happy" ending. But there is a further, hidden and insidious level of the story's skepticism; for besides questioning the equation of moral correctness and human value, the story also blurs and complicates the issue of moral right and wrong so that it becomes difficult to make unequivocal moral judgments. There is a sense in which Friedrich and Littegarde are themselves agents of villainy while, on the other hand, the Count's position has a kind of justice of its own. This is the paradoxical result of the device of the outer frame and its being the apparent occasion for the story of Friedrich and Littegarde; to this aspect of the text we must now turn.

The frame has seemed to many critics to be only loosely connected to the main story. It might at first sight seem that the duel had begun as a small part of a plot concerning the succession to the throne and the murder of the Duke and had then gotten out of hand, so becoming the main issue of the story while the original main issue of the plot—the murder—is only briefly mentioned at the end to tie up the loose ends created by this untidy and undisciplined narrative. But we should be cautious about such a judgment; Kleist uses this technique of apparently losing the thread of his plot elsewhere in his stories, always as a way of making us see the events of the story in a new light. If we look carefully at what happens in the outer frame and juxtapose the issues of that frame to those of the central story of Friedrich and Littegarde, we shall have to conclude that the first part of the story, far from being a mere "Sprungbrett" for the rest, is thematically essential to it.[9]

The most important thing about the outer frame is that it touches on a number of issues that are centrally involved in the duel itself, in a way that undermines the system of values that is the subject of the duel. For example, extramarital affairs are outrageous in the context of the duel; the occasion of the total breakdown of Littegarde's way of life is simply the accusation that she has spent a night with a man, though that man is of such high social rank that he is first in line of succession to the throne. Even if the accusation were true, it would scarcely be evidence of a generally immoral way of life, and the relationship would be, for her, a considerable move up the social scale. But once we put the possible relationship of the Count and Littegarde in these terms, we must be reminded of the story's opening words, where the Duke and the (eventual) Duchess (who had been "unter seinem Rang") seem a parallel instance. In fact, they seem to be a more extreme case; they had had a child before the marriage, which suggests that the relationship must have lasted some time. It is an amusing comment on the ostensible issue of the duel (a slander against Littegarde's moral purity) that the present occupant of the throne is the result of just such a situation as that which is so unthinkable for the purpose of the duel. But this is only one example of the thematic continuity between the frame of the story and the duel and the uncomfortable nature of that continuity when closer attention is brought to bear on it. A more important aspect of this continuity consists in the fact that if we now take the story as a whole, we can see an original antagonism between two people becoming transformed several times, each time concerning itself with a new issue and involving new people yet always preserving aspects of its previous shape.

The dispute between the Count and the Duchess concerning the investigation of the murder of the Duke is recognizably the continuation of the struggle between the two brothers over the succession to the throne. The Duke had been trying to maneuver his brother out of the succession by legitimizing his illegitimate child, and the Count had responded by arranging his brother's murder. After the Duke's death, the uneasy maneuvering between the Duchess and the Count fundamentally concerns the same issue of the succession. The Duchess fears that she might only succeed in provoking a popular move in the Count's direction if she prosecutes him; he waits for her to make the mistake that may have the effect of putting him on the throne. But next, in a further transformation of the original antagonism, the Duchess's part in the struggle is assumed by Friedrich and Littegarde and they become the means by which Count Jakob is prosecuted for the murder of his brother. Thus the Duke, the Duchess, Friedrich, and Littegarde are all successively involved in a struggle against the Count. It is a delightful irony of the story that Littegarde in her struggle against the Count to vindicate her honor is the lineal descendant and in a sense the instrument of the original attempt to promote to the throne the child who is the issue of that very sin at which she recoils! As a coprosecutor of the Count, she places herself in the same camp as the kind of woman from whom she wishes to distinguish herself—the Duchess. Her struggle for her moral values indirectly, but importantly, rewards their opposite; in this way she is really achieving the opposite result to the one she thinks she is achieving.

The ending of the story can only be regarded as a resolution of all its issues if an important fact is ignored: that in the whole course of the events of the story, the first sin and the first injustice were both committed by the Duke. The narrator points out that "Jakob der Rotbart verschmerzte, in kluger Erwägung der obwaltenden Umstände, das Unrecht, das ihm sein Bruder zugefügt hatte" (230). The Count was guilty of murder but was at least provoked by a great "Unrecht" and thus not motivated simply by his own greed. And at the end of the story he performs an action that has no other motivation than a concern for justice. By contrast, the Duchess never seems to act for any reason other than her own advantage, and she subordinates to that consideration any possible wish to bring her husband's murderer to justice, even though she has good reason to believe that the Count is the murderer. All of this means that Littegarde and Friedrich, in their pursuit of justice and virtue, are allied with (and in the long term serve the interests of) a woman who is less concerned with those values than any other person in the story.

The last words of the text provide a final, and decisive, undermining of its apparently positive ending: "Der Kaiser aber hing Herrn Friedrich, nach der Trauung, eine Gnadenkette um den Hals; und sobald er, nach Vollendung seiner Geschäfte mit der Schweiz, wieder in Worms angekommen war, ließ er in die Statuten des geheiligten göttlichen Zweikampfs, überall wo vorausgesetzt wird, daß die Schuld dadurch unmittelbar ans Tageslichte komme, die Worte einrücken: 'wenn es Gottes Wille ist'" (261). An acceptance of the convention of the trial by combat and its revelation of God's judgment is of course unavoidable, for that convention is an integral part of the story. Just as there is no point in reading ghost stories unless we are prepared to accept the convention used (in spite of our normal unwillingness to believe in ghosts), so here we must accept the framework of a simple medieval faith, for otherwise we can make no sense of what happens in the duel, why Friedrich and Littegarde are in such distress about it, or why as readers we too should be puzzled at the apparent outcome and then satisfied when further developments show that after all no mistake was involved.[10] We see the convention threatened and then surviving apparently intact. Why, then, the change in the statutes of the duel? That the change is dealt with in the last sentence of the story is a guarantee that it is of some importance; and in fact this apparently insignificant change of wording has the effect of destroying any possibility that the duel can be relied upon to reveal the truth in future.[11] Once the possibility is granted that the truth may not come to light "unmittelbar," the question then arises, "How long must we wait?" And we cannot know. It may be two days, two weeks, two months, two years, two decades. Once it is granted that the truth may not always be immediately visible on the conclusion of the duel, we have lost everything that the duel was supposed to guarantee; its whole point was that one could rely on it. Once it is assumed that in some cases we may not know right away what the truth is, it follows that we cannot know for certain in any case. It will never be possible again to look at the outcome of any duel and say simply: there is the truth. Since we never know God's will (even granted the convention of the story that this will exists and is benevolent), the phrase "Wenn es Gottes Wille ist" is as good as saying "Perhaps." The truth-discovering function of the duel had seemed to be saved after being doubted for a while; but the apparently innocuous change of wording now destroys it. The paradoxical position results: even granted a faith in the truth-revealing function of the duel, we still cannot see what it reveals!

In *Der Zweikampf*, Kleist uses a conventional framework that is built on simple and familiar ideas such as the vindication of faith, the triumph of virtue and justice, the presence of an omnipotent and benevolent God, and the hero and heroine after their trials living happily ever after, to do something very intriguing with it: he assimilates it to a pessimistic and skeptical outlook. The end result is not a story that attacks these stereotypes directly but one that accepts them only to question whether, even granted that acceptance, they have real positive value. We cannot of course ignore the interpretation of the story that seems to be there at its surface level and that I have set out at the beginning of this chapter. Yet neither can we ignore another interpretation that offers itself just as persistently throughout the story: the tiresome and ineffectual simpleton, more by good luck than good management and not without having made a fool of himself, at last wins the priggish girl in a marriage that looks to be uninteresting and to be based less on love than on her dutiful acceptance of the savior of her reputation—the only thing that seems to concern her. Virtue and faith not only look unattractive as a result, but worse still their representatives assist the larger triumph of immorality and injustice and help to keep the scheming Duchess and her son, the issue of her immoral behavior, on the throne. An alliance of ambition, immorality, and injustice on the one hand and priggish simpletons on the other has indeed eliminated the villainous Count from the scene. But he was the one character in the story who, for all his faults, had any human warmth, dignity, or impersonal concern for justice; and the wrong done him—that which set the whole sequence of events in motion—goes unavenged. Falsehood and trickery have prospered while God's truth and goodness, even granted they exist, have become inaccessible and obscured. Perhaps the story is not so untypical of Kleist after all.

V

Michael Kohlhaas

Kleist's *Michael Kohlhaas* is among the most celebrated works in German literature, and it has been the subject of extensive critical discussion that is, however, far from producing any consensus.[1] Two much disputed issues are always at the center of the critical discussion: first, the question of how we should judge Kohlhaas and his actions—positively, negatively, or some combination of the two and with what emphasis—and second, the question of the gypsy episode's place in (or even relevance to) the story or, to be more precise, the place of the sequence of events that in the narrative begins with Kohlhaas's journey to Brandenburg and ends with the conclusion of the story itself.

The first of these two questions can have a deceptive simplicity that has often allowed its interpreters to think they were making statements that were self-evident—only to be contradicted by others equally convinced of their own correctness in a diametrically opposite view. And it seems that the debate is becoming sharper: recent studies have been more uncompromising both in negative and positive judgments of Kohlhaas than ever before. Karl Schultze-Jahde's very plausible positive evaluation of Kohlhaas in one of the earliest studies of the story provides a good introduction to the focal point of the discussion. Schultze-Jahde explained carefully that Kohlhaas's violence in the story had a legal basis; since the law is ultimately an agreement between people to regulate their dealings with each other, and governmental power is also the result of an agreement entered into for the protection of individuals, society's action in denying him justice breaks its agreement with Kohlhaas and releases him from his obligation to keep to his side of the bargain. He is then back in a state of nature, in which each man is the protector of what is rightfully his, and must respond to any forcible seizure of it with an attempt to seize it back again by force.[2] Gerhard Fricke in a later article rounded out this picture of the wholly admirable Kohlhaas by stressing that Kleist goes to some lengths early in the story to show Kohlhaas as a man of great patience and reason. Fricke points to the number of provocations that Kohlhaas ignores, the careful way he proceeds, and stresses that Kohlhaas takes matters into his own hands only after all other possible remedies are exhausted; and with a great deal of textual

evidence at his disposal, by no means taken out of context or misin-
terpreted, he makes a very good case for the conclusion: "So hat der
Dichter alles nur Mögliche getan, um seinen Helden als das Gegenteil
eines Rechtsfanatikers, Absolutisten oder radikalen Weltverbesserers
zu erweisen."[3] Richard Matthias Müller, in one of the most recent
articles on the story, and well aware that this view has in the meantime provoked much dissent, takes the most uncompromising position to date, insisting that Kohlhaas does *nothing* for which we might
even partially disapprove of him. The obvious textual reasons for
doubt over the thesis of Fricke or Schultze-Jahde had been that Kohlhaas takes the law into his own hands by violent means that involve
the death of innocent people. Müller sees this as merely "ein Stück
Pathologie und Naturgeschichte der Revolution" and says that Kleist
wants to show us just what can result from even the noblest motives.[4] But this begins to sound considerably less plausible than
Schultze-Jahde or Fricke did: can Kohlhaas's indiscriminate lashing
out at bystanders in his search for the Junker be separated from his
intent and his moral stance when the results of his actions are visible
to and predictable by him?

Small wonder, then, that critical voices have been raised that are
very much less sympathetic to Kohlhaas. Many have viewed him as a
basically good man with a good cause who, degenerating under strain,
does regrettable things in pursuit of that cause. But recently a much
more totally negative view of Kohlhaas has appeared. R. S. Lucas
argues that Kohlhaas is not a reasonable man at all, accuses him of
dishonesty, opportunism, and of breaking the amnesty agreement;
and his general view is that Kleist, in Kohlhaas, has "laid bare, one
after another, the illusory objective grounds of revenge and shown
the thing up for the personal and irrational satisfaction it is."[5]

This kind of view is the complete counterpart of Müller's; it can
find some genuine support in certain passages of the text (what happens at the Tronkenburg and at the convent, for example), but like
Müller, though coming from the opposite direction, Lucas tries to
make the whole text consistent with the impressions legitimately
gained from particular parts of it, and that leads again to some highly
implausible interpretation. It is very hard to deny that there is *some*
justice in Kohlhaas's case, but that is what Lucas feels he has to deny.
The text contains a great deal of evidence that the Saxon government
is repeatedly corrupt and unjust in its dealings with Kohlhaas; Lucas
either disregards the evidence or twists it beyond recognition. The
Elector of Saxony promotes his corrupt officials after he has been
confronted with their corruption, but Lucas argues that since Nagelschmidt's letter is the occasion for the Elector's action, Kohlhaas bears

this responsibility for sending the government from bad to worse. And whereas the text makes it clear that Kohlhaas only writes to Nagelschmidt *after* the amnesty has been broken, Lucas rewrites this by saying that "the amnesty is not broken until Kohlhaas puts himself in the wrong by fresh association with the new crimes of Nagelschmidt."[6] Now such blatant misreading of Kleist's text would be of no interest were it not for the fact that the simultaneous appearances of Müller and Lucas underline an important fact about the story that will not go away and must be faced: it is that a great deal of the text seems to show Kohlhaas as an exemplary man with a patient and reasonable attitude to justice, while other parts of it seem to show him as vengeful and indiscriminately violent; we must not lose sight of this apparent inconsistency by attempting, as Müller and Lucas do, to ignore or distort either set of passages in order to simplify the text and to allow the interpreter to rely wholly on the one as if the other did not exist. This may make life easier for the interpreter, but it avoids the real point of the story. The challenge it presents to us as readers is precisely that Kohlhaas is both exemplary and repellent in the story: how can a man who displays such genuine respect for the law, such patience and such honorableness, also be capable of indiscriminate violence, of killing innocent people, and of descending at the end of the story to a vengefulness that in his final words to the Elector of Saxony ("Ich aber kann dir weh tun, und ich wills!" [86]) looks almost petty?[7] What is Kleist doing in giving us such a clash between these two appearances of Kohlhaas? What thematic point underlies this conflict in the text?

It is of course clear from the first that the conflict is a central and well-considered feature of the story. Kleist's narrator makes the point for us in his opening sentence when he says that Kohlhaas is "einer der rechtschaffensten zugleich und entsetzlichsten Menschen seiner Zeit," and when he claims a little later, "Das Rechtgefühl aber machte ihn zum Räuber und Mörder" (9). But after this summary opening evaluation, the narrator does little more to help us solve the problem of how to conceive of the relation of the two sides of Kohlhaas. He does indeed continue to express attitudes; the clear negative evaluation of Kohlhaas's "Mandat" as a "Schwärmerei krankhafter und mißgeschaffener Art" (36) is an obvious case, but that this cannot be used as any kind of final judgment is shown when somewhat later in the text the narrator is still calling him "den ehrlichen Kohlhaas" (58). The inconsistency shows that here Kleist's narrator, as always, judges impressionistically and not in an authoritative way that might provide a secure point of orientation for the reader.[8]

Some critics have attempted to do justice to both images of Kohl-

haas, but have done so in a way that seems curiously inappropriate to
the intensity of Kleist's texts. They have tried to take a judiciously
balanced view of the whole and to reconcile the two extreme positions by seeing Kohlhaas as a basically good man who admittedly
makes some mistakes. Ludwig Büttner, for example, in an article
entitled "Michael Kohlhaas—eine paranoische oder heroische Gestalt?" cautions against either simple view but then goes on to say
that Kleist gives us here"ein Bild des wirklichen unverfälschten Menschen mit seinen Tugenden und seinen Lastern."[9] But this keeps
negative and positive aspects of Kohlhaas in sight only at the cost of
removing the crucial tension between them; they are not so easily to
be reconciled without losing much of the story's force, for in Kleist's
text they are felt to be contradictory and apparently irreconcilable.
Kohlhaas is both scrupulously just and blind to justice, both conspicuously patient and conspicuously impatient, both grand and petty
in his actions. An easy compromise between the two is too complacent
a solution; the story has been made to seem much more tame than it
is. Kohlhaas is drawn on too grand a scale for us to regard him as an
ordinary man with the same faults and virtues as the rest of us.

One way to sharpen the issues here is for the reader to ask himself
what *he* would have done in identical circumstances to those in which
Kohlhaas finds himself. Not surprisingly, there is rarely any easy
answer. Would it have been best to take the horses back at the beginning and accept the fact that there is no way to get justice where the
nobility is an adversary, or instead to take them back after the law-
suits failed and accept the fact that the courts are irrevocably corrupt,
and that two horses are not worth the total disruption of one's life?
Assuming, on the other hand, that the matter should not be dropped,
was it then best to pursue the Junker while scrupulously avoiding
harm to the innocent? Alternatively, was Kohlhaas's mistake writing
the letter to Nagelschmidt or perhaps his refusing the possibility of
saving his life by giving up the "Kapsel"? This seems to be a fairly
complete list of all major points where different decisions were possible, but there are obvious objections to all of the alternative courses
of action. To drop the matter is to acquiesce in and encourage a
corrupt system, and we commonly regard men who have taken on
and beaten corrupt systems as heroes. Carefully limited force is probably impossible—the Junker has an established place in the society,
and his using that position to protect himself will mean that an attack
on him will automatically involve others. When Kohlhaas wrote to
Nagelschmidt, he seemed to be without resource in face of a broken
amnesty, and failure to act could easily have seemed like a passive
acceptance of death. As for giving up the "Kapsel," after so much

suffering it would seem like a very unsatisfying surrender, an anti-
climactic event leaving Kohlhaas and the reader at least with a strong
sense of unfinished business and of a continuation of corrupt government. There is, then, no easy answer to the question "What should
Kohlhaas have done?"—but that does not remove the sense that he is
indeed "entsetzlich" nonetheless.

Having set out the dimensions and the issues of the first of the two
major interpretative problems of the story, I wish now to consider the
second, that of the relevance of the gypsy episode. In so doing I do
not mean to abandon the first, because ultimately the two problems
become the same and require the same solution; the apparent discrepancy between the two faces of Kohlhaas has much to do with that
other apparent discrepancy between the earlier and later parts of the
story.

The chief problem of the gypsy episode has always been that it is
not clear how this episode could or should occur at all with the rest of
the text.[10] Late in the story—four-fifths of the way through it, in
fact—we go from a text that has been concerned exclusively with
realistic description and problems in the real world of real people into
a strange world of supernatural events; the story begins firmly with
the kind of motivation that we can all understand and relate to the
world in which we live, and yet suddenly, near the end, that is no
longer true. One kind of critical response has been the view that,
quite simply, the unity of the work is disturbed by this sudden change:
Heinrich Meyer-Benfey says that the two parts of the story are "miteinander unverträglich," Karl Otto Conrady that they are not organi-
cally related.[11] A common explanation of this mismatch is derived
from the genesis of the text: when writing the ending of the story,
Kleist apparently forgot what his convention at the beginning had
been, since he wrote the ending much later than the earlier part. But
the contrast in the two parts is so strong that it is hardly plausible to
suggest that Kleist did not notice it.

The first significant attempt to look at the relation of the gypsy
episode to the rest of the text in terms of a possible thematic function
was by Schultze-Jahde. He thought that Lisbeth introduced a divine
perspective to emphasize that justice could not be achieved in this
world; meanwhile, from a divine perspective, Kohlhaas is a good and
just man. Interesting as Schultze-Jahde's account is, it is not convincing. The means chosen by Kleist (soothsaying, magic, etc.) are not
Christian; Kohlhaas's concern with vengeance at the end of the story
is most un-Christian; most important of all, the explanation offered
seems too lame to do justice to the radical jolting that Kleist inflicts on
his readers as the style and kind of motivation of the story abruptly

change. A shift from a human to a divine perspective could surely have been achieved by other and clearer means. Moreover, the means chosen seem to be very much concerned with this world, rather than the next; that is, with the issue of the Elector of Saxony's succession and Kohlhaas's receiving and satisfying the justice of this world.

Schultze-Jahde's has remained the only serious and reasonably well-developed attempt to interpret the function of the gypsy episode in the story.[12] Fricke explicitly decided to keep it out of his discussion on the grounds that it contributed nothing to the central question: "Wer war und was wollte Kohlhaas?"[13] But, on the contrary, the confusion sown by this episode is a confusion in just those issues which Fricke wants to talk about. Instead of waiting until the issues of Kohlhaas's character and actions have been settled and only then facing the issue of the function of the gypsy, we must take the two issues together and ask at the outset: what kind of confusion does the gypsy introduce into the judgment of Kohlhaas and why?

The full extent of the change in the story bears careful attention—it involves much more than merely the introduction of magical elements. There is, first of all, a change in the principal antagonism, which now becomes Kohlhaas against the Elector rather than against the Junker. The second change is in the object that is the ostensible focus of the antagonism; this was the pair of horses but now becomes the "Kapsel." Third, the search for justice becomes a pursuit of vengeance in that Kohlhaas seeks now to harm the Elector rather than achieve a fair settlement of his dispute with the Junker. Fourth, there is a change in the kind of events admitted into the story; these can now include supernatural and irrational events whereas formerly they had been restricted to objective businesslike dealings in the everyday world of ordinary people. Fifth, the narration begins to include fairy tale elements: for example, fortune telling and the kind of rags-to-riches transformation (of Kohlhaas's children) that frequently occurs in fairy tales.

It is important to see that we have here not merely a change of style or a sudden inclusion of the supernatural but a *series* of changes at all levels of the story (including significantly its dominant issues and principal characters) that must be taken together, each one seen as part of the whole complex of changes. It is perhaps natural that one element in the complex has caused the most puzzlement—the magic associated with the gypsy—and that this has deflected attention from the others. And yet the first of the changes to appear is *not* the introduction of magic; before that happens, there has already begun the process of changing the focus on the main characters and on the dominant antagonism of the story. It is, in fact, the scene of the hunt at the estate of Aloysius von Kallheim that clearly opens the final and markedly different episode of the story:

Es traf sich daß der Kurfürst von Sachsen auf die Einladung des Landdrosts, Grafen Aloysius von Kallheim, der damals an der Grenze von Sachsen beträchtliche Besitzungen hatte, in Gesellschaft des Kämmerers, Herrn Kunz, und seiner Gemahlin, der Dame Heloise, Tochter des Landdrosts und Schwester des Präsidenten, andrer glänzenden Herren und Damen, Jagdjunker und Hofherren, die dabei waren, nicht zu erwähnen, zu einem großen Hirschjagen, das man, um ihn zu erheitern, angestellt hatte, nach Dahme gereist war. (79)

There follows a description of the festivities, but soon the text returns to give us even more information about Lady Heloise: "Der Kurfürst, der mit halboffener Brust, den Federhut, nach Art der Jäger, mit Tannenzweigen geschmückt, neben der Dame Heloise saß, die, in Zeiten früherer Jugend, seine erste Liebe gewesen war . . ." (80). In a fashion typical of Kleist, there is here much cramming in of circumstantial detail: some overly precise description of the Elector's hat, some throwaway comments about the numbers of splendid lords and ladies present at the hunt. All this creates the familiar impression that the narrator is eager to get on with the main outline of his story, pausing for a brief descriptive comment only in order to help us visualize the scene. But the odd thing is that both these passages, which look as if they aim only to give a colorful impression of the immediate scene, give us vital information about the relationships among the main actors that is unexpected and that had curiously been withheld from us until so late a stage in the story. In both cases the focus on Heloise is striking. Almost as a cover, the narrator stresses that many other lords and ladies are there, but it is she that is singled out in both passages, and each time a new piece of information is dropped in about her relationship to the Elector, the Tronkas, and the Kallheims. Why are we suddenly given this information about a hitherto unseen woman, and why is it slipped into the text as part of the irrelevant detail used to evoke a colorful scene? These questions will test just how carefully the reader has followed the details of the alliances between various families; if he has been attentive to those details and to the conclusions that they seem to have suggested, he will now see that this new information changes everything. What we learn about Heloise may not be immediately striking, but if we consider its bearing on how and why the major events of the story have taken place, its impact is shattering. It changes the whole thematic basis of the story. This almost hidden but enormously significant change ushers in all the more obvious changes because it is really the basis of them all. To see how this is so, we must go back into those earlier parts of the story to which this new one is directly relevant;[14] we must be clear about the kinds of impressions that had been built up of the central issues and personalities of the story before we can see just how this new information renders those impressions seriously inadequate.

A central question throughout the story has been the reason for the failure of justice in Kohlhaas's lawsuit. In general, we have been given an impression of a conspiracy of a few interrelated families who cooperate to their mutual advantage by forming a corrupt establishment that is able to deny justice to any outsider if he is in conflict with an insider. But this impression does not arise from any one point in the story, nor does it occur in explicit form. On the contrary, it is an impression gained from various small pieces of information spread out over the text, and it develops and is rounded out slowly with each new textual detail that is added to it. Just as in Kleist's other stories, the notion of a sequence of impressions is a very important one; as readers, we are actively involved in reconstructing what they all add up to, and we must always be prepared to see that later information will show a tempting conclusion earlier in the story to have been a mistake. It is important, therefore, to trace carefully the sequence of our impressions of the nature of Kohlhaas's cause.

Our very first impression is that of a simple legal struggle against the Junker, but very soon it begins to seem that what he is really up against is a shadowy establishment network. As our understanding of that larger and more sinister adversary develops, our view of Kohlhaas's moral position develops with it, since the two are interdependent: our judgment of the appropriateness of Kohlhaas's response to his adversary depends on just how we conceive of that adversary. The first hint that Kohlhaas is up against something much bigger and more important than Junker Wenzel occurs when Kohlhaas inquires as to why his first complaint to the Dresden tribunal has been rejected and learns in reply, "daß der Junker Wenzel von Tronka mit zwei Jungherren, Hinz und Kunz von Tronka, verwandt sei, deren einer, bei der Person des Herrn, Mundschenk, der andre gar Kämmerer sei" (22). Here is no statement of motives or of who stood to gain and how; we get the bare fact and must imagine the rest. Kohlhaas then turns to Berlin, taking his case to the ruler of his own state, and when it is rejected again, he finds out as before not how or why it happened but just the bare fact, "daß der Graf Kallheim mit dem Hause derer von Tronka verschwägert sei" (24). The long arm of the establishment reaches even further, we now assume, crossing even state lines. The illusion starts to grow of the mafialike quality of the establishment, with eyes and arms everywhere, a quiet but efficient network of men whose collective power can ensure that the interests of any one of them are protected against outsiders.

We have no more information about the establishment until much later, and it is against the background of his and our knowing only this much that Kohlhaas sets out in pursuit of justice; we (and he) therefore see the situation now not as Kohlhaas against the Junker over two horses, but instead as Kohlhaas against the governmental establishment over large-scale corruption and injustice. This change— a major broadening of the issues—makes all the difference in the world to our judgment of Kohlhaas's actions and motives, and we must recall this important fact when Lady Heloise enters the picture. It may seem foolish to disrupt his life and family from the first point of view but heroic to do so from the second. What Kohlhaas does next requires a feeling that the issues are on a sufficiently grand scale; Kohlhaas himself says that he is "auf große Dinge gestellt" (25), and his conversation with his wife again stresses the scale of what he is to do. What is at stake is not his own personal situation but the nature of the society in which he and others live. Others have suffered and will suffer, and it might be Kohlhaas's *duty* to take up the fight on behalf of all. So far so good: the stakes are high, the extent of the evil looks great, the courage to take on so large an issue is admirable.

But even so, we, and the narrator, still find Kohlhaas's next series of acts disturbing. Those comments of the narrator that betray this disturbance are in fact concerned with just this question of the scale of importance of Kohlhaas's mission. The series of manifestoes that Kohlhaas publishes shows a constant escalation of his sense of its importance. The first is a simple set of instructions to the people of the state not to harbor the Junker "bei Strafe Leibes und des Lebens" (34), which shows that Kohlhaas has arrogated to himself the power of the law to judge and punish. Later he calls himself "einen Reichs- und Weltfreien, Gott allein unterworfenen Herrn" (36), which seems to imply a claim to act in accordance with God's law. The narrator clearly displays anxiety over Kohlhaas's exaggerated sense of his mission and terms the wording of this manifesto a "Schwärmerei krankhafter und mißgeschaffener Art." But the claim becomes more explicit in the next manifesto, where Kohlhaas calls himself "einen Statthalter Michaels, des Erzengels" (41). Whenever anxiety over Kohlhaas's grandiose claims emerges, it raises with it the nagging question: were two stolen horses worth all this? Or, to be more correct, but even more disturbing: two forcibly borrowed horses. We need more to justify the grandiosity of the claim to be a "Statthalter Michaels." If Kohlhaas succeeds in overthrowing a corrupt government, his sense of himself and his mission might seem justified; he would have achieved something magnificent. But still, Saxony is not the world, so that Kohlhaas's signing the last manifesto "auf dem Sitz unserer provisorischen Weltregierung" will still seem disproportionate to what he is doing, even on the most favorable interpretation of what that is. The stage is not big enough for this language.

The violence of Kohlhaas's pursuit of the Junker also makes it necessary for the reader to think about the scale of importance of his cause. Some of the Junker's servants die a brutal death; some of the inhabitants of Wittenberg have their houses burned. According to the more trivial view of Kohlhaas's mission, these are innocent bystanders who have no connection with the Junker's stealing the horses, and they are the victims of Kohlhaas's indiscriminate, senseless rage. According to the grander view, they could be seen as the people who serve and acquiesce in the corrupt regime and so allow it to continue; the violence may be necessary for the social change that is the real point of what Kohlhaas is doing. Kohlhaas's apparent readiness to burn the convent at Erlabrunn might seem needlessly savage. But since its abbess turns out to be Wenzel's aunt, Antonia von Tronka, the same issue arises of how we are to conceive of what is at stake. Would this be the destruction of an arm of the corrupt establishment that seems to be everywhere and the removal of a part of the system by which the Tronka network maintains its oppressive power—or the senseless burning of a convent over a few horses by a man crazed with indiscriminate anger?

The next occasion on which we learn more about what it is that Kohlhaas opposes occurs when the Saxon court considers the letter from Luther. Another member of the establishment appears, a Count Kallheim who is the Saxon "Präsident der Staatskanzlei." Kleist does not even bother to tell us precisely who he is, to whom he is related, or how he fits into the corrupt network. We know that a Brandenburg official named Kallheim has been instrumental in dismissing Kohlhaas's complaint there, and that he is related by marriage to the Tronkas; all the narrator needs to do is to bring out another Kallheim without even giving him a first name (we never do learn it), and the reader simply raises his eyebrows and thinks: "Another one of them." And the more extensive the system of the corrupt establishment, the better Kohlhaas's cause looks. The narrator's giving us no information on this Kallheim seems to suggest that what we have seen is as yet only a small part of what there is to know—the mere tip of the iceberg.

At this point in the story Kohlhaas and his cause in any case begin to look better for other reasons. He disarms himself and his men, goes back into the courts, and a clear distinction begins to emerge between the honest men of the Saxon court, Count Wrede and Prince Christiern von Meissen, and the criminals, the Tronkas and Kallheims. His mission seems even to have been partly successful already: he has indeed forced the issue of corruption out into the open and in so doing may already have weakened the power of the Tronka-Kallheim complex.

The next development in our conception of Kohlhaas's adversary comes with the introduction of a new name: von Wenk. A von Wenk appears in the market place (60), and he is said to be a friend of Kunz. It is therefore distressing when we learn that after Prince von Meissen goes to spend some time at his estates his duties have been given to "dem Schloßhauptmann Freiherrn Siegfried von Wenk, einem Vetter des oben erwähnten Herren gleiches Namens" (70). What is most disturbing about this is not just that the man who appeared to be Kohlhaas's chief protector is replaced for the moment by a friend of Kunz; the darkest and thematically most important aspect of this fact is that one more arm of the establishment has appeared, another strand in the net of friends and families forming the system that Kohlhaas is up against. Another gloomy aspect of the situation is that the appearance of one honest man in a high position seems to have been a rare and temporary phenomenon on which we cannot rely. Behind such men, waiting to take their place and close the breach in the wall of the establishment, there are, it now seems, countless cousins, brothers-in-law, and cronies. The establishment network looks tighter and more menacing than ever. Kohlhaas seems to be in great danger, but on the other hand the reader is now more inclined to view him in a positive light, since the more extensive the corruption of the establishment, the more Kohlhaas's mission can be seen as a heroic and valuable one. Kohlhaas is understandably anxious when he sees that the character of the guard on him has suddenly changed from a few men acting as his bodyguards for his own protection to a greater number watching over him as if he were under arrest (72). His interview with Siegfried von Wenk establishes that their orders have indeed been deliberately changed, and thus that the amnesty has been broken. When Kohlhaas asks whether he is a prisoner, von Wenk confirms that he is.[15]

At this point we have the impression that the establishment easily bounces back just when great effort by dedicated men had managed to get it even partly under control. Kohlhaas's letter to Nagelschmidt is sometimes seen as a fatal error, but from Kohlhaas's point of view, and even that of the reader at this point in the story, it seems quite reasonable. It now appears that the establishment will never honor its promises or play by any rules, and that Kohlhaas made a mistake in divesting himself of the one thing that the corrupt system ever took seriously—armed force; and that impression only makes his earlier behavior seem the more justifiable.

What happens next only serves to reinforce this attitude. When the letter is captured, it shows clearly that Kohlhaas has written it only because he believes that the amnesty is broken. The Elector can now be in no doubt that his subordinates have broken the agreement between himself and Kohlhaas, and that Kohlhaas's action is not a breach of the agreement but a response to one on the Elector's side. But he seizes the excuse to proceed against Kohlhaas as if he were at fault. And instead of proceeding against those who broke the agreement and so dishonored him and his word, he promotes them and rids himself of one of the only two honest men in his administration! Wrede is removed, Kallheim is given his position, and Kunz is promoted to Kallheim's old post.[16] It is as if a flaw in the establishment network had been seen and quickly repaired.

The effect of all this is to allow the grand view of Kohlhaas's cause (a heroic challenge to a corrupt system) to gain ground at the expense of the more trivial version (excessive vengefulness over a few horses). And yet, we have curiously little information about the network of the establishment; its members seem to interlock by friendships and marriages and to conspire to protect their common interests, and so we assume that their motive is that of any corrupt oligarchy—the preservation and further aggrandizement of the power and wealth of those who already have it in great measure.

It is against this background of where the story and the reader stand that the revelations that open the strange final episode must be seen. We suddenly see the real shape of the relationships and motives that had seemed to constitute an evil, ever-present establishment of greedy and corrupt men, and we now realize that that impression was completely wrong. Kohlhaas is dealing not with an extensive and sinister network but with a few silly, weak people whose motives are trivial. From an interpretative standpoint, nothing could be more serious than this change; it alters everything.

The first important piece of information we are given is that Heloise is the wife of Kunz and sister of Count Kallheim of the Saxon court. At last we see the link between the Tronkas and the Kallheims, and it turns out not to be another greedy establishment power broker but instead a flirtatious woman. Instead of our former vague impression of a far-flung circle, we now have precise knowledge of one particular individual who is the actual link, and who turns out to be not another of the powerful male governmental figures but only a woman without office or personal power.

The establishment already seems much smaller and less threatening as a result of this first piece of information about Heloise; yet the second changes not merely our view of the extent of the alliance against Kohlhaas but more importantly still our impression of its nature and its motivation. That irrevocably changes the entire story. The information itself is simple: merely that Heloise had been the first love of the Elector's youth. But whereas Kohlhaas's whole moral position has depended on the gradual build-up of the impression that the state of Saxony was dominated by an evil and avaricious government mafia, we now see instead that the source of all the trouble is only the vague affection which the Elector feels for his first love, Heloise. There *is* no organized avaricious conspiracy. And as for the extent of the network of allegiances of interlocking families—it really goes not much further than Heloise's closest possible personal ties: her husband, her brother, her former lover. What lies behind Kohlhaas's troubles is not even a strong relationship with any great passion in it—it is only a vague warmth. Kleist deliberately makes the basis of the whole situation a trivial emotion and a trivial set of circumstances. The motive is not power or wealth but merely a weak man's sentimental attachment. The source of the Tronkas' and Kallheims' power lies not in their being part of a conspiratorial network but in their being the closest relatives of Heloise. This, then, is the reason for the Elector's always seeming strangely embarrassed by the Tronkas' and Kallheims' misdeeds instead of being wholeheartedly behind them: he is not a cruel tyrant but only a man trying weakly not to do anything to upset the Tronkas and Kallheims because he wants to protect his warm sentimental relationship with Heloise.

The information about Heloise, therefore, causes a wholesale retrospective reinterpretation of the value of Kohlhaas's cause and of the appropriateness of his behavior. But for the reader who has retained all the details of the earlier part of the story in his mind, things are now much, much worse than this; he will see with alarm that Kleist now shows that the trouble all arose because the Tronkas have essentially exploited a set of circumstances almost identical to circumstances that Kohlhaas himself tried to exploit earlier—and we did not think of that as corruption when it happened. That Wenzel's cousin secures favorable treatment at court by exploiting the Elector's still warm feelings towards his wife has a very uncomfortable precedent involving Kohlhaas himself. For Kohlhaas had happily acquiesced in his wife's plan to exploit a former admirer's similarly still warm feelings towards her to gain access to the Elector of Brandenburg. The parallel is frighteningly exact. Lisbeth told Kohlhaas that "der Kastellan des

kurfürstlichen Schlosses" (29) had formerly wooed her; that though
she and he were now married to others, "sie aber immer noch nicht
ganz vergessen wäre"; and that Kohlhaas should leave it to her "aus
diesem und manchem anderen Umstand . . . Vorteil zu ziehen." At
that earlier point in the story, the reader had been inclined to think
that this was only taking advantage of a fortunate accident; but we
must now accept the fact that Kohlhaas himself has readily agreed to
become tainted by an attempt to exploit an old flame's connection in
order to get a more favorable hearing at court. And this is exactly how
the Tronkas had managed to cheat him in the first place! Not only is
Kohlhaas guilty of the same shoddy morality that was the ultimate
source of the bad treatment he received in the courts, but that kind of
offense had seemed at worst a minor one when it had been reported
in Kohlhaas's case early in the story. And aside from Kohlhaas's
similar culpability, the scale of the offense is a vital issue in itself.
Even if we do condemn the Tronkas' behavior as corrupt, and even if
we overlook Kohlhaas's involvement in the same kind of behavior, all
of this now looks far too much like a question of human weakness
and far too trivial to support the notion of Kohlhaas's grand pursuit
of justice, his "große Dinge" that were needed to justify his total
commitment to a cause. The introduction of Heloise has changed the
entire thematic structure by opening up a huge disproportion between Kohlhaas's avenging angel behavior and the target against
which it is directed. Kohlhaas set out heroically to slay a dragon and
to root out corruption, avarice, injustice, and great evil, but instead
he finds a mouse and a mild weakness for a former love. After this,
the question of judging Kohlhaas as just or unjust simply cannot be
raised in the same way any more. The disproportion between his
actions and the real situation he was up against is not one that invites
a judgment about the justice of his position at all: what is most striking here is simply the absurdity of the discrepancy. An avenging
angel must have a grand opponent, but Kohlhaas, we now find, has
only a trivial man with a trivial motive. Was this something that could
justify the setting up of a new provisional world government?

A nicely calculated point is that there is not even an affair between
Heloise and the Elector, for that might seem a stronger factor in the
situation. Instead, a low-key situation is all Kleist allows to exist: the
Elector still feels affection for Heloise and likes her company, but that
is all. The Elector is a weakling in all that he does, bowing to pressures rather than making decisions, and his relationship with Heloise
is evidently much less than passionate. When Heloise wishes to see
the captive Kohlhaas, the Elector seems powerless to do anything
other than indulge her whim; and as he does so, he pronounces the

most important truth in the whole story: "Torheit, du regierst die Welt, und dein Sitz ist ein schöner weiblicher Mund!" (81). This apparently insignificant remark is the key to what was wrong with Kohlhaas's view of the world, and all the actions that sprang from that view. Foolishness does indeed rule the world and is the source of Kohlhaas's troubles; yet his whole stance has required that injustice rule the world. He has set out on a grand mission with sword in hand to root out injustice, bringing fire and destruction to those who resist, but all that is there to be rooted out is foolishness and susceptibility to the whims of a pretty woman. He seeks a tyrant to make a terrible example of him—but how can a frivolous weakling match up to the role that Kohlhaas's attitude assigns to him? The problem here is not that the Elector is guiltless, for he is not; what is thematically vital is that he operates on too trivial a level to be an appropriate target for Kohlhaas's righteous fury. The tragedy of Kohlhaas at the end of the story is not that he falls from being a model of perfect justice, or that he is sacrificed in the name of justice. It is that the world is too inconsistent, too disorganized, and too much influenced by whims and foolishness to be able to find a place for Kohlhaas's grandiose sense of mission.

It is, then, the introduction of Heloise and the consequent revelations about Kohlhaas's adversary—what had seemed to be the corrupt establishment—that produce a fundamental change in our concept of the story's thematic structure. The series of radical changes at all levels of the text that now follow serve to dramatize the point that this is no longer the story we thought it was. A profound conceptual change is reflected immediately in many changes at the surface level of the text. And the point of the bizarre impression of the story's later parts lies surely in its stressing that the world, society, and even Kohlhaas himself are not organized in so logical and consistent a manner as had seemed to be the case: the inconsequential and irrational are now allowed to appear.

Kohlhaas had always behaved as if the world were rational and consistent: if it misbehaves, it can be called to account; if it malfunctions, the malfunction must be located, diagnosed, and corrected; somewhere, there are people who are clearly in the wrong, and they can be distinguished from those who are not. The conversation with his wife (27) spelled out a logical and compelling case for his acts of protest and for the impossibility and even immorality of remaining silent, of allowing the defect in the state to go uncorrected. Kohlhaas's concern in that conversation was with the magnificent abstraction "Recht," but whenever there was any mention of the person who was withholding it from Kohlhaas, it was the impersonal "man" who seemed to be responsible. Later, Kohlhaas's conversation with Luther is again a clear and logical exposition of his reasoning; he argues that the individual gives up some of his own freedom in return for the protection of law, and if that protection is withdrawn, it follows logically that the resulting situation "gibt mir, wie wollt Ihr das leugnen, die Keule, die mich selbst schützt, in die Hand" (45). But Heloise's appearance changes everything; no longer can we think of what has happened as an individual's struggle against a cohesive group that acts consistently and with a clear understanding of what it is doing, as well as with a clear motive for doing so. Instead, there is only a disorganized, incoherent situation, in which the actors are just individuals who do not think very clearly, and whose motives are rather haphazard and trivial. It no longer seems possible to abstract from them an impersonal "man" who has a single-minded intent to deny "Recht" to Kohlhaas. And suddenly, the world looks very different: it is now a place full of strange irrational events, where superstition, coincidence and unexplained oddities prevail,[17] where men act on whim or out of sentiment rather than on the basis of consistent reasoning, where actions result not from grand principles but from smaller scale—even petty and trivial—motives, where anger and a desire to get even predominate, instead of a pursuit of abstract justice. The "magical" elements may at first sight make this world seem less realistic than it had formerly seemed, but that is an illusion; the point of the change is that that plausible earlier world is the unreal one that does not exist, and that the second world, for all its surface oddities, is the real world in which we and Kohlhaas live. As a result Kohlhaas himself does not seem to be the man he was—one who acted consistently and always on the basis of clear principles; that too was part of an illusion.

It is in the character of what Kohlhaas seeks that he seems most changed. Formerly he seemed to seek only justice: a just punishment for the Junker and a more just condition for society, one in which the legal system operates fairly. But the last section of the story has Kohlhaas doing something very different;[18] here he refuses to buy his own life by giving the Elector the capsule and tells him instead: "Ich aber kann dir weh tun, und ich wills!" (86). The emphasis is not on Kohlhaas's having abandoned his former regard for the principle of justice; the punishment the Elector will suffer is certain and is in the future, and Kohlhaas's act has *nothing to do* with bringing that punishment about. This is not an unjust action, then, but it is a petty action and as such contrasts with the formerly grand and noble pursuit of justice. All that is involved here is the Elector's anxiety about when and where he and his line will die out; Kohlhaas simply enjoys the thought that the Elector will suffer anxiety over what his punishment is to be. Kohlhaas himself has not necessarily changed, but the image presented of him does, and in just the same way that the story has changed. Formerly, he seemed to be above all a man who was ruled by an abstract idea of great importance, and who sought personal satisfaction in the notion that he was making the world a better place. Now he seems merely to be a human being capable of enjoying a much more local and immediate kind of satisfaction.[19]

To say that the Elector of Saxony is an insufficiently grand villain to allow room for Kohlhaas's grand heroism, and that the former in a way removes any place in the world for the latter, is not of course the same thing as saying that the Elector of Saxony is not the villain of the story—he is more centrally responsible than anyone and is the ultimate source of the injustice to Kohlhaas. Some critics have radically misconceived this scaling down and trivializing of the nature of his motivation and have seen it as absolving the Elector from responsibility.[20] But all that is changed here is the way in which he bears responsibility, not the fact of that responsibility. It is made abundantly clear that the Elector knows of the misdeeds committed in his name, that he does nothing to stop them, that he promotes those who commit them, that he avoids steps that will set things right at the cost of jeopardizing the wrongdoer, and that he takes steps that correspond to a just course of action only when he is compelled to or has no alternative that is not immediately more dangerous for him. The discussion at court of Luther's letter to the Elector, for example (49), makes clear that the Elector knows everything, that he is not surprised or outraged by it, and that he is concerned to protect the wrongdoers, while never once expressing disapproval of what they have done. Kohlhaas's letter to Nagelschmidt makes clear to him that the amnesty has been broken by his subordinates. This is further confirmed when he fails to use the Nagelschmidt letter in his complaint against Kohlhaas to the Imperial court "wegen der zweideutigen und unklaren Umstände, unter welchen er geschrieben war" (79). Yet he had earlier had no scruples about those "unclear" circumstances when using the letter as a pretext to condemn Kohlhaas and to remove the honest Wrede from the government. The clearest demonstration of the fact that weakness is not the same as innocence of responsibility can be seen in his response, which is only embarrassment, when he learns of the crimes committed in his name; again and again he is "verlegen." When Christiern von Meissen asserts bluntly that Kunz must be brought to trial, the Elector "wandte sich, indem er über das ganze Gesicht rot ward, und trat ans Fenster" (51). He clearly does not *like* what Kunz does; but how would he face

Heloise if he had to prosecute her husband? The thought is evidently too much for him.

When the Elector decides to take the course of action proposed by Count Wrede, he might seem to side with the opinions of a just man, but the text makes it clear that his motives are very different from Wrede's. First and foremost, he thinks this the best way to avoid the prosecution of Kunz. And in other respects, Wrede's view seems to him the most *expedient* ("zweckmäßig" [52]); military confrontation with Kohlhaas could be dangerous since the "Unziemlichkeiten" of Kunz's rule had caused much unrest in the state, and that could work to Kohlhaas's advantage. Remarkably enough, then, the Elector's reasons include a clear recognition of Kunz's corruptness quite apart from Kohlhaas's case *and* a desire to protect Kunz and keep him in his office nonetheless! The Elector evidently has no political judgment, no concern with justice, and would really like people to stop bothering him with issues that interefere with what he really cares about: his friends, his parties, and Heloise. As such, he is really very like Wenzel von Tronka. Both sin through omission more than through commission. Both know of their corrupt subordinates' acts and try to protest that they were not responsible. Both are weak men, who when called on to face issues become "verlegen," or blush, or go pale. Both are more worthy of contempt than hate; and both are usually seen to be interested in trivial pursuits. Like the Elector, Wenzel is too concerned with a hunt in the company of his cronies to accept responsibility for what is being done in his name.

The Elector of Brandenburg is in clear contrast to the Elector of Saxony. He can make a mistake (in his appointment of Kallheim) but moves to correct that mistake as soon as he knows of it. To argue that Brandenburg's mistake makes the two Electors comparable would be to miss the point that the initial similarity (a corrupt official in the court of each) is used precisely to distinguish them. Brandenburg's Kallheim is an isolated instance and is quickly removed. By contrast, the Elector of Saxony makes a *practice* of hiring corrupt officials—the Tronkas, the Kallheims, the Wenks—and does not regard them as mistakes when their corrupt actions become visible; he promotes them in light of their characteristic kind of service, and roots out *his* few "mistakes"—the appointment of an honest man now and then—as soon as he has an excuse to do so.[21] The execution of Kohlhaas might at first sight seem a disappointing action on the part of the Elector of Brandenburg in that it distances him from Kohlhaas. But precisely the reverse is the case, for it is by this act that the Elector shows himself fully to share Kohlhaas's perspective. Like Kohlhaas, he is a man who places principles before people. Consider, for example, the narrator's saying that Kohlhaas's sentence was one, "das die ganze Stadt, bei dem Wohlwollen das der Kurfürst für den Kohlhaas trug, unfehlbar durch ein Machtwort desselben, in eine bloße, vielleicht beschwerliche und langwierige Gefängnisstrafe verwandelt zu sehen hoffte" (94–95). We see the point of this comment if we remember the narrator's prior remark about the Elector of Saxony having a "für Freundschaft sehr empfängliches Herz" (52), and we realize that the Elector of Brandenburg will act out of pure regard for justice and not be swayed at all by his liking for Kohlhaas. If he acted otherwise, he would be doing what the Elector of Saxony has done and distancing himself from Kohlhaas in a more fundamental way. Kohlhaas himself recognizes this and, far from protesting, is at last at peace in his last few days. He even acknowledges that he is satisfied with the actions of his ruler—more, he is overcome with joy by them. The ending is not simply pure justice—it is Kohlhaas's own kind of justice, administered by Kohlhaas's own kind of man. The Elector even speaks to Kohlhaas in his own language: "Nun, Kohlhaas, heut ist der Tag, an dem dir dein Recht geschieht!" (101). Small wonder that Kohlhaas is satisfied with a ruler who is almost a copy of himself. It is an important paradox that this man of meticulous principle is the one who finally executes Kohlhaas; his severity has of course something dreadful about it, but that just shows again that all men of principle can be, like Kohlhaas, both "rechtschaffen" and "entsetzlich."

The Martin Luther of the story may not seem like Kohlhaas, but his place in the thematic structure also depends on a certain kind of similarity with him. Clifford A. Bernd is certainly correct in arguing that Luther's positions in his argument with Kohlhaas are inconsistent and illogical, emotional and altogether indefensible.[22] His letter confuses the two Electors, his offer to Kohlhaas of conditional absolution is theologically and morally indefensible, and his reasoning is confused when he equates Kohlhaas's forgiving Wenzel with dropping the lawsuit against him. But why does Kleist use such a Luther in his story? The answer lies surely in Silz's perception that Luther himself is a kind of former Kohlhaas, a man who followed his own sense of what was right in spite of opposition from the organized church, and who led a rebellion against the establishment on grounds of conscience.[23] Kohlhaas and Luther both defy the system because of a strong conviction within themselves of what is right. But there is an ironic side to this identity of the two, for Luther is a successful rebel whose rebellion against the system has now become the system, and he is now just as resentful of and impatient with any challenge to the status quo as any of his former foes were. The just rebellion has become the establishment, and it too soon begins to lose sight of its

first concern with natural justice; Luther responds to Kohlhaas's simple logic with confused and muddled emotional arguments for expediency and conformity. How to get rid of an embarrassing problem is
now the main concern of this man who once believed in following
one's conscience wherever it may lead. How soon would Kohlhaas
too become complacent if he were to be as successful as Luther? The
thematic significance of Luther in the story lies in yet another undermining of the demand implicit in all that Kohlhaas does that the
world and everyone in it behave consistently and logically. If Luther,
of all people, can tell Kohlhaas that he should not have rebelled
against higher authority, how can we hope that Kohlhaas will retain
his keen sense of justice once his own crusade is over, and when he
has no personal stake in a given situation? Inertia, confusion, and
simple comfort—not necessarily evil and injustice—are the real problems with which idealists like Kohlhaas cannot deal, but they are so
much part of the human scene that even a man conspicuously like
Kohlhaas in temperament can embody them, whereby they represent
a major problem for him. Luther's response can be summed up as a
feeling that Kohlhaas, however much right is on his side, is a nui-
sance; and that he should feel so means that the text has given heavy
stress to the notion that human beings find great causes a disturbance
to their comfort.

Yet even if the end of *Michael Kohlhaas* seems to drive a wedge
between Kohlhaas's grandiose sense of mission and the trivial reality
of the Elector's weakness and frivolity, and to stress the disproportion
between the two and therefore the inappropriateness of what he
does, it still expresses a different and more positive judgment on him
by means of a curious and surprisingly consistent series of rewards
and punishments for the main actors of the story: his behavior may
not be vindicated, but he is still, in a way, admirable. Wenzel's punishment is trivial and ignominious, entirely in keeping with his character
and his offense. For Kohlhaas himself, the situation is complicated
but still intelligible. There is for him a grand final scene: its grandeur
is a comment on him and his having aspired to something that might
have been a great mission. Yet he is still executed, which underlines
the sad fact that what he aspired to was not ultimately well directed.
The most appropriate judgment of Kohlhaas's actions is not that they
were just *or* unjust, but that they were inappropriate for the disorganized world that exists, one in which the adversary he required to
make sense of his actions could not be found. In an unjust world,
Kohlhaas could have been a hero; but in the much more normal
situation of a foolish world, he is out of place. It may be partly a
matter of luck: Kohlhaas might have run into one of those historically

much rarer situations (much more recent German history provides an example) in which a sinister and evil conspiracy really existed, but instead he could only find a group of weak, inconsistent people. Even so, in the contrast between his end and that of the Elector of Saxony, the story gives full weight and value to his grandeur as opposed to the Elector's triviality. In contrast to the magnificent scene of Kohlhaas's death, the Elector suffers a slow and ignominious fading from the scene, a fitting end for an ignominious man who never could face up to issues squarely, always avoiding them and trying to put them off. Now his own death, though certain, eludes him, and he suffers the anxiety of not being allowed to face that issue squarely either, as though it were temporizing with him just as he had always temporized with every serious issue that had come before him in the past.

An even more important element in the final rewards and punishments is seen in the fates of Kohlhaas and the two Electors: it concerns the future of their names and their descendants. The Elector of Brandenburg will reign long, as will his whole line; his descendants will "zu Macht gelangen, vor allen Fürsten und Herren der Welt!" as the gypsy says (91). Meanwhile, Kohlhaas's sons are knighted, and the last words of the story tell of the long survival of his family into the eighteenth century. The Elector of Saxony, on the other hand, will have his line die out. This set of punishments and rewards is a classic one in the Old Testament.[24] The God of the Old Testament is at His most severe when He not only destroys a man but obliterates all traces of him by having him leave no descendants and therefore no name behind him. On the other hand, His greatest reward is a prophesy that a man's children and his children's children will prosper; a long and thriving line is the highest sign of God's blessing. Without necessarily bearing any theological weight, this system of punishment and reward is peculiarly appropriate to the kinds of good and bad features displayed by the characters throughout the story. The Elector of Saxony is a weak man who allows his government to operate corruptly, but though he is as a ruler ultimately responsible, he is not guilty of direct malicious action; and so he meets no direct and immediate punishment other than being made to suffer all the anxiety that he had tried to avoid by ruling carelessly and thoughtlessly. Ultimately, however, he suffers a punishment that is severe and appropriate: he is to fade away without a trace, into the oblivion that so trivial a man richly deserves. He and his descendants are to be removed from the throne and disappear from sight. Kohlhaas is a misfit who badly misjudges how the world works, and whose pursuit of a clearly diagnosable fault causes havoc in a world that is too disorganized and inconsistent to present him with a target worthy of

his mission; his execution is a necessary result of that discrepancy.
And yet he does make an impact on the world; he might in different
circumstances even have been a legendary hero. It is fitting then that
he will have an impact on posterity, and that he will be remembered.
Though his actions were so inappropriate to the world as it was that
he was justly executed by his alter ego, the Elector of Brandenburg,
the story registers its admiration for him by allowing him a future
comparable to that of the Elector—his name and his line will flourish
well into the future.

VI

Prinz Friedrich von Homburg

Few other works of German literature have aroused as much critical interest as *Prinz Friedrich von Homburg*,[1] but even fewer can have been the subject of such persistent and basic disagreement among its interpreters. Nevertheless, there has at least been a kind of consensus as to where the focus of debate should be; what has always divided the critics has been the question whether the values represented by the Elector or those associated with the Prince prevail at the end of the play, and what those contrasting values are. A majority have seen the Elector's values as prevailing, but a significant minority judge that the Prince's are really the dominant values; and even those who have preferrred a compromise solution in which both sets of values contribute to the play's solution, while avoiding the usual choice, have still accepted the terms of reference of their predecessors—that is, a concern with the question who of the two men is right and who is wrong.

The outlines of the main attitudes to the play so far can be set out easily enough in terms of the debate about the predominance of the values of one or the other of its main figures. The Elector has been praised as a wise and farsighted man, as a representative of impartial justice, as the embodiment of the law, as an advocate of self-discipline and restraint, as one who acts prudently and responsibly while encouraging others to do likewise, as a clever educator of the Prince, as a great leader and statesman, as a champion of reason, as one who shows the claims of the state to be higher than those of the individual, as a splendid example of the Kantian ethic, as an embodiment of the best Prussian values, and as a German national figure. The Prince is then judged to be irresponsible, impetuous, selfish, undisciplined, careless of his duty to society, imprudent and foolish, immature, and the Elector's apprentice. The Prince, in the contrasting view, has been valued as the gifted individual who is above the dictates of society, as one who respects the spirit rather than the letter of the law, as a man who values human feeling more than cold reason, as an advocate of the superiority of individual judgment over mere obedience, as a human being who refuses to be a mere pawn in the Elector's game, as a figure who shows the need for the exercise of free will, as a colorful personality instead of a lifeless abstraction (which, by implication, the Elector is), as a creative rather than an imitative person, and (also) as a German national figure.

Both sides have been able plausibly enough to claim some support from the text, but that also means that both have found it hard to deal with those parts of the text usually cited by the other side. The first view has never really been able to explain away the fact that the Elector we see in the text is often "verwirrt," sometimes displays unwarranted anger, plays a dubious joke on the Prince that evidently embarrasses him enough to make him want to conceal it, and takes no action to remove from an important command a commander who is obviously unreliable. The second view has even more trouble with the Prinz Friedrich of the text, who is too obviously selfish and ego-centric for him to be plausibly considered the central figure in the value system of the play. Gerhard Fricke, by far the most dominant of this group of interpreters, justifies his stance by a retreat into a meta-physical discussion that is mostly woolly, abstruse, and often incomprehensible;[2] it is all too obvious that his discussion would not have been easily conducted in close proximity to Kleist's text.

The regrettable fact is, however, that *both* sides in this perennial dispute have tended to lead the discussion away from the detail of what Kleist wrote—Fricke into general metaphysics and those more sympathetic to the Elector into equally general discussions of legal issues (e.g., should one always obey orders?) that have also soon lost sight of the context of Kleist's play. The result is that all kinds of details of the text—those that were not of immediate relevance to a rather narrowly rationalistic discussion of the question which of the two men was to be preferred to the other—have been completely ignored. A dramatic example of this can be seen in a remarkable set of parallel passages from the first and last acts of the play. In the first, the following scene takes place:

DER KURFÜRST *über ihn gebeugt.*
Was für ein Laub denn flicht er?—Laub der Weide?

HOHENZOLLERN.
Was! Laub der Weid, o Herr!—Der Lorbeer ists,
Wie ers gesehn hat, an der Helden Bildern,
Die zu Berlin im Rüstsaal aufgehängt.

DER KURFÜRST.—Wo fand er den in meinem märkschen Sand?

HOHENZOLLERN. Das mögen die gerechten Götter wissen!

DER HOFKAVALIER. Vielleicht im Garten hinten, wo der Gärtner
Mehr noch der fremden Pflanzen auferzieht.

(46–53)

To this there is a striking parallel in the last act:

DER PRINZ VON HOMBURG.
Ach, wie die Nachtviole lieblich duftet!
—Spürst du es nicht?
Stranz kommt wieder zu ihm zurück.

STRANZ. Es sind Levkojn und Nelken.

DER PRINZ VON HOMBURG.
Levkojn?—Wie kommen die hierher?

STRANZ. Ich weiß nicht.—
Es scheint, ein Mädchen hat sie hier gepflanzt.
—Kann ich dir eine Nelke reichen?

DER PRINZ VON HOMBURG. Lieber!—
Ich will zu Hause sie in Wasser setzen.

(1840–45)

Among the many parallels between the first and last acts of the
play, this is surely one of the most intriguing. Both passages are
seemingly irrelevant, occur in a garden setting, and include a discussion of plants. Both are question-and-answer sequences in which one
character mistakes the identity of a plant, is corrected by the other,
and then asks how the plant came to be growing there; and in both
the answer given is strangely vague. Equally striking are the changes
highlighted by these parallels: in the first passage the plants are trees,
in the second, flowers; the questioner in the first is the Elector, in the
second, the Prince; the "Gärtner" of the first exchange has become a
girl in the second; and the use made of the plants in the first is absent
in the second. It would seem that this very obtrusive and apparently
systematic series of similarities and differences is intended to provide
some clue to the meaning of the play.

But, obtrusive as this is, only one of the many hundreds of critics of
the play has ever seen and commented on it, and he wrote over forty
years ago.[3] There is in fact a great deal in this play that is not directly
and immediately relevant to the debate over the moral and legal
rectitude of the Prince and Elector, and it has received scant attention
from critics whose main concern was that debate.

There is, of course, a level of the play that is concerned with the
rational discussion of moral and legal issues, and if we read the play

only on that level, we can easily reach conclusions such
ing: when the Prince is ordered to play a certain part in
duty is made clear to him, but he disobeys orders, there
ing the outcome of the battle. Whether he does so wilfu
misunderstanding would not matter, for a general ig
orders is guilty of gross negligence, and in any case
reminded of them. The result of his disobedience is to
Elector's plan that no significant part of the opposing
able to escape. The Prince's action may have necessita
battle, and hence caused the loss of many lives in the a
denburg. The Elector wished to save these lives; the Prir
sible for them. He is therefore accused by his commande
found guilty in a court of his fellow officers. The accuser,
could not have acted otherwise without endangering the state; the
Elector would have failed in his duty to protect his subjects and
soldiers had he not prosecuted the Prince. The Prince is pardoned
only when it becomes clear that he is no longer a danger to the state
but will instead be a useful part of its protective apparatus.

There is nothing wrong with such an argument as far as it goes; yet
the crucial point here is that this is not an interpretation of the play
but instead only one element of the text, a part to be taken together
with other parts if an overall interpretation is to be achieved. The play
constantly hints that this is only one of its levels, and that another
level contrasts with it and has an equal right to be taken into account.
In a great variety of ways, Kleist makes it clear that his play has a dual
structure, and that the overt, rational discussion of moral and legal
issues represents only one side of that structure.

The first and most obvious way in which the contrasting levels are
suggested lies in the settings of the play, which place the middle part
of the drama in strong contrast to the first and final scenes. The
former, which includes the major plot events of the play, takes place
in the daytime; the latter at night. The contrast is between light and
dark both physically and metaphorically. In the daylight scenes the
actions of the characters seem to be in plain view with no conceal-
ment; but in the garden at night a darker side of human nature becomes visible. In these two settings are also contrasted the realm of
nature and that of civilization. The setting of buildings and battle
orders is harshly real and linked with the existence of the state and its
security; the garden scene is one of exotic fantasy. In the one sphere
things are apparently orderly and predictable, man-made and given
shape by his conscious planning; in the other sphere there is growth
according to the laws of nature, which are less predictable. As we
shall see, natural growth serves as a symbol of that area of human

behavior that can never be controlled. A further contrast implicit in this division of scenes lies in the behavior of the characters. Outside the garden there is much rational discussion guided by apparently clear and conscious motivation: the plans for the battle, the arguments toward the end of the play, the analysis of the battle, and so forth. By contrast, we see in the garden a display of emotions, desires, and unconsciously held attitudes.

It is commonly observed that the Prince allows his unconscious mind and emotions to be seen in the garden; but the same is no less true of the otherwise highly rational Elector. He is at first curious, then plays an odd and tantalizing, even cruel jest; after that he speaks aggressively with his admonition "Ins Nichts" (74) and later seems embarrassed at how he has behaved. Once out of the garden, his rational side asserts itself and he sends a message to Hohenzollern not to tell the Prince anything of what has happened. Both Prince and Elector were unaware of themselves, behaving irrationally, and allowing their deepest feelings and attitudes to come to the surface. The difference—a very interesting and important one—is that the Elector immediately moves to cover up what has appeared in the garden with his message to Hohenzollern.

Part of the play's concern with the coexistence of two levels of behavior can also be seen in the way that relationships between two characters always have a private and a public aspect. They relate to each other as one state or military functionary to another but are also conspicuously friends and relatives. They have public duties and private loyalties, responsibilities involved in their positions but also responsibilities to friends and relatives. The former are comparatively clear and easily formulated while the latter are more complex and less easily understood. That the double relationships complicate matters in the play is obvious. Consider Natalie's relationship to the Prince: he is to her a loved one, a brother officer, and a relative. That of the Prince to the Elector is even more complex, in fact intolerably complicated: they are commander in chief and subordinate officer, relatives, head of state and subject, and also judge and accused. Even more important are two strands of the situation that are matters of attitude rather than of hard fact: the relationship is similar to that of father and son (e.g., lines 67 and 1784) and as a result creates the impression of also being that of head of state and heir apparent (e.g., lines 585–86). Part of the strategy of the play is evidently to introduce so many elements into their relationship that the personal and the public interests cannot be separated from each other.

Once again, it is most clearly the Prince who allows personal matters to interfere with public duties. But, equally, a somewhat closer

look at the Elector's behavior shows a similar situation. Take, for
example, the scene in which the orders for the coming battle are read
out. We may well wonder why the Elector allows a family group to be
present at a conference of his general staff. But even more strange is
the fact that he intersperses a series of questions, commands, and
exclamations during the reading of the battle orders, all having to do
with the family group (267, 285, 287, 289, 312, 315), and that in so
doing he persistently diverts the Prince's attention from his orders,
for these interruptions always occur at key points in the instructions
to the Prince. Take the first example of those cited:

FELDMARSCHALL. Der Prinz von Homburg—

DER KURFÜRST *erhebt sich gleichfalls.*   —Ist Ramin bereit?
                                                          (267)

Just as the Prince's orders are to begin, the Elector interrupts; in lines
281–83 the Prince's position on the battlefield is being dictated, and in
line 285 the Elector causes another diversion by interrupting to ask
what is troubling Natalie; and as he is moving offstage with the
women, he draws attention to the glove, which leaves the Prince
completely confused and repeating, but not understanding, the line
"Dann wird er die Fanfare blasen lassen" (322).

Just as in Act I, it is the Elector who creates the situation that leads
to the Prince's downfall; here he draws the Prince's attention away
from the battle orders three times, and previously he had given added
impetus to the Prince's dreams of glory. We must surely wonder what
the Elector is doing, for he seems to be inviting the behavior for
which he will condemn the Prince.

Another indicator of the play's dual structure can be seen in the
two different ways in which it moves forward. On the one hand,
there is a clear plot outline, a story of a subordinate who disobeys an
order and is condemned to death for it. It is possible to give a scene-
by-scene résumé of the way the plot moves forward and tells this
story, very much as one might summarize the historical source. Yet
on the other hand, this clear outline is interspersed with numerous
enigmatic episodes that do not (apparently) contribute to the development of the plot and are not even clearly motivated. From the
standpoint of the "objective" plot events (disobedience, judgment,
battle, state, etc.), they might be and sometimes have been considered
redundant. They certainly arrest the main action. Examples of such
episodes are the parallel question and answer sequences that I have
cited above; another outstanding example is the conversation between
the Prince and Hohenzollern in which the former relates his sup-

posed dream (Act I, Scene 4). This conversation is concerned mostly with the Prince's failure to remember the identity of the figure in the dream, who was in fact Natalie. The scene lasts from lines 87 to 218, and the question comes up repeatedly from line 146 to 203. After the eventful but much shorter first scene, this one seems slow and perhaps irrelevant. It moves in a halting and confused way:

DER PRINZ VON HOMBURG.
. . . .

Der Kurfürst und die Fürstin und die—dritte,
—Wie heißt sie schon?

HOHENZOLLERN.   Wer?

DER PRINZ VON HOMBURG *er scheint zu suchen*.
                              Jene—die ich meine!
Ein Stummgeborner würd sie nennen können!

HOHENZOLLERN. Die Platen?

DER PRINZ VON HOMBURG.   Nicht doch, Lieber!

HOHENZOLLERN.   Die Ramin?

DER PRINZ VON HOMBURG.
Nicht, nicht doch, Freund!

                                        (146–50)

This confused search for the name continues, is dropped, is then picked up again (165–70), is dropped again, and then taken up once more (192–94). All of this looks aimless, repetitive, and unnecessary; but if we are attentive, we can discover an underlying logic. In lines 146–56, the Prince denies that the name he seeks is Platen or Ramin, but after his cry "Lieber" (164) things change; he then consistently says it may be one of those two, while Hohenzollern badgers him for the correct name. What this exchange really shows is the Prince first trying to remember, finally succeeding in line 164, now realizing that it is dangerous to admit the name, and covering up what he has remembered. Meanwhile, Hohenzollern is anxious because he knows the name, does not want the Prince to remember, and is alarmed because there are signs that he has. Thus Kleist makes us concerned with what is happening in the minds of his characters when odd, inconsequential exchanges occur; if we confine ourselves to the rational, explicit argument of the play without careful attention to the many odd little episodes that apparently arrest its action, we shall miss the entire other level of its meaning.

The play itself draws attention to the question how oddness of behavior in its characters is to be regarded. Already in Act I, we see contrasting attitudes taken to the Prince's sleepwalking. Natalie and the Electress both take it very seriously and say that the young man is sick. But Hohenzollern retorts that this is "eine bloße Unart seines Geistes" (39), a narrowly rationalist disregard for the possible significance of irrational behavior. It is of great importance that Hohenzollern, of all people, should later become the chief spokesman for the opposing point of view, that the odd behavior in the garden should have been taken much more seriously; the play shows him learning to understand much more of what is happening than he was at first willing to see. But by contrast, the Elector is shown to be very reluctant to progress beyond his rationalist disregard for the significance of the oddities of the Prince's behavior—or of his own. He regards his action in the garden as merely a "Scherz" (83) in the first act and still sees it as a harmless joke in the last act (1717). But his attempt to cover up what has happened shows that he is really more worried by what he has done than he will admit, and his uncharacteristic anger in the last act shows that he is still worried then; he surely senses that his making fun of the Prince had a serious side to it because it related to his own sensitivity to the Prince's grandiose dreams and his wish to cut them down.

The very language of the play constantly stresses it dual structure. Passages constituting prosaic accounts of military or legal matters alternate with striking imagery; and clear, explicit, and well-formed language expressing coherent reasoning can alternate with obscure, enigmatic, and dislocated language whose unstated implications must be thought over carefully.

By a variety of means, then, the play makes us aware that much is happening beneath the surface in the relationship of the Prince and the Elector, and that we should be careful to see through that surface and the simple view of the Prince's guilt that it suggests. The play's dual structure requires us to take the explicit, legalistic argument over the Prince's action in the context of all that is less clear and explicit in the text. If we wish to gain a more inclusive view of the central relationship that does justice to both levels of the play, there is no better way to begin than by looking at all that is *implicit* in the situation with which the play begins.

By the end of the second scene of Act II, the Prince has disobeyed orders, but even earlier, in Act I, his disobedience seems not improbable. How does this initial situation come about, and who is instrumental in producing it? In Act I, the Elector complains that the Prince has recently thrown away ("verscherzt") two victories (349–52).

But this judgment by the Elector contrasts strangely with Dörfling's announcement that the Elector will entrust the cavalry to the command of the Prince, "ruhmvoll, wie bei Rathenow" (274). Why does the Elector persevere with so irresponsible a commander? His behavior continues to suggest irresponsibility (21); and Dörfling obviously thinks that his failing to follow his orders is likely once more (340–42). Quite apart from his proven and continuing lack of responsibility, there is also some question as to the Prince's suitability for a tactical role in the battle. All that we see of the Prince at this early stage suggests that he is a bold and vigorous leader in a direct assault (e.g., line 3) rather than a shrewd tactician, and this is entirely consistent with his later actions, in which we see him lead a cavalry charge with more gusto than intelligence. The Prince is neither disciplined nor skilled in strategy, but he is a brave and inspiring fighter; he should obviously be used to lead a frontal assault, not given a tactical waiting role.

By contrast, the Elector himself is an older and wiser man, an experienced strategist with a wide vision. He has an eye not merely to this battle but to past and future ones. He is the opposite of the Prince in his usefulness to the army. He is unlikely to be a good leader in a spearhead attack and is much better employed in a strategic role. Their roles are naturally opposed.

If we were to ask which role is the most vital, the answer would have to be that of the Elector; an excellent strategist is worth far more to an army than one courageous and inspiring attacker. If, on the other hand, we ask which is the more appealing role, which is more celebrated when victory occurs and wins the admiration of the public, the answer will be that of the Prince. The image of the vigorous, courageous young cavalry leader has greater appeal than that of the schemer who controls the battle from behind the lines.

We must bear all this in mind when considering a very strange fact about the Elector's battle plan: he reverses what, according to their abilities, would be the natural order of their roles. The Prince is placed in a waiting role; the Elector, on the other hand, takes a leading part in the main assault.[4] The battle will be decided by the time the Prince comes into it, and he and his men are to be used not in a spearhead attack on the enemy but as a tactical reserve with which the broken remnants of the Swedish army are to be finished off. The Prince's efforts are to be directed not toward the victory of this particular day but to preventing the possibility of a future Swedish army arising to regroup and attack again. The opposite is true of the Elector, who must lead the glorious main assault that will win or lose the battle. The Elector's reversal of their roles is puzzling behavior; the Prince behaves strangely too, but, unlike the Elector, his oddities are more obvious. The oddness of the Elector's behavior only becomes fully apparent when we think about it. Why should such a brilliant strategist make such a bad mistake in using the various talents available to him?

The inappropriateness of the initial positions assigned to the Prince and the Elector in the battle is emphasized by the fact that *both* reverse their positions during the course of the battle. It is more obvious that the Prince does not finish the battle as he was intended to. But equally, the Elector does not remain the leader of the main assault. Froben sees how unwise this is and persuades him to dismount from his conspicuous horse, after which he "kehrt zurück, wohin sein Amt ihn ruft" (672). His "Amt" is commander in chief, not front-line attack, and he fades out of the battle. Both, then, revert from their initial inappropriate roles to their natural roles. Sparren's later account stresses how unwise it was for the Elector to be in this conspicuous position, and how he was "jeder Warnung taub" (641). And this surely gives the game away: the Elector wants the glamorous role for himself, and his battle plan is in part designed to keep his dashing young relative well clear of that role, waiting on the sidelines until the main part of the battle is over. And we should notice also that a small detail of Sparren's account ("wie bis heut noch stets geschah" [644]) emphasizes that this attempt to seize the center of the battle is a compulsive habit of the Elector's; he always wants to be there. The answer to the question why so shrewd a strategist should make such a bad mistake in his command assignments—and indeed the key to all the other strange things the Elector does—must lie in the considerable competitiveness and rivalry revealed in the Elector's attitude to the Prince. The older man is jealous of the public acclaim that the dashing young cavalry leader receives. It is obvious on the surface that the Prince's dreams of glory make him neglect his duty to the state; what is less obvious but no less true is that the Elector's personal ambitions and feelings cause him to fail in his responsibility to the state. The Elector may seem at first to be a man who represents law, reason, and public responsibility, and at the conscious level he may be; but at a deeper level his behavior is as irrational and irresponsible as that of the Prince, and just as dangerous.[5] The legal argument as to the Prince's guilt for disobeying his orders is of course absolutely watertight; but the point is that the Elector has, consciously or unconsciously, set up a situation in which that would almost predictably happen. He assigns to a habitually disobedient and irresponsible general a role in which he can only exercise his natural abilities (and win the acclaim that those abilities would naturally earn) *if* he disobeys his orders. The Prince deceives no one but himself into believing that the interests of the state and his own coincide; but when the Elector confuses his own wishes with the good of the state, he is indulging in a far more subtle form of self-deception that is more plausible to everyone else, and so deceives them too. His irrational acts have at their service a superb rationalism that can cover and defend them, and the Prince is by contrast quite defenseless. The play is in fact built on the contrast between the obviously irrational and irresponsible man and the highly rational, responsible ruler whose underlying irrationality is the real source of the trouble.

The very excuses which some critics have made for the strangeness of what the Elector does in his battle assignments only underline their irrationality.[6] Some have argued that his placing the older Kottwitz at the Prince's side is a safeguard against the young man's irresponsibility. But that only draws more attention to the Elector's ineptitude; he knows Kottwitz well, and it can surely be no surprise that Kottwitz is so like the Prince that, far from restraining him, he joins in the charge with gusto. To assign Kottwitz to the Prince's side is more likely to bring out irresponsibility in the Prince than suppress it. Antoher excuse sometimes put forward has been that the Elector is magnanimously giving the Prince another chance after his two prior failures. But that only makes us ponder another oddness of what the Elector does: a third chance is a big risk, and a commander in chief who does such a thing takes upon himself a big responsibility. How strange it is that so lucid and reasonable a man as the Elector never considers his own record of command, his own misjudgment, his own repeated failure to serve the state by managing its military affairs competently, his own risking the security of the state over and over again with a commander who has a proven record of irresponsibility! A third debacle must surely be more the responsibility of the Elector as commander in chief than that of the Prince himself.

The fundamental basis of the clash between Prince and Elector lies in their both wanting to occupy the same position, a fact that is emphasized by their both bearing the name "Friedrich"; and this is obviously the reason for the Elector's curiosity about the Prince's ambition in the first act ("Ich muß doch sehn, wie weit er's treibt" [64]) as well as the emphatic and contemptuous rejection of that ambition:

> Ins Nichts mit dir zurück, Herr Prinz von Homburg,
> Ins Nichts, ins Nichts! In dem Gefild der Schlacht,
> Sehn wir, wenns dir gefällig ist, uns wieder!
> Im Traum erringt man solche Dinge nicht!

(74–77)

The Elector's final comment here is not only completely discrepant in tone with his later characterization of the whole incident in the garden as a "Scherz" (1709); it is also discrepant with his plan for the battle. Having taunted the Prince with the fact that he must win fame and glory in the harsh reality of the battlefield, not in dreams, the Elector then assigns him a role in the battle that effectively precludes his winning "solche Dinge."

The early scene in the garden is unique as far as the figure of the Elector is concerned; we do not see his emotional response to a situation displayed to the same extent at any other point in the play. Yet this early scene should make us skeptical of the Elector's rational exterior, and if we look closely at his actions, we can see remarkable inconsistencies. Take, for example, his attitude to the law. Many critics have thought him admirable in his placing respect for the law above personal considerations, even to the extent of condemning his young cousin to death. But he is actually very inconsistent in this respect. Natalie forges an order from him without authorization (1486–97), but he covers up this deliberate act of insurrection on his niece's part and does not allow it to come to a court-martial. A little earlier, the Elector has good reason to suspect Kottwitz of mutiny but in relaxed fashion says that there is no reason here to talk of a death sentence (1414), which only a tyrant like the "Dei von Tunis" would do in such circumstances:

> Doch weils Hans Kottwitz aus der Priegnitz ist,
> Der sich mir naht, willkürlich, eigenmächtig,
> So will ich mich auf märksche Weise fassen:
> Von den drei Locken, die man silberglänzig,
> Auf seinem Schädel sieht, faß ich die eine,
> Und führ ihn still, mit seinen zwölf Schwadronen,
> Nach Arnstein, in sein Hauptquartier, zurück.
>
> (1417–23)

But where the Prince is concerned, the Elector *reverses* this argument; the way of a ruler who acts "auf märksche Weise" is here impartial application of the law without favor to anyone and total respect for the law in itself; he tells Natalie that he could only act otherwise if he were a different kind of ruler: "Wär ich ein Tyrann . . . " (1112). The references to tyrants in both cases make it unavoidable that we should compare the two and see the Elector's inconsistency; and the similar description of the offenses of Kottwitz and the Prince by the Elector ("eigenmächtig" refers to the Prince in line 1562, to Kottwitz in line 1418) further stresses the need to compare the two situations. In Kottwitz's case, his argument is that only a tyrant would take so strict a view of the law as to prosecute; in the Prince's case, it is instead that only a tyrant would *not* consider himself bound to apply the law strictly. Evidently the Elector is not impartial at all in his application of the law. His condemnation of the Prince occurs not in spite of their personal relationship but because of it. The full apparatus of the law need not be invoked to deal with rebellion or dishonesty on the part of those he loves unambiguously; but it is invoked with a great display of righteousness if a young man steals honor and glory in battle when the Elector had tried to prevent this.

There is no reason to believe that the Elector is not sincere in his action. The point of Kleist's making his motivation not at all obvious and of his allowing the Elector to seem eminently reasonable on the surface (at least after the first scene) is precisely that the Elector must seem reasonable to himself. His feelings of resentment and rivalry cannot be construed as conscious malice, and his part in bringing about the situation in which the Prince stands condemned must not be thought of as conscious entrapment. Kleist's Elector is a man who sees things very plainly on the surface but is subject to pressures that he does not fully understand. His conscious sense of doing right and his well-meaning handling of situations obscure his instinctive responses to challenges to his prerogatives. And this is why by the end of Act II he has produced the situation in which he can respond to these challenges by prosecuting the Prince and have an objective reason for doing so.

The Prince is in some ways a more simple and easily understood character. He is a young man behaving expansively and trying, so to speak, to increase his personal territory. In his dream he tries to gain prestige as a victor in battle, and on the following day he forcibly takes the dominant position in that battle. On the report of the Elector's death he quickly assumes the role of the Elector as Natalie's protector and as the protector of the state. It is this pressure to expand and extend his sphere of influence and acclaim that produces the crisis; the dispute over the Prince's disobedience is a late symptom, not a cause, of the underlying conflict between the two men. The most general context of the disobedience is the classic situation in which the status quo of the older generation is disturbed by a vigorous young man who instinctively exerts pressure to make it yield a more important place for him. As a result the older man is torn between his regard for the younger as a loved son and his fear of him as an aggressive competitor. Part of the Elector's instinctive reaction is a destructive one, and yet he cannot react unambiguously and consciously; even when he condemns the Prince for his entry into the battle, he still has the Prince named as the victor in that battle (810–12).

The Prince, too, is no more aware of the complexities of their relationship than the Elector; he naively only expects praise from the Elector for assuming the role of the hero-figure in the battle and is obviously unaware of pressure to which the Elector is being subjected by his ambitions. His danger is that he uses only the superficial concepts of everyday consciousness ("Edelmut und Liebe" [785]) in thinking about his relationship with the Elector and never senses its competitive undercurrents.

The irrational side of the relationship between Prince and Elector is significantly elucidated by the play's striking imagery, which often shows deeper motives and attitudes than the surface level of the dialogue can convey. The importance of the images can be seen most clearly if they are taken in groups, and the most significant and striking group is that involving plants and their cultivation. The enigmatic parallel passages that I have cited above are part of this group, and their meaning can only become clear if we place them in the context of the entire group of such images. Take, for example, the odd reference to the gardener and the strange plants he raises (52–53); this takes on added meaning when we see the Prince's comment on his relationship to the Elector following his arrest:

> Schien er am Wachstum meines jungen Ruhms
> Nicht mehr fast, als ich selbst, sich zu erfreun?
> Bin ich nicht alles, was ich bin, durch ihn?
> Und er, er sollte lieblos jetzt die Pflanze,
> Die er selbst zog, bloß, weil sie sich ein wenig
> Zu rasch und üppig in die Blume warf,
> Mißgünstig in den Staub daniedertreten?
>
> (833–39)

The development of this imagery becomes even more interesting when Natalie, pleading for the Prince's life, says to the Elector:

> Ich will nur, daß er da sei, lieber Onkel,
> Für sich, selbständig, frei und unabhängig,
> Wie eine Blume, die mir wohlgefällt.
>
> (1087–89)

It seems that the Elector is the gardener and has raised a plant—the Prince. The Prince acknowledges his dependence on the one who has raised him, but Natalie emphasizes the independence of the flower, arguing that it must be allowed to exist for itself. And the Prince too thinks that the trouble lies in the plant's flowering before the gardener was ready for it, thus asserting its independence of the gardener's control. When he is crushed at the thought of death, he suggests a complete withdrawal from the scene and of his claim to Natalie, and the withdrawal is put in terms of his going to his own garden, that is, removing himself from the Elector's sphere of influence and from competing within that sphere:

> Nataliens, das vergiß nicht, ihm zu melden,
> Begehr ich gar nicht mehr, in meinem Busen
> Ist alle Zärtlichkeit für sie verlöscht.
>
> . . . .
>
> Ich will auf meine Güter gehn am Rhein,
> Da will ich bauen, will ich niederreißen,
> Daß mir der Schweiß herabtrieft, säen, ernten.
>
> (1023–32)

The horticultural imagery has an obvious general place in the thematic structure of the play: it is the sphere where reason and nature meet. Gardening may be a science but not an exact one; plants can be guided but not controlled. One would expect "der Gärtner" to be identifiable as the Elector, the planner and reasoner who attempts to control and direct everything; and he does in fact appear in the role of the gardener in the plant imagery throughout the play. He plans the battle, in which his soldiers are a "Saat" (533), victory is the carefully nurtured blossom (1788), and he "mows" the flags of the enemy (753–54). But his battle plans go wrong as the "Eisenregen" mows down his men (531). A more important aspect of his activity as the gardener is his control of people. The image of the Prince as a flower planted and nurtured by the Elector, but one which cannot be totally controlled by him, occurs twice in the play. The image suggests that the Elector's treatment of the Prince and expectations of him do not reckon with the laws of nature. He has vainly tried to prevent the growth of the Prince in an unwelcome direction. In the language of the image, personalities and flowers can be encouraged but not molded; their independence of the gardener is a fact he must acknowledge.

The gardener must have a garden, and here the horticultural images broaden to include the question of sphere of influence. When the Prince turns to thoughts of escaping from his sentence, he must, at some level of his mind, realize that his attempt to expand his influence within the Elector's sphere of authority has been the cause of his downfall, for he now proposes to avoid the problem by going off to a country estate to sow and reap there; he knows that he must get out of the master-gardener's territory to leave the latter's authority there undisputed.

The general background of plant imagery in the play has provided

several obvious clues to the interpretation of the parallel sequences in
the first and last acts. In general, the question-and-answer sequences
are indicative of the confusion of both Prince and Elector: each, in
turn, is the questioner and is mistaken about the plant's identity. But
the *particular* mistake in each case, and the kind of confusion it indicates, is instructive. The Elector mistakes the laurel for a willow and
in so doing shows an instinctive tendency to associate the Prince with
a symbol of mourning rather than one of victory. In a curious way this
foreshadows Act II, for here he first condemns the Prince to death,
only later acclaiming him as a victor in the battle. This aspect of the
exchange in Act I, coming as it does before the Prince's crime, suggests again that the later developments involve the Elector's predis-
positions as well as those of the Prince.

When corrected, the Elector questions the right of the offending
plant to be in "meinem märkschen Sand." The slightly strange use of
the possessive here makes this query also a complaint against an
encroachment on his personal sphere of authority. But he is told that
it was "der Gärtner" who put it there, together with other "fremde
Pflanzen." There is much in the play that identifies "der Gärtner" as
the Elector, and this suggests that he is actually querying his own
action. He has taken two children into his house who are not his own
and are therefore in a sense "fremd"—that is, Natalie and the Prince,
the latter twice referred to metaphorically as a plant "raised" by the
Elector. While the laurel functions as the symbol of the Prince's ambition, it seems also to symbolize the unacceptable side of the Prince.
When all this has been considered, the imagery suggests that it is the
Elector who has nurtured this challenge to himself within his own
sphere, without realizing what he was doing.

The second of the parallel sequences is more complex and difficult.
It is in some ways similar to the first sequence, and in other ways
contrasted with it. As before, there is confusion and then recognition,
the replacement of one name by others, and a question of the hand
behind it all. The changed identity of the gardener from the Elector to
"ein Mädchen" suggests that some aspect of Natalie or something
associated with her has become dominant to the point of replacing
the equivalent aspect of the Elector. This change will be important for
an understanding of the play's ending, and I shall return to it. The
change from trees to flowers seems to be consistent with the change
from Elector to Natalie. There is, however, a change within the Prince:
he had used the laurel as the symbol of his aspirations in the first
scene, but he now admires flowers for themselves; they are no longer
fashioned into a crown. This links with Natalie's earlier demand that
a flower be allowed to grow "frei und unabhängig," and with the
significance of the Prince's intention of putting them in water; they

are now to exist purely for their beauty. All this suggests the rejection of the notion of spheres of influence and of the authority and control over others associated with the Elector in the plant imagery. In the language of the symbol, the second of the parallel sequences rejects the Elector's theory of gardening and the relation of gardener to plant and switches to Natalie's.

What now of the three flowers and their confusion? In Act I an identification is suggested by the Elector and then rejected in favor of another. This time it is the Prince who thinks he smells the "Nachtviole," a deep purple flower that smells strongly at night. One obvious factor that links this with the corresponding plant in Act I is mourning, traditionally associated with both deep purple and the willow. On both occasions, sadness and mourning are first impressions that are then rejected. In Act I the first impression is the Elector's; in Act V it is that of the Prince, who at this point wishes to die. But the Prince's suggestion and its basis are rejected in favor of the bright colors of the "Nelke" (primarily red)—the brightness of life rather than death. At the same time the darkness of night associated with the "Nachtviole," both by its name and by its smelling sweetly primarily at night, is rejected in favor of the light of day: the "Levkoje" is a white pseudoviolet (the Greek word is literally "white violet") just as the "Nachtviole" is a dark pseudoviolet. Thus the flower of death and darkness is replaced by flowers of life and light.

There is one other major group of images that tells us a good deal about the quality of the relationship between the Prince and the Elector—that involving horses and riding. There are three horses in the play. The first is that of Kottwitz; the second is the "Schimmel" of the Elector, which he exchanges under pressure from Froben for another of a different color; and the third is that of the Prince, which causes an accident that is variously reported, and which seems to change color in the process. The links among the three are thematically very interesting.

Having asked for help in dismounting from his horse, Kottwitz is assisted by Golz and Hohenzollern and then utters these interesting lines:

> Habt Dank!—Ouf! Daß die Pest mich!
> —Ein edler Sohn, für euren Dienst, jedwedem,
> Der euch, wenn ihr zerfallt, ein Gleiches tut!
>
> . . . .
>
> Ja, auf dem Roß fühl ich voll Jugend mich;
> Doch sitz ich ab, da hebt ein Strauß sich an,
> Als ob sich Leib und Seele kämpfend trennten!
>
> (368–73)

Kottwitz feels full of youth and vigor when mounted but feels his age when he dismounts. To understand the point of what Kottwitz says here, we must look at two further passages. In the first, Sparren gives his account of how Froben persuades the Elector to dismount from his "Schimmel":

> Er naht, voll heißer Sorge, ihm und spricht:
> "Hoheit, dein Pferd ist scheu, du mußt verstatten,
> Daß ichs noch einmal in die Schule nehme!"
> Mit diesem Wort entsitzt er seinem Fuchs,
> Und fällt dem Tier des Herren in den Zaum.
> Der Herr steigt ab, still lächelnd, und versetzt:
> "Die Kunst, die du ihn, Alter, lehren willst,
> Wird er, solang es Tag ist, schwerlich lernen."
>   (661–68)

In the second, the Elector complains that Kottwitz does not understand how the security of the state must be served:

> Mit welchem Recht, du Tor, erhoffst du das,
> Wenn auf dem Schlachtenwagen, eigenmächtig,
> Mir in die Zügel jeder greifen darf?
>   (1561–63)

The point of the whole series is that for the Elector, the Prince's disobedience is an attempt to seize from him the reins, and therefore the overriding control of the situation. He cannot accept, as Kottwitz can, that a noble son should help him down from this central position and assume the reins of power when he is too old ("Wenn ihr zerfallt" [370]). All that enables him to abandon his foolish insistence on a dangerous central position in the battle is that the advice to dismount comes not from a young rival but from the *old* man, Froben: the Elector addresses him as such, and the situation seems to become one in which the Elector is the headstrong youth, to whom the older man gives wise counsel. The Elector is almost pretending that he is the Prince; his reply to Froben actually revels in the fact that Froben will never teach him to be more circumspect (the obvious thrust of the veiled remarks on what Froben wants to do with his horse) and is more to be expected of a younger man obsessed by bravado than a mature ruler.

Everything about the horses stresses the parallelism of Prince and Elector. Even the fact that the horses are "scheu" at or before the beginning of the battle points symbolically to the inappropriateness of their positions in the battle. Contrast and parallelism are present in the colors of the horses, for both men apparently change the color of their horses: they begin as opposites (black and white) but finish the battle on horses that are merely different shades of brown, "Fuchs" and "Goldfuchs" respectively. A general pattern of the relations of the two is shown as contrast ends in identification, and their initial opposition turns out to be illusory; at first they seem quite different in character, but as the play progresses their underlying similarity becomes increasingly apparent. The horse image raises the questions of jursidiction, control, and supremacy, as does the image of the gardener and his plants. Just as the plant image occurs when the Prince talks of going away to sow and reap elsewhere in order to get out of the Elector's sphere of influence, so the horse image occurs in a similar way when the Prince speaks to the Electress:

> Du scheinst mit Himmelskräften, rettenden,
> Du mir, das Fräulein, deine Fraun, begabt,
> Mir alles rings umher, dem Troßknecht könnt ich,
> Dem schlechtesten, der deiner Pferde pflegt,
> Gehängt am Halse flehen: rette mich!
>
> (973–77)

To remove any suggestion that he is challenging the Elector for the reins of power, the Prince will make himself subservient even to the lowliest boy who minds the horses; in other words, he will make himself as remote from claiming the horse as his own as he possibly can.

There are various aspects of losing control of the reins: a man can be resigned that he needs to be helped from his horse by a noble son (the case of Kottwitz); or he can have the reins grasped by a son who wishes to assume control (the Elector and the Prince); or he can be persuaded by an older person that it is foolhardy to keep them (the Elector and Froben); or, as in the Prince's case, to which I shall now turn, he can be thrown from the horse.

It is not easy to decide what actually happened to the Prince. Hohenzollern, when questioned by Kottwitz about the fall, answers:

> Nichts von Bedeutung!
> Sein Rappe scheute an der Mühle sich,
> Jedoch, leichthin zur Seite niedergleitend,
> Tat er auch nicht den mindsten Schaden sich.
> Es ist den Odem keiner Sorge wert.
>
> (379–83)

Yet the stage direction at his entry a few lines later has him "mit einem schwarzen Band um die linke Hand," a fact that is remarked by no one present; and he is evasive about what he has been doing:

> Ich—war in der Kapelle,
> Die aus des Dörfchens stillen Büschen blinkte.
>
> (408–09)

Truchß's later account, just after the battle, is entirely different:

> Der Prinz hat mit dem Pferd sich überschlagen,
> Man hat verwundet schwer, an Haupt und Schenkeln,
> In einer Kirche ihn verbinden sehn.
>
> (726–28)

But Truchß is busy denying that the Prince could have led the cavalry in the battle. When the Prince arrives on the scene, Dörfling evidently suspects Truchß of lying ("Truchß! Was machtet Ihr?" [739]), and the Prince replies to the Elector's comment on his reported severe injury:

> Mein Goldfuchs fiel, vor Anbeginn der Schlacht;
> Die Hand hier, die ein Feldarzt mir verband,
> Verdient nicht, daß du sie verwundet taufst.
>
> (744–46)

There seems here to be yet another parallel between Prince and Elector: the erroneous report of the Prince's injury recalls the erroneous report of the Elector's death. But what are we to make of the inconsistency of these three reports? Hohenzollern minimizes the Prince's wound while Truchß maximizes it—and it seems that the constant factor is the need to cover up for the Prince. The different situations and ways in which the Prince needs protection dictate the details of their accounts. Hohenzollern wants to counter any implication that the Prince might not be fit to lead in battle, while for Truchß the need is to believe that he could not have been fit enough to lead—a striking example of how the Prince is kept from individual responsibility by the shortsightedness of his friends, and how they sacrifice any larger concerns to immediate demands of the present situation. They too contribute to creating the crisis in the relations of Prince and Elector. But the thematic point of the Prince's being thrown by his horse is clear enough: if the Elector is not yet willing to give up the reins and admit that he is now too old, the Prince is unable to take them because he is not yet able to exercise intelligent control of them.

So far, I have discussed the general character of the relationship between the Prince and the Elector, and the way in which it produces the situation that is the main focus of the play; I want now to consider how the relationship develops during the play, and especially how the ending comes about and what it means. Criticism of the play has always had to deal with the fact that it is not at all easy to judge the responses of either main character at the end. We are given no clear sign as to how the Prince responds in the play's final lines, nor is the Elector's state of mind or judgment of the situation entirely obvious during the whole last act. And judging his attitudes entails a much more complex and varied set of issues than, for example, the common critical puzzle: at what point does the Elector decide to pardon the Prince?

Let us return once more to the parallel passages from the first and last acts. They occur within fifty lines of the beginning and the end of the play respectively; one would expect them to constitute a kind of summary comment on what has happened meantime. Many features of the first sequence recur in the second, but there are significant changes. The most significant of them all is the change from "der Gärtner" to "ein Mädchen." The point of this is that the ending is dominated neither by the Prince nor by the Elector, but by Natalie; her influence and her thinking prevail. It is largely during the last half of Act III and all of Act IV—a stretch of the text where she is clearly the most important character—that she is active; and to understand what she does there we must first go back to Hohenzollern's role at the beginning of Act III.

The Hohenzollern of Act I was inclined to simplistic dismissal of anything that was not immediately obvious, and he was especially opposed to taking the Prince's state as seriously as the female characters did; he rejected their notion that the Prince was sick and needed help. But by Act III, Hohenzollern is beginning to see the need for more serious thought, looks "bedenklich," and asks the Prince:

> Hast du vielleicht je einen Schritt getan,
> Seis wissentlich, seis unbewußt,
> Der seinem stolzen Geist zu nah getreten?
>   (911–13)

It is surely important that Hohenzollern, formerly insistent that no hidden significance should be sought below the surface of events, now realizes that he and the Prince must look to the source of this problematic situation in some offense to the Elector's pride that the Prince may even have committed unconsciously. Hohenzollern's formulation is very sophisticated and cautious, as is his further question to the Prince:

> Ein Wort, das die Kurfürstin Tante sprach,
> Hat aufs empfindlichste den Herrn getroffen;
> Man sagt, das Fräulein habe schon gewählt.
> Bist du auf keine Weise hier im Spiele?
>   (920–23)

The Prince assumes that what he has done is to upset a political deal
with the Swedes involving marriage of Natalie, and that this is the
real source of the Elector's anger. This represents a swing on the
Prince's part from a previous overconfident view of the Elector's benevolence toward him to the opposite extreme of a very low view of
the Elector's motivation as being merely deviously political. But that
is the Prince's view, not Hohenzollern's—a point the critics of the
play have consistently missed. Hohenzollern pointed on the contrary
to the Elector's pride being hurt and to his sensitive reaction to what
his wife told him. What Hohenzollern is getting at is more likely that
the Elector was annoyed because the Prince had made a proposal of
marriage to Natalie as soon as he thought the Elector dead, hastily
seizing the chance to replace the Elector as her protector.

It is already clear in Act II that Natalie senses how the Prince's
advances to her while the Elector was presumed dead will constitute
a problem. She was formerly most eager to accept those advances, in
fact directly provoked them (577–80), but as soon as news arrives that
the Elector still lives, she hastily pulls back (704), sensing the danger.
Natalie is essentially practical in character. She is never taken in by
the unreal clichés that the Prince thinks so important ("Edelmut und
Liebe"); she understands the complex motivations of both Prince and
Elector far too well for that. It was a practical matter for her immediately to invite the Prince to assume the Elector's role, rather than to
continue to lament the Elector's death; and when she now sees the
Prince collapse in fear of death, she is equally practical about the
situation. She is far too shrewd to be insulted that the Prince would
give her up to remain alive or to lament *his* lack of "Edelmut und
Liebe"; instead she sees in his state of degradation a weapon that she
may be able to use in order to free him, and she is "mutig" (1053)
rather than disappointed.

When she goes to the Elector to ask for the Prince's life, she speaks
very openly about his present condition:

> Der denkt jetzt nichts, als nur dies eine: Rettung!
> Den schaun die Röhren, an der Schützen Schultern,
> So gräßlich an, daß überrascht und schwindelnd,
> Ihm jeder Wunsch, als nur zu leben, schweigt.
> . . . .
> Schau her, ein Weib bin ich, und schaudere
> Dem Wurm zurück, der meiner Ferse naht:
> Doch so zermalmt, so fassungslos, so ganz
> Unheldenmütig träfe mich der Tod,
> In eines scheußlichen Leun Gestalt nicht an!

—Ach, was ist Menschengröße, Menschenruhm!
(1148–51; 1169–74)

We might think it strange that Natalie should not only advertise the
disgrace of the man she loves but actually go so far as to say that even
a timid woman would not be so craven. But Natalie senses intuitively
that this is the one approach that may work, for it is the one thing that
will replace the Elector firmly in a dominant position. In the competi-
tion for supremacy, for public acclaim, and for the position of hero,
the Elector has now won and the Prince has lost; the Prince's image as
the courageous and valiant hero in battle has been severely damaged.
Sure enough, the Elector is fascinated by the news, asks twice, "Er
fleht um Gnade?" (1157 and 1159) (which Natalie wisely never answers), and abruptly says, "So ist er frei" (1176)—forgetting, in the
process, all of his scruples about legal and constitutional action! Natalie has managed to set in motion the events that lead up to the
pardoning of the Prince.

But the Elector cannot resist giving the situation one last twist. He
offers the Prince a choice: he may either grant himself, unilaterally, a
pardon, or he may consent to die if he believes that the sentence has
been just. Thus the Prince can live only if discredited both by his
unheroic behavior and by *his avoidance of the law*—not even as the
beneficiary of a pardon. If, on the other hand, the Prince admits that
he was justly condemned, the Elector can still pardon him since he
will have acknowledged the Elector's authority and justice.

Still the Elector cannot resist further humiliation for the Prince. He
asks Natalie to carry his letter to the Prince and then says: "So kann
er, für sein Leben, gleich dir danken" (1198): The Elector, to complete
the Prince's destruction as a hero figure, wants to make quite clear
that he has a woman to thank for his life.

In the conflict between the two men, the Elector seems to be gain-
ing ground. That his letter is not premeditated is indicated by the
stage directions that show his surprise and confusion. He had not
thought that he would win the struggle so quickly and easily. Natalie
is suspicious:

DER KURFÜRST.
  Mein liebes Kind! Bist du mir wieder gut?

NATALIE *nach einer Pause.*
  Was deine Huld, o Herr, so rasch erweckt,
  Ich weiß es nicht und untersuch es nicht.
  Das aber, sieh, das fühl ich in der Brust,
  Unedel meiner spotten wirst du nicht:
  Der Brief enthalte, was es immer sei,

Ich glaube Rettung—und ich danke dir!
Sie kußt ihm die Hand.

DER KURFÜRST.
Gewiß, mein Töchterchen, gewiß! So sicher,
Als sie in Vetter Homburgs Wünschen liegt.

(1199–1207)

Only on the surface is this an affectionate conversation between father
and daughter; scarcely hidden beneath it is a cunning game of double
talk, in which each tries to outmaneuver the other. Natalie, aware of
the sting in the Elector's words, attempts to bind him to a favorable
interpretation of what he has said, asserting that any other would be
a mockery of her, and virtually dares him to deny it; but he is evasive.

The Elector appears to have secured the complete deflation of the
Prince whatever happens; but during the course of Act V, it becomes
clear that he has in fact miscalculated. To begin with, the Prince
chooses a course that the Elector had not foreseen: a hero's death.
And then Natalie sets up the confrontation between the Elector and
his senior officers by giving forged orders to Count Reuß as soon as
she sees what the Prince intends. (That Natalie's pragmatism will
stop at nothing is shown when she tries to persuade the Prince to
believe that the Elector's "Großmut" is boundless, which she clearly
does not believe, any more than she believed her appeal to his nobility
in line 1203; such concepts evidently do not form part of her own
analysis of what is happening, but she is quite happy to use them,
quite dishonestly, for debating purposes.)

The Prince's response to the Elector's letter shows that he too is not
happy with it:

Ich will ihm, der so würdig vor mir steht,
Nicht, ein Unwürdger, gegenüber stehn!
Schuld ruht, bedeutende, mir auf der Brust,
Wie ich es wohl erkenne; kann er mir
Vergeben nur, wenn ich mit ihm drum streite,
So mag ich nichts von seiner Gnade wissen.

(1380–85)

The last lines indicate that the first two are a sarcastic expression of
dissatisfaction at what the Elector has offered: the Prince did not want
to be told that he could pretend he was innocent (he acknowledged
his legal guilt in line 870) but to be forgiven for his crime. What the
Elector offers is *not*, in fact, "Gnade." The tone of the last line is
important; the Prince is saying that he wants nothing to do with a
pardon if it is not freely given. The Prince thus responds as if to a
challenge to that element of the Elector's letter that was a move in the
game. On the surface, the Elector's offer seems reasonable, even

noble, and the Prince's answer equally so. Critics have traditionally regarded both men's actions in this way. In one sense this is not a mistake: it matters in the play and to the two men that their actions at this point should appear noble. Yet it would be a mistake not to consider the devious, calculating element in their actions too; we must remember that the object of the game they are playing is to achieve their desires while seeming impressive.

Even at this point we cannot view the Prince and Elector as being simply hostile toward each other; in the emotionally confused situation there is still much that indicates their concern for each other. The Elector refers to the Prince as his son and as a young hero; the Prince acts deferentially and speaks of his personal relationship with the Elector in a way that implies its value for him (e.g., line 1765). But it is by no means clear whether the object of the Prince's deferential speech might not be to carry the hidden barb that emerges in his last request of the Elector. The request recalls the Elector's political negotiations with the Swedes involving Natalie; there is surely veiled criticism of the Elector in the Prince's asking him not to conclude such a dishonorable bargain, since the request assumes precisely that the Elector was indeed planning to do something dishonorable. This also gives the Prince an opportunity to attribute Natalie's rescue from the Elector's machinations to his own intervention; he will die and in so doing wring from the Elector the concession that will save her. Thus he subtly reverses the Elector's previous assertion that the Prince could thank Natalie for his life—she can now thank him for saving her from the Elector's plan. The Elector's reply is defensive: he concedes the prior existence of the bargain but explains that it was due to the misfortunes of war. That, however, is a riposte in similarly veiled fashion; the misfortune to which he refers is the Prince's disobedience, without which the Elector thinks he would have won so decisive a victory that no concession to the Swedes would have been necessary. The Elector is really saying that it was all due to the Prince. At the surface level of this scene is a noble last wish, magnanimously granted; beneath that surface is an unpleasant game of accusation and counteraccusation.

Towards the end of Act V, the situation is no longer as comfortable for the Elector as was his position at the end of Act IV, when the Prince was crushed and degraded. The Prince has managed to repair his own damaged image, and his public request that the Elector not sacrifice Natalie to political expediency damages the Elector's image. The senior military officers are displaying coolness toward the Elector and siding with the Prince against him; and Hohenzollern has raised the issue of the Elector's part in provoking the crisis. We can see how uncomfortable he is by his uncharacteristic anger at Hohenzollern's well-reasoned statement and his confessing to being affected by Kott-

witz's sentimental but insubstantial remarks. When, under the pressure of this situation, he decides to pardon the Prince, he still does so
hesitantly, tries to make others bear responsibility for the decision
(1823), and cannot actually bring himself to say that he is doing so.
His announcement, such as it is, is in the form of a not entirely clear
question to his officers (1818–23) whether *they* will want to take the
risk of rehabilitating such an irresponsible commander. And he still
plays another joke on the Prince in the garden, one which has a cruel
side to it.

It is also doubtful whether the Prince has changed for the better.
His irrational ambition for glory has not disappeared; the only difference is that victory in battle has given way to martyrdom as a means
of achieving it, as the terms of line 1850, suggesting Christ, seem to
indicate: "Schlug meiner Leiden letzte Stunde?" Thus the change in
sophistication is not matched by a change in direction. The grandiose
imagery of his early speeches is still present in lines 1830–34:

> Nun, o Unsterblichkeit, bist du ganz mein!
> Du strahlst mir, durch die Binde meiner Augen,
> Mit Glanz der tausendfachen Sonne zu!
> Es wachsen Flügel mir an beiden Schultern,
> Durch stille Ätherräume schwingt mein Geist.

It is also doubtful whether he welcomes the outcome, which robs him
of the glory he thought he was to achieve. There is an enormous
discrepancy between the Prince's ecstatic readiness for death and the
assumption made by all the other characters that he does not want to
die.

The ending of the play provides a surface resolution, but at bottom
resolves nothing. In Kottwitz's affirmation, in response to the Prince's
question, that this is all "ein Traum," the notion of dream is ambiguous; it may refer either to a dream come true or to an illusion. And the
joining of all voices in condemning the enemies of Brandenburg (1858)
is possible only because it is not at all clear who those enemies are;
the Prince and the Elector may also in their different ways have acted
contrary to the interests of the state. Appeals to patriotism have always been linked in the play with the kind of simple-minded, superficial thinking that helped to obscure the real basis of the situations in
which they occurred, and they have served mainly to make self-
deception easier for both Prince and Elector. The basis of the conflict
between Prince and Elector cannot be removed, and the relation between reasoned behavior and underlying motives will continue to be
obscure and problematic. The play has probed but not solved the
problem, nor could it.

VII

The Character of
Kleist's Literary Work

In the first six chapters of this book I have examined and interpreted six of Kleist's most important works at some length instead of attempting to survey his whole output. In doing so, I have proceeded on the assumption, elaborated both in my introduction and in the last chapter of this book, that a close look at a manageable number of the best works is a much better foundation for a general discussion of the character of his writing than a more superficial survey of everything that Kleist wrote. There are a small number of basic questions that must be central to a general discussion of a writer: What are the fundamental concerns of his writing? What is most characteristic of him? What is the importance of his work? In discussing these questions I shall be drawing mainly, though not exclusively, on the results of the first six chapters; on occasion, I shall refer also to the major plays that I have not chosen to analyze in detail.

In his well-known and much reprinted literary history, Fritz Martini begins his discussion of Kleist by referring to Goethe's negative response to Kleist's "pathologisch erscheinende Neigung zum Grausamen, Entsetzlichen."[1] With variations of emphasis, this judgment is still the basis of the predominant critical attitude to Kleist's work. Critics commonly mention above all else the emotional intensity of his work, its preoccupation with violent passions such as rage and vengeance, and its consequent strong, immediate impact on the reader. They point also to the tendency of his work to deal with extreme situations and people of equally extreme character, and to the resulting image of a world in which no well-ordered life can be secure against the sudden eruption of violence and chaos.

As a surface description of some of the events that occur in Kleist's work, this account has of course some limited validity; but it is far from being an accurate general discription of his work and even farther from being a valid interpretation of Kleist's meaning. My point in introducing this predominant critical stereotype of Kleist here is to make a contrast with the direction in which my own argument will lead in this chapter. I shall argue that Kleist's work is essentially of

a much more thoughtful kind than this; it has the character of a series of thematic studies, in which the occasionally intense or violent
scenes always function to serve thematic purposes rather than simply
to shock the reader or to create a world that is inherently violent.

Kleist's work has indeed a highly characteristic quality, and that
quality can be seen in every aspect of his writing—his style, his
choice of themes, the personalities that he created, and the kinds of
events that take place in his work. But it would be difficult if not
impossible to discuss these characteristic features of his writing in
any really useful way without taking them in their wider context of
what he was actually trying to do with them. Only a discussion of the
fundamental strategy and concerns of Kleist's writing can provide the
context in which his use of certain kinds of people, events, language,
or motifs can be understood. For this reason, I want to begin by
pointing to a typical thematic structure in Kleist's work.

Consider, for example, how often the stories begin with a clear
presentation of a set of circumstances or issues but later veer off in a
surprising new direction that seems at first hard to reconcile with the
initial part of the text. Usually the change of direction is set in motion
by a jolting episode that introduces fundamentally new issues, characters, or events that may even seem so out of place in the text as it
has developed to this point that the episode seems not to belong in
the same story.[2] But, as we have seen in the preceding interpretations, the change of direction has the effect of making the reader
question whether he really understood the issues that were presented
at the beginning of the text, and whether those issues were indeed as
simple and straightforward as they at first had seemed. In short, the
unexpected episodes suddenly introduce much more thematic complexity into the story and make us retroactively see the beginning of
the text in a more complex light too. Let us look briefly at how this
works in some of the texts that I have discussed.

In *Michael Kohlhaas*, the early part of the story sets out the issue of
justice fairly clearly, with the just Kohlhaas apparently pitted against
a corrupt nobility and an unjust legal system. But the gypsy episode
seems to be completely inconsistent with such a framework; it appears to depart from the world of real people and the concern of that
world with law and social justice and to take the story instead into a
world of magic and the supernatural. Yet gradually the effect of this
jolting episode becomes clearer: it brings with it a more fundamental
challenge to the earlier framework of the story than even appeared to
be the case at first sight, for it destroys the whole notion of a corrupt
establishment that was necessary for Kohlhaas's stance to make any
sense. The later episode thus has the effect of showing how the

earlier part had been built on assumptions that were merely illusions, the chief revelation being that the world is a much more untidy and inconsistent place than clear, consistent thinkers like Kohlhaas can deal with. In *Der Findling*, the simple notion in the early part of the story that this is about a benevolent old man and his ungrateful adopted son begins to crumble as soon as we see something that seems at first not to bear on that earlier framework at all, namely, that his wife has a horrendous personal history that still haunts her. Slowly, this new factor changes everything, including our view of the old man, who no longer seems so unambiguously benevolent. In *Das Erdbeben in Chili*, there is a series of upsets to the reader's impression of what the story means and where it is going, but the entry of Don Fernando must be judged an especially puzzling episode at the time it happens; what had seemed to be the story of two young lovers, first gravely imperiled, then joyously reunited, is suddenly complicated by the appearance of a major new figure just when it seemed that the events of the story had already run their course. And, sure enough, at the end of the story he turns out to have been a central figure, even though he appeared so late in the work. Introducing a major new figure at so late a stage was evidently Kleist's way of making the reader wonder if he had been mistaken in his impression that he had already grasped the point of the story; he is not to be allowed to go on thinking that this is a tale simply about two lovers and their fate.

Der Zweikampf is an especially interesting example, for its entire plot seems to be radically reshaped and redirected in the middle of the story. It begins on one issue—the murder of the Duke and the prosecution of the murderer—and then suddenly veers off in a new direction; the story then begins to focus almost exclusively on the issue of sexual morality and the fate of Friedrich and Littegarde. The Regent and the Duke are almost forgotten, and what had seemed the main plot issue of the story is taken up again only briefly at the very end. It is only after thinking carefully about what has happened that we see the important thematic links between the apparently separate areas of the plot and notice the really intriguing fact that the values of one half of the plot seem to negate those of the other half. Again, Kleist has used an apparent break in the continuity of his text to throw a fundamentally new light on it.

Die Marquise von O . . . seems to have resolved its major issue before the disturbing new episode appears. The Count seems about to be rehabilitated after his earlier unacceptable behavior, and the story therefore appears to be about to close, when the extraordinary scene between father and daughter occurs. This time it is not the introduction of a major new character that produces the jolt to the reader, nor is it the introduction of a major and unexpected turn in the plot events; what happens here is that the tactful and elegant tone of the story and its entire narrative convention are shattered by a grossly explicit description of father and daughter embracing. The point of this is that we must now think again about the whole question of illicit desires and their place in the elegant aristocratic world of these people; the Count's transgression is suddenly given a new context that must make us seriously rethink how it is to be judged. The thematic basis of the story is changed by an apparently irrelevant scene, and where formerly only the Count had seemed problematic, the whole family group including the Marquise herself must now be thought of as equally problematic.

If we look at these five cases together, then, we find that in each case the reader's sense of what the text is and what it is about is disturbed at a late stage, and that the means of accomplishing this are one or more of the following: a break with the tone and narrative convention of what has gone before (*Michael Kohlhaas* and *Die Marquise von O . . .*); a major new turn in the plot events, or indeed a transformation of the plot and of the issues with which it seems to be concerned (*Der Zweikampf, Der Findling,* and *Michael Kohlhaas*); or the introduction of major new figures and changes in the relative importance of existing figures (*Das Erdbeben in Chili* and *Michael Kohlhaas*).

So far, I have looked only at the stories, and indeed, this particular pattern is characteristic *only* of the stories. But its fundamental purpose is one that the plays share, though they realize that purpose in different ways. Therefore, before going on to discuss the plays, I want first to consider what Kleist's purpose is in constructing his stories as he does.

Critics of Kleist's work have on occasion noted that it is characteristic of him to introduce new material late in his stories, but they have generally minimized the importance of this practice, as well as the unexpected character of the new material. Helmut Koopmann, for example, thought of all this purely in terms of a technique of exposition.[3] Kleist, he thought, was fond of a "flashback" kind of expository technique, and that was why he introduced late in the story material that belonged at the beginning. And, Koopmann thought, the fundamental reason Kleist did this was that he was a pedantic storyteller, who kept feeling the urge to motivate all that happened more thoroughly by giving a good deal of the prehistory of the events that he narrated. Now there is obviously much more to the unexpected new material than mere flashbacks—the most disturbing episode in *Die Marquise von O . . .* , for example, is chronologically in its correct sequence in the text, even though it completes our understanding of what has been a factor in the family situation throughout the story. But Koopmann has not really dealt with the flashbacks either, for they do not simply provide more exposition—they change the whole shape of the events. What we learn about Elvire in *Der Findling* completely changes our view of the entire household. More simply, it changes the character of all the rest of the exposition up to that point in the story. This is not merely more exposition but in a sense the reverse, an overturning of the shape of the prior exposition.

Max Kommerell, on the other hand, stressed that Kleist's work was full of puzzling episodes, but he thought of them merely as puzzling in themselves, not puzzling against the background of the rest of the text in which they occurred.[4] That led him to concentrate more on the Marquise's pregnancy as a puzzling fact (which, in the context of the story, it is not) than on the Marquise's behavior with her father, which, when it occurs, is utterly puzzling and causes a reinterpretation of the whole story.[5] What is most important about the unexpected episodes in Kleist's stories is not their intrinsic oddity, but their being part of a sequence of events and of narration against which they are unexpected because they take the events and the narrative in unexpected new directions. *Das Erdbeben in Chili* is the best example of how a Kleist narrative can constantly change direction. The reader forms an initial impression of the general shape of the situation, but as new events occur, he must continually change that impression and even revise his impression of the initial pages. The interpretation of the text constantly shifts as new events and emphases compel it to shift.

An important consequence of this is the danger in trying to abstract any meaning from a particular page until we have seen what the rest of the text does to the impression gained on that page; Kleist's stories do not stand still long enough for that—they develop thematically all the time. At particular points in his stories, for example, we may get a strong suggestion of ideas derived from Rousseau. In *Das Erdbeben in Chili* the middle section gives the reader the impression of a return to a natural state in which man is naturally innocent as soon as he is no longer corrupted by the institutions of society. And in *Michael Kohlhaas*, Kohlhaas's arguments in support of his action sound like a page out of *Du Contrat Social*; the thesis that the implicit contract between himself and the government is broken and that he is then free to pursue justice by his own individual means coincides exactly with Rousseau's own argument. Many critics have concluded that Kleist was simply advocating Rousseau's ideas in these texts, but they have missed the way in which his writings use certain ideas as thematic material but then move on from those ideas. If the critic becomes too impressed with the atmosphere of a particular page, he is in danger of focusing narrowly on a single idea that the text abandons to go in a different direction. This principle is true regardless of how enthusiastically the narrator seems to embrace a particular viewpoint. Near the end of *Das Erdbeben in Chili*, for example, the narrator is evidently tremendously impressed with Don Fernando's dignified and courageous stoicism, but the attentive reader will see that, only a page or so later, there is a subtle questioning of his role in what has happened; it may be that his concern with courage and dignity led to the final disaster because it precluded a more prudent and reasoned approach to the situation.

The stories constantly use ideas and then cast them aside; the purpose of the unexpected episodes lies in their jolting a story out of one set of ideas and sending it in a new direction. The point of this recurring phenomenon in Kleist's stories lies in a fundamental aspect of the meaning of his work: above all, Kleist's writings are about the *process* of coming to terms with the world, of interpreting and then reinterpreting it, of trying out different ideas and attitudes to it. The situations and often the characters in his work are ambiguous and difficult to grasp, and several possible ways of looking at them are exploited by the text at various times. There is constant movement in the text among the various possibilities, a continual search for attitudes that will work, and an equally continual stumbling into new aspects of the characters and situations that make a given attitude difficult to maintain. It was this quality of a continual intellectual and emotional searching for the "right" attitude to the world that led me to call *Das Erdbeben in Chili* a kind of "detective story on a cosmic scale."[6]

To say that Kleist's work is ambiguous is not nearly enough, and does not get at its really characteristic quality.[7] It is after all something of a cliché in literary criticism to say that works of literature are full of ambiguity. It would still be far too static a view of Kleist to think merely of his work as having more than one level of meaning. What characterizes him is the active movement from one explanation or attitude to another, the constant search for meaning in events and for a secure judgment of people and their behavior. Meanings are not just ambiguous and left that way in *Das Erdbeben in Chili*, for example; they are set up initially as highly probable and then left behind in the wake of the story as it discards them, one by one, as failures.

It is this general structural pattern, and the attitude towards meaning that it represents, that is truly typical of Kleist. But within the pattern there is in fact considerable variety. Though they share the same kind of strategy for thematic development and exploration, his works do not all treat the same thematic areas. *Das Erdbeben in Chili* explores in Kleist's characteristic fashion the most general problem of man's relationship to the world around him; the text is continually concerned with the interrelated questions of how he should understand it and how he should behave towards it. The story is a study that has both epistemological and ethical aspects. The thematic material of *Michael Kohlhaas*, on the other hand, lies in the area of social life and social justice, and the text is concerned with the problem of what an individual can expect from a society and the various ways in which he can interpret and respond to its failures to provide protection and justice. *Der Findling* is about the way people relate to each other, their roles in each others' lives, and the different possible evaluations of one person's role in the life of another—in particular the peculiar relationship between generosity towards and exploitation of another human being.

Die Marquise von O . . . and *Der Zweikampf* both concern the area of virtue and morality, yet in very different ways. In the former, the emphasis is on the positive and negative aspects of social norms, social elegance and social inhibitions generally, and on the extraordinarily arbitrary quality of these notions; in the latter, it is on the different attitudes that are possible to virtuousness and moral impeccability. All the stories, then, have the stamp of Kleist's particular kind of thematic study, yet they are also about very different subjects.

So far, I have spoken only of the stories. The dramas, it seems to me, are more various. Some are quite different from what we have seen in the stories and lack that characteristic quality of a Kleistian thematic study—the exploration of all sides of a thematic area. *Die Hermannsschlacht*, for example, though a late work (dating from 1808), appears to be a predominantly patriotic play, not to be considered in the same category as the rest of Kleist's output, and consequently it has not received the same critical attention as his other work. *Die Familie Schroffenstein*, Kleist's earliest play (1802), has evidently not yet embodied his most characteristic features. But the most well-known and best received of his plays are indeed characteristically Kleistian thematic studies that share the same basic strategy and purposes of the stories, though those purposes are realized somewhat differently.

The stories use the *sequence* of narration to move from one situation (and interpretative attitude) to the next. The reader's understanding develops by a distinct feeling of moving on and occasionally, as we have seen, by being jolted into a new direction by enigmatic episodes that, as we think about them, effect a big change in the way we understand the entire story. By contrast, the plays tend to focus on a single situation and to proceed to a deeper analysis of it by making most of its levels visible in some way from the very beginning. *Prinz Friedrich von Homburg*, for example, is evidently a study of the many layers of complexity in the relation of Prince and Elector. We do not, however, move in sequence from one layer to the next, as is the manner of the stories, but instead see the two main strata of the relationship at the very beginning of the play; and during the rest of the play we watch the increasingly complex interaction of those strata.

A striking demonstration of the difference of strategy between this play and the stories lies in the position of the most obvious "puzzling" episode in the *Prinz von Homburg*. The analogue of, say, the gypsy episode in *Michael Kohlhaas* is the strange garden scene, but this begins the play and then recurs at the very end. The puzzling episode here, then, is in a sense ever-present: it is no less than the encircling framework for the entire play and the episode we must remember during the progress of the rest of the play. Instead of jolting us out of a viewpoint that is to be discarded, it constitutes an odd and puzzling scene which must color all we see. This is because the play is about the relation between conscious, reasoned behavior and the instinctive, less well-understood feelings and tendencies that underlie it. The structure of *Prinz Friedrich* makes us aware that all of the reasonable and rational argument and planning of the middle of the play takes place literally within the framework of unconscious or half-conscious dreams and wishes, as well as fears and anxieties. Here, then, we have the same characteristic concern with different ways of looking at people and events, and with interpreting and re-interpreting what is actually happening between these two characters. But instead of presenting that concern by proceeding sequentially from one interpretation to the next, Kleist develops simultaneously all the possible levels of understanding the situation. Whereas the stories proceed from one view to another, the play moves back and forth between two predominant modes; in place of the searching and discarding of the former, the latter has a process of progressive illumination of the relationship between public acts and private wishes. But, in common with the stories, the focus of interest is on the continuing process of interpreting and understanding the behavior of both men; and, again like the stories, the movement from one mode to another is partly signaled by a change in dramatic convention and style, though it can work in both directions: the harsh reality of the battle or of the general staff meeting at the end of Act I clashes with the prior fantasylike garden scene, just as the return to the garden in Act V clashes with the preceding legalistic argument between the

Elector and his senior officers.

The fundamental continuity of purpose behind the different means of presentation can be seen by looking at the thematic similarity between *Michael Kohlhaas* and the *Prinz von Homburg*. The contrast of Kohlhaas's concern with perfect justice on the one hand and the strange irrationalism of the gypsy episode on the other is rather like the contrast between the Elector's concern with the law and the exotic fantasy world of the garden. The thematic point of the two contrasts is also similar: in both, a reasonable, articulate, and logical way of looking at the world, which seems at first sight self-sufficient, is suddenly complicated by the appearance of less rational factors that strike at the basis of that whole system of thinking.

Kleist's three other major plays—*Der zerbrochne Krug*, *Amphitryon*, and *Penthesilea*—all show his characteristic concern with different ways of looking at the same situation, with interpreting behavior, and with understanding the many levels of a given situation, though perhaps not developed to the same degree shown in the stories and the *Prinz von Homburg*.

Der zerbrochne Krug is a relatively simple example. The plot looks easy enough to interpret, and it might seem that there is no difficulty in deciding where our sympathies should lie. The village judge, Adam, is not only incompetent but misuses his position to try to intimidate Eve into accepting his advances. He sows discord, temporarily, between the young lovers Eve and Ruprecht; and the pretty young Eve is obviously well matched with Ruprecht, but not at all with a rather ugly man at least twice her age. The honest and decent inspector, Walter, comes to set the whole situation straight, and Adam is deposed. So far, so good, but many details suggest another way of looking at things, making it not quite so clear who deserves our sympathy. The most obvious textual feature that, in a manner typical of Kleist, jars with the obvious surface interpretation is the naming of the characters. At the surface plot level, the natural pair is Eve and Ruprecht, but the names suggest the pairing Adam and Eve. And that fact immediately suggests several other details of the setting, imagery, and even plot events that link with it. For example, Ruprecht is not an exemplary young man or the ideal match for Eve. Throughout the play, he repeatedly calls Eve a whore, and though of course he thinks he has reason to feel suspicious of and disappointed in her, he is clearly far more verbally violent than is either necessary or accounted for merely by his disappointment; for example, his "Verflucht bin ich, wenn ich die Metze nehme" (444) does not make him seem a very appealing choice for Eve. Nor, we feel, should any reasonably acceptable mate for Eve ever try to kick her, as Ruprecht

does (1019) when blinded by the sand that Adam has thrown in his
face. Kleist is obviously doing much more than showing a disappointed lover; he is portraying Ruprecht as an ill-tempered, incon-
siderate, and unimaginative clod who can behave abominably toward
the woman whom he supposedly loves. His boorishness and simplemindedness are conveyed too in both the sound of his second name
and the names with which Adam confuses it: "Ach, Gimpel! Sim-
pel! Tümpel heißt der Ruprecht" (2160). Ruprecht and Eve would of
course make a rustic and relatively unsophisticated pair, but that
cannot be the point of Kleist's characterization of Ruprecht, for Eve
herself is shown to be quite different to him; she is loyal even when
abused, gentle, and considerate. The marriage of the two, then, is
scarcely an unambiguously good conclusion of the play; they do not
look as if they belong together, Ruprecht does not seem worthy of
Eve, and we are left with the feeling that she deserves much better
than this unattractive individual.

Still, the Adam and Eve of the play, however their names are
matched, do not seem a good match either; but that is not the point.
The names are there to send the reader's thoughts in a different
direction when he considers Adam. Like his counterpart in the Garden of Eden, Adam meets Eve in the garden and is tempted by her;
and as a result—though in more physical and even grotesque fashion
—he too falls, out of the window. This puts much more emphasis on
Eve as temptress than would seem to be there on the plot's surface
and much more emphasis on Adam's sin as a universal human weakness of the male for the female. Now this kind of emphasis might not
seem to be easily reconcilable with the plot, in which Adam seems to
demand of Eve that she give herself to him sexually as the price of his
intervening to prevent Ruprecht's being conscripted for service with
the army in Batavia, an event which Adam has in any case invented
in order to frighten her. Human susceptibility is one thing; forgery
and extortion are another.

Here it is critical to recall that this is true only of the second, shortened version of the play. Criticism of the Weimar performance in 1808
had centered on the long explanations at the end, and so Kleist shortened them, in the process compressing Eve's long narrative to a very
brief explanation of her silence and statement of Adam's demands:
"So Schändliches, ihr Herren, von mir fordernd, / Daß es kein Mäd-
chenmund wagt auszusprechen!" (1946–47). But though he shortened
the play's ending, Kleist still subsequently published, in the edition
of 1811, the original ending as a "Variant." He still wanted that original ending as a possible alternative, then, and did not concede that
the original, longer version had simply been improved by the revi-

sion. The reason is not hard to see if we examine the two endings and compare them. The second version not only shortened Eve's explanation, it changed the character of that explanation and made Adam's sin very different from that of the original version. The longer version has Adam use his forged document about Ruprecht only as an excuse to meet Eve in her room in the evening, where all he does is take her by the hand and look at her. He does not threaten her, nor does he demand that she submit to him. In the original, then, Adam uses the false story about Ruprecht as an excuse to have a secret evening meeting with a pretty girl, and that may well be as far as it goes; he takes her hand and looks at her just as Ruprecht is heard outside, and the scene cannot develop further. Of course we can speculate about what might have happened, but there are many possibilities: perhaps he would have declared his fondness for her; perhaps he would have asked her to show her gratitude for his saving Ruprecht by kissing him; perhaps he would have excused his looking at her and taking her hand by claiming a paternal fondness for her as a close friend of her dead father; and perhaps something more serious might have occurred. The one thing that is certain is that we do *not* see him crudely threaten and extort. Indeed, it is difficult in the shorter version to understand Walter's kindly, forgiving tone at the end of the play, when he says that he will only remove Adam as judge but do no more provided his accounts are in order. In the longer version that makes sense—Adam has been only indiscreet and silly. But in the shorter version, Adam has behaved criminally towards Eve, and further punishment would be indicated. My own feeling here is that Kleist said what he wanted to say in the longer version, bowed, after the failure of the performance, to critical pressure for a punchier, more dramatic ending, but always wanted his original to stand— which is why he printed the original version as a full alternative reading, available for any director who felt that length was not a great problem.

The original version certainly contains the same potentiality for entertaining two different versions of what has gone on that is present in his best and most mature work. The surface meaning of the play is that which I first described; but the meaning that keeps intruding in all kinds of ways has Adam as a man sinning in very human fashion and falling from grace, while the young man who is to marry Eve is an unattractive person who does not deserve her. That view has Adam as a pathetic figure, cruelly vulnerable to the most human of all attractions and temptations, the temptation of Eve, while the reader has no sympathy at all for the utterly unattractive Ruprecht. Typical of Kleist here, then, is the way that details of setting, imagery and langauge all work *against* the overt plot events to undermine the superficial view that those events suggest and to substitute a completely different interpretation of what happens in the play.

Amphitryon, too, is full of ironic reversals in the way events are perceived, though they are of a relatively uncomplicated kind. The obvious deceit in the play, for example, is Jupiter's deceiving Alkmene by pretending to be Amphitryon; but quite late in the text we find that the reverse has been just as true. Alkmene, when praying to Jupiter, has in fact been visualizing Amphitryon; and so where at first it seems that Jupiter has substituted himself for Amphitryon, in fact Alkmene has all along been substituting Amphitryon for Jupiter. Another curious reversal of what might seem to be the case lies in the question of the apparent wrong done to Amphitryon. At first sight it might seem that he has been cuckolded by Jupiter and so dishonored; but Kleist eventually has things the other way round: what an honor for Amphitryon and what an amazing proof of his wife's total faithfulness to him, that even Jupiter himself, the master of the universe, must pretend to be Amphitryon before he can make love to Alkmene!

Yet another reversal is seen in the difference between the obvious, superficial view of Jupiter's intrusion into the lives of Alkmene and Amphitryon and what reveals itself when we look deeper. The surface tends to let Jupiter be seen as the spoiled all-powerful one who takes whatever he wants, in the process trampling on the wishes and the happiness of mere mortals; this is consistent with the traditional view of Jupiter's sexual exploits in the classical legends. He is a kind of celestial sinner, always intent on being unfaithful to his queen Juno. But there is also something of the reversal here that we see in *Der zerbrochne Krug*; there is something of Ruprecht in Amphitryon. When Alkmene first tells Amphitryon that another has visited her in his guise, he abuses her, calling her "Verräterin" (971) and "Treulose! Undankbare!" (975) to the point where she eventually calls him an "unedelmütger Gatte" (980). This is reminiscent of the exchanges between Ruprecht and Eve, in which he is willing to believe the worst of her very quickly. And like Ruprecht, Amphitryon is content to advertise his wife's embarrassment and his opinion of her. He actually says that he will call witnesses: "Zeugen doch / Jetzt ruf ich, . . . Ich rufe deinen Bruder mir, die Feldherrn, / Das ganze Heer mir der Thebaner auf" (996–99). The impression here is that of a selfish man who is concerned only with his own image and his honor, not with his wife's distress. No wonder Jupiter (still disguised as Amphitryon) insists that he (Jupiter) is the one who is deceived:

Er war

Der Hintergangene, mein Abgott! *Ihn*
Hat seine böse Kunst, nicht dich getäuscht,
Nicht dein unfehlbares Gefühl! Wenn er
In seinem Arm dich wähnte, lagst du an
Amphitryons geliebter Brust, wenn er
Von Küssen träumte, drücktest du die Lippe
Auf des Amphitryon geliebten Mund.
O einen Stachel trägt er.

(1287–95)

To be taken for such a man and to have to resemble him in order to
be loved is indeed no great compliment. And meanwhile there is a
strange sense in which Alkmene is only recognized for what she is
when given Jupiter's attention. The insensitive Amphitryon cannot
see what he has in Alkmene and so cannot appreciate her value; but
when she is visited by Jupiter, she is seen as the divine creature
among women that she really is. In a sense, Jupiter takes the form of
a mortal so that Alkmene can then emerge as something ethereal
among mortals.

Penthesilea is in many ways the strangest of all Kleist's works, and
its savage ending has unfortunately done most to support the widespread and mistaken notion that Kleist's work is in general obsessed
with violence and brutality. In fact, this is not even entirely true of
Penthesilea. While it is, to be sure, markedly different from anything
else that he wrote, it still has the characteristic thoughtful quality of a
thematic study that plays with many different ways of conceiving its
subject—in this case the love relationship between Penthesilea and
Achilles. The literal battle between the two is not something that
takes us outside of, and makes the play irrelevant to, the range of
normal experience in relations between men and women generally,
nor does it simply reduce that experience to a lowest level of violence;
on the contrary, it is used by Kleist to bring out all of the complexities
of relations between the sexes and to allow the two to express a great
number of different emotional responses to what is happening to
them as they gravitate towards each other. The tone of the relationship between them and its many levels of response is set firmly when
Odysseus, reporting their first meeting, says of Penthesilea that she is
"verwirrt und stolz und wild zugleich" (99). The symbolism of the
battle situation projects the atmosphere of challenge involved in the
beginning of a love relationship, the dangerous feeling of emotional
vulnerability, as well as the excitement and exhilaration that accom-
pany those dangers. The very act of seeking each other out to fight is
for Penthesilea and Achilles a kind of commitment to each other, a

decision to prove themselves a match for the other, and a provocative
gesture that challenges each to accept the dangers and put aside fear
in order to come to terms with the other; if both can stand the test, the
relationship can progress. Mixed up with this already very complicated set of emotions is the urge, which both show, to conquer the
other, to carry him or her off as a prize that has been won, and to
display the capture proudly to friends and countrymen; but both also
show the opposite emotion, the wish to be captured by the other.
Achilles is willing to make an elaborate pretense of Penthesilea's having won, in order for her to carry him off to her capital as a captive;
while Penthesilea herself, in spite of her expressed obsession with
capturing Achilles and her resolve never to take a man that she has
not captured by the sword (1580–81), is actually furious when she is
rescued by her women from captivity in Achilles' hands (2298 ff.).

Quite how precarious the balance is between these opposing wishes
to conquer and yet be conquered is shown on a number of occasions.
Early in the play, Achilles is menaced by the sword of a Trojan; Penthesilea, though still nominally also in battle against Achilles, grows
pale at the sight and kills the Trojan to protect Achilles, whose reaction may seem ungrateful:

> Er jetzt, zum Dank, will ihr, der Peleïde,
> Ein Gleiches tun; doch sie bis auf den Hals
> Gebückt, den mähnumflossenen, des Schecken,
> Der, in den Goldzaum beißend, sich herumwirft,
> Weicht seinem Mordhieb aus, und schießt die Zügel,
> Und sieht sich um, und lächelt, und ist fort.
>
> (187–92)

The point is, however, that Penthesilea has disturbed the balance of
emotions—she has saved him and in so doing has asserted dominance and superiority over him at the same time as expressing concern for him; she has satisfied both needs (she smiles, aware of her
dominance), but he, now disoriented, can only lash out at her to try
to redress that crucial balance of mutual dependence.

If the play ends violently, that is surely a matter of the breakdown
of the balance. Penthesilea recoils from sustaining the tremendous
emotional complexity of the situation by engaging in a simple, uncomplicated act. The precariousness of the emotional situation has
proved too much for her, the situation too difficult for her to maintain
at so complex a level emotionally. The final savage act is above all a
resort to simplifying the situation, letting one emotion take over and
crowd out all the others that have formed a whole of unbearable
complexity. She breaks down under the sheer effort of maintaining a

grasp of the situation that can keep its various parts in their proper perspective; what gets out of hand is her feeling of vulnerability to Achilles, to the possibility that he only wants to take her without any deeper commitment to her then merely the desire to show her off as a captive "mit Hohngelächter" (1571). Because she lets her view of Achilles' attitude to her become so reduced, a corresponding reduction of her emotions to a need for self-protection in the face of great emotional vulnerability is the result.

Since Kleist's texts move so conspicuously among different attitudes and interpretations, it follows that the one quality critics of his work most need in order to do it justice is flexibility; but, as we shall see in the next chapter, that quality has been rare in Kleist scholarship. Kleist's critics have generally, like Penthesilea herself, recoiled from ambiguity into a single rigid attitude.

More often than not, Kleist's text moves from initially simple and superficial attitudes to more complex ones. One particular version of this is found in both *Das Erdbeben in Chili* and in *Michael Kohlhaas*, which begin with ideas about the structure of the world (in the one case) and of society (in the other) that are, to be sure, grandiose but are also naive and simplistic. In both cases these neat, clear-cut ideas come to grief as it becomes evident that the world and society do not lend themselves to such tidy summarization. In both, grandiose philosophical and juridical notions are eventually rendered obsolete by a trivial circumstance, so that a card-house of theological and sociological theorizing is destroyed by the reality of actual people and events. In the former case, the trivial circumstance that triggers the final disaster occurs when the priest lets his tongue run away with him. In the latter, the circumstance is the person of Heloise and the Elector's vague affection for her, which turn out to have been the trigger for Kohlhaas's entire series of actions—neither a vast conspiracy nor a fundamental injustice in the society in which he lives.

On the other hand, the movement in *Penthesilea* is really the other way round; here we see not the breakdown of simple, clear ideas, but instead the breakdown of the equilibrium of a complicated situation and a retreat from that complexity into the simplicity and directness of savage violence. The situation seems unable to maintain itself in the precarious balance of emotions that had existed for most of the text, and the ending represents a resolution on the part of Penthesilea that is always the most tempting in a complex situation—a reduction to the stark simplicity of death and destruction. Both patterns can be seen in *Der Findling*: an initially simple interpretation of the situation (that the kindly old Piachi is wronged by his ungrateful adopted son) is complicated by the addition of new levels of interpretation, but then the resulting complexity is reduced to simplicity by an ending like that of *Penthesilea*. An emotionally precarious and complex situation is resolved only by violence and destruction.

There is really no facet of Kleist's work—whether language, imagery, narrative style, or recurrent motifs—that can be treated except in the context of the general framework of his fundamental concerns as a writer and the most basic strategy and structure of his work. Let us look, for example, at some of the most commonly identified recurring motifs in his writing. One such observed motif is that of error, deceptive appearances, and mistakes. It crops up frequently in criticism of Kleist, and the motif is indeed common in his work. But estimating what this recurrence means can only be a matter of setting it in the context of what his work is really about; and if we do that, we do not find Kleist to be obsessed with error and deceit per se, as many of his critics have thought.[8] Nor is his point the trivial one that people often make mistakes. This motif has to be taken as an integral part of Kleist's concern with the development of understanding and interpretation; his emphasis is not on human fallibility but instead on the way life demands that we continually attempt to understand and interpret what we see, and that we be prepared to abandon unsuccessful attempts to interpret it in order to rethink the situations we face. Mistakes are a part of this process, not the point of the whole, and in saying this I do not mean that there is in Kleist's work a sense of finding the right answers: the emphasis is only on the search for them.

"Gefühl" is another watchword of Kleist criticism that has on occasion been made an absolute value in his work, and the word itself is indeed another recurring motif. But its recurrence does not mean that Kleist embraces a heart-over-head, feeling-rather-than-intellect position.[9] Sometimes intuitive certainty turns out to be correct, sometimes incorrect—a point we can see proven when, late in *Das Erdbeben in Chili*, Josephe feels strongly that everyone should go to pray in the Dominican Church, while Elisabeth's intuition points just as strongly in the reverse direction. The reason for the prominence of references to "Gefühl" is simply that intuition and feelings are one way in which characters might respond to the situations in the stories. But the emphasis is on the continual need to respond—and intuition as one kind of response—not on it as the exclusive way to grasp the essence of a given situation. Typically, Kleist uses intuitive responses as a counterpoint to more reasoned ones simply in order to introduce conflicting attitudes to a situation; no issue is made of the value of intuitive feelings per se, either positively or negatively.

The case is much the same with another of the well-worn words of Kleist criticism: "Vertrauen." Complete trust seems to work well sometimes (the case of Friedrich von Trota in *Der Zweikampf*), might have worked at other times (the case of Gustav in *Die Verlobung in St. Domingo*), and is disastrous at still other times (the case of Achilles in *Penthesilea* and Josephe in the *Erdbeben*). In itself, it is viewed neither negatively nor positively; again, it is important only as another possible response to people or situations and thus another source for the various attitudes and interpretations that Kleist's texts play on and move among.

The recurring motif of chance in Kleist's work does not mean that in his world chance is all-powerful and fate blind (though that notion can of course be part of the "Stoff"—the material *used* in a particular text).[10] Within the context of Kleist's characteristic concerns, unexpected, chance events need to be seen primarily as challenges to the reader; they move the story in suddenly different directions so that he must rethink what is happening and conceivably alter his interpretation of the situation. By the very fact that they seem to lack a clear place in the structure of the text, and thus a clear motivation within it, they invite attempts to search for their significance and purpose. The *Erdbeben in Chili* is the clearest example of this. The first few pages present a large number of events explicitly referred to as chance events: for example, Jeronimo's managing to see Josephe again after she is sent to the nunnery, his finding a rope when in his cell, and finally his finding a means of escape, which is only possible because he is able to go underneath a "zufällige Wölbung" (146) made by two houses as they collapse towards each other—a remarkable coincidence indeed. But of course this very insistence on chance invites the reader to wonder whether more than chance is involved: is this divine providence? In *Der Findling*, the chance return of Piachi similarly provides food for thought: had Piachi been so apprehensive about the whole situation in his household that he had begun to spy on Elvire and Nicolo? Far from dismissing these events as having no significance for the structure of the situation, this harping on chance invites us to think about what their possible place in that structure might be. The frequent invoking of chance, then, is all part of Kleist's strategy of making his reader continually think about the shape of what is happening.[11] Where several attitudes are possible, a chance event often provides a temptation for us to fit it into a possible structure and reach an interpretative conclusion about how to look at what is happening; but we must be prepared—most notably in the *Erdbeben*—to go back and abandon this construction that we have put on the event and resign ourselves to the fact that the event in question was, after all, mere chance. At other times, even when chance events do remain

in the realm of the genuinely fortuitous, they may still seem to have
been in a sense invited by a given situation. Such is the case, for
example, in *Die Marquise von O . . .* , where there is a peculiar symmetry between the withdrawn and overprotected state of the Marquise and the extreme means by which she is wrenched from that
state.

The critical investigation of Kleist's style and language might at first
sight seem a more purely descriptive matter than those that I have
been discussing, but it too can only be pursued within an interpretative framework. From the point of view of the framework I have
proposed, for example, Kleist's critics have been seriously mistaken
even when they have tried to be merely descriptive. A common view
of Kleist's style is that it is highly objective and factual, even sober,
that it avoids subjectivity and either coloring or commentary by the
narrator, that it is highly realistic, and that it is economical and direct,
keeping description to an absolute minimum. In short, it is thought
that he gives us the facts as they are and nothing besides.[12] This is at
one and the same time a very good account of the surface impression
that Kleist makes on his reader and a disastrous misconception about
what he is really doing. There is, in the telling of the stories, an
overall sense of directness; for example, facts speak for themselves
rather than being colored or commented on by a narrator. (Even on
the surface level, this is only partially true of the plays.) And this
overall impression seems to put the onus on the reader to form his
own judgment of those facts, which of course he must constantly
do. But this cleverly maintained general impression soon disappears
when we look more closely, for then we find that Kleist is constantly
violating that convention and in so doing raising the issue of how to
interpret the facts, suggesting possible ways to do so, often dwelling
on the need for thought and interpretation, and just as often knocking down interpretations that had seemed tempting.

The chief characteristic of Kleist's prose style lies in a constant tension between factualness and interpretation. This is achieved partly
by a fairly overt violation of his general convention of factualness and
economy at critical points in the texts and also through a more subtle
manipulation of the convention that is harder to see. The first phenomenon occurs when Kleist violates his convention of an economical, fast-moving narrative by suddenly dwelling on and expanding
the description of an apparently unimportant event, thereby arresting
the normally rapid succession of plot events, or when his narrator
uses some striking imagery or some equally obtrusive evaluative language. But the second is found largely in the way the selection and
formulation of events give them a particular direction, and this is

something that must be abstracted from a long stretch of the text, rather than an effect that has a dramatic quality that emerges visibly at a particular juncture. In this category we must also place those many instances where selection is a matter of omitting information that the reader needs, whether this consists in failure to tell us what someone whispers to another character, or failure to include any explanatory comment in situations that remain puzzling without it, or withholding from us until very late in the text a fact that was needed much earlier if we were to make sense of what was happening. All of this means that it is simply not true to say that Kleist tells the story directly and economically without any coloring of the facts; we miss the most important quality of his narrative if we see it this way. Yet paradoxically, it is also true that the nonfactual side of his narrative achieves its importance only through the general impression of factualness. By this means, Kleist gives the impression that he is merely giving us the facts, unadorned, but at the same time is always jogging the reader to do something with those facts—to see how they hang together, to think about particular facts more than others, to worry about facts that are not there and what they might prove if he knew them, to guess at facts that are hinted at but not really stated, and to grasp what really happened in passages that are left ambiguous. In short, the reader is always required to be active, to move and to think, to shape events and to interpret them. The surface impression of factualness, then, is precisely the reverse of what Kleist's real concern is in these stories; evaluation of the facts is an ever-present problem.

Let us next consider examples of how this actually works. The most easily visible examples of what I have been discussing are the overt violations of the convention of factualness and economy. There are at least two examples of a complete breakdown of the economy of narration in the otherwise breathlessly economical *Erdbeben in Chili*: the first devotes a whole page to Jeronimo's changes of attitude to the earthquake itself, and the second a comparable amount of space to Donna Elisabeth's misgivings about the plan to return to the city to pray. Both these passages arrest the action of the story and in so doing create a hiatus where the focus of attention is clearly not on what is happening but on the significance of what is happening. The *Marquise von O . . .* , too, contains a section that is slow and relatively devoid of events, namely the pages leading up to the end of the story. But in these we get the extraordinary scene between father and daughter, which dwells on the tenor of their reconciliation at great length instead of merely reporting it. However, in so doing, it covertly introduces issues that completely alter the basis of the text. Another example is the odd description of the duel in *Der Zweikampf*, in which the narrator is strangely long-winded about telling us that Friedrich seems not to be a very spirited fighter. This part of the story should be the high-point of its action—the duel itself. But Kleist evidently has something in mind in making it drag so much that the spectators think the whole thing a bore—a fact that the narrator seems to find embarrassing but only makes worse by his attempts to explain away Friedrich's incompetent performance, in the process making it actually ludicrous. Obviously, Kleist uses the possibility of retarding or accelerating the action as a way of drawing attention to key issues in his story, but it is only the general impression of rapid narration that allows him to do this. When it suits him to do so, he glosses over huge areas of plot events—notably in the first page of *Das Erdbeben in Chili*, where the entire history of the romance between Josephe and Jeronimo is compressed into a few lines. But he can also expand a single point in the events and describe it at great length: description is surely *not* consistently kept to a minimum in Kleist.

Striking violations of the general convention of factual language are also quite common, and once more each occurrence derives its impact largely from its being a departure from a norm. A fine example is the appearance of the evaluative word "Bigotterie" (201) in *Der Findling*. This seems to jump at us from nowhere, without any secure position either among the facts we have been given or in the style of the story up to that point. The language of the scene between the Marquise and her father is similarly unexpected, a complete change in the tone of a narrative that has not only seemed factual, but also tactful up to that point. Elegance is suddenly replaced by a description that is nothing short of repellent. Some of the most striking examples of lapses into highly evaluative and evocative language come again from the *Erdbeben*; the central section provides the well-known example of a consciously "poetic" language (the description of the night scene), while the narrator's response to Don Fernando's behavior as he fights off the mob at the end of the story is an unusually direct and forceful evaluation: "dieser göttliche Held" (158). These dramatic examples of a break in the factual style could be multiplied, and they show all too clearly that subjectivity, narrator comment, and evaluation are not at all excluded by Kleist's style: on the contrary, they are actually highlighted and used with greater effect by that style.

Nevertheless, the subtler kinds of manipulations of facts, those that do not call attention to themselves as breaks with the surface convention, are the most interesting. In *Das Erdbeben in Chili*, for example, it may not at first sight seem to be evaluative, rather than simply informative, to refer to Josephe's brother as "stolz" (144); but that adjective, together with "hämisch," also applied to him, and "zärtlich," this time applied to the character of the relationship between the lovers, all give a particular shape to the whole situation that unfolds at the beginning of the text; the formulations have given the situation a distinct shape in the reader's mind. To be sure, having established that, Kleist then gives it a jolt with the phrase "zum Schauplatze seines vollen Glückes," which does not agree with our impression so far of the situation. In similar fashion, the words "jagte" and "trieb" (146), used when Jeronimo is escaping from his prison, give that situation a distinct feeling too. This is anything but factual storytelling—it is constant manipulation. The same is true of those cases where Kleist deemphasizes critical facts, like a writer of a detective story who wants to draw a clue past the reader's nose without the reader immediately recognizing the answer to the mystery.[13] For example, Kleist will sometimes go to great lengths to justify the introduction of crucial information with an utterly trivial excuse. In this category, for example, are the introduction of Heloise and the vital information that this gives about how all the establishment figures in the story are linked. The two critical facts about her are introduced as if merely the background information needed to set the stage for a colorful hunt party. The reader must look beyond the trivializing context of this information and make his own estimate of its actual importance. Or in *Das Erdbeben in Chili*, the shattering information about the hanging of an innocent man and of the continuing looting and thieving—all of which conveys the thematically vital fact that the world is actually no better than it was before, in spite of the previous appearances to the contrary—is introduced almost as a footnote to Josephe's anxiety about the appearance of friends who know of her status as a woman condemned to death. This understating of important facts is carried even further in *Der Findling*, where it is crucial to know that Nicolo's "mother" Elvire is actually in her twenties, just as he is. But to discover that, the reader has to put together several pieces of information that are scattered throughout the story. All of this kind of manipulation of the stories' "facts" functions to keep the reader thinking and interpreting; he can never passively accept what is offered him but must constantly judge the significance of what is narrated and how it is narrated.

Another kind of manipulation consists in the withholding of facts about which the reader will naturally be curious, and which the narrator could easily have given us. In *Der Findling*, Nicolo's returning to his room and finding it locked is very odd; why should it be locked, and why should not Nicolo have a key to it? Why does Elvire have the key on her person? And how does this strange situation relate to the odd coincidence that Elvire is still up and about at so late an hour, as Nicolo is returning? Is she deliberately watching over his movements? Does she faint on seeing him because she thinks she sees Colino or because she sees the resemblance between the two? None of this is explained; Kleist obviously wants us to puzzle over this for ourselves, but there is a good reason for his doing so. The nature of Elvire's feelings about Nicolo is the issue in these unanswered questions, and if we think enough about that issue, we should also come to think about the related question of why those feelings exist. From there we should be led to think about Piachi's role in Elvire's life and finally about the entire structure of Piachi's oppressive household.

There is a great deal of information withheld from the reader in *Michael Kohlhaas*. From the day after Kohlhaas's wife dies, all of the events involving the gypsy are withheld, for example, until very late in the text; and the crucial fact that Heloise is the link among the various governmental figures who thwart Kohlhaas is revealed equally late in the story. Kleist here manipulates the facts of his story by initially withholding all those that do not fit with Kohlhaas's own view of the situation, and when he later fills in those gaps, it becomes clear that the shape of the situation is completely different from that we and Kohlhaas himself had imagined. Having given us the facts that will predispose us to one view of the situation, Kleist then gives us those that are inconsistent with that view and thus changes the direction of our thinking.

Critics have on occasion thought of the way Kleist obtrusively omits information as part of his tendency to give us action and external description rather than giving us the responses and thoughts of his characters. This would all be consistent with the notion that he is a factual writer, one who shows us what happened but does not comment on it or let his characters' reactions to it show either. But this too is an untenable view except as a description of a superficial impression that Kleist creates in order to exploit it. The truth is that Kleist *does* report the thoughts and responses of his characters over and over again. Even in *Michael Kohlhaas*, the story most frequently cited to demonstrate Kleist's allegedly purely external description of people and events, there is a great deal of comment on the state of mind of Kohlhaas and others, including even such explicit mind reading as: "Kohlhaas dachte: 'So möge mir Gott nie vergeben, wie ich dem Junker vergebe!'" (30). There is, as we have seen, a great deal of space devoted to the thoughts of Jeronimo in the *Erdbeben*, as well as frequent comment on the state of mind of others, including of course the absolutely all-important last sentence of the story, which reports Don Fernando's *thought* about what has happened. And in *Der Find-*

ling, there is a continuous commentary on the tortuous progress of Nicolo's thoughts and emotions. Yet even though there is no question that this kind of comment that goes beyond the visible events is extremely common in Kleist's works, it still often suits his purposes to pretend that this is not the case and to stay at the visible surface of what happens, pointedly omitting any other kind of comment. These are cases that present open invitations to the reader to ponder what the withheld information might have been, and they are all cases that take the reader, through that process, into the heart of the issues of the text. We do not hear what Elvire says to Piachi at the end of the story just before Piachi throws Nicolo out of his house. Kleist makes us think about what she might have said, which in turn will make us think about her whole state of mind at that stage and all the pressures that weigh upon her. The point is, of course, that nothing that she could actually have uttered would be as complicated as what is going on in her mind. By withholding from us something that seems important enough for us to guess, Kleist has actually made us enter a realm of thought that is far deeper and more important than the few missing words that instigated the process of pondering in the reader. The words are almost a kind of bait; we chase them and end up grappling with something far bigger and more valuable.

Similarly, there is the instance in the *Erdbeben* in which we are not allowed to overhear what Donna Elisabeth whispers to Don Fernando. We have to guess what she might have said in order to form some idea of what his visible and audible response means, while the narrator pretends, in a manner quite inconsistent with his procedure up to this point, that he is in no better position to know what the words were than any other spectator to the scene. Once more, the result is different to, and more important than, what we would have learnt from the missing words; to guess at what was said will involve thinking about what kind of man Don Fernando is, and that will take us to the important thematic issue of his insistence on dignity rather than on calculation of what the future holds.

One more example is the wordless gesture of the Marquise's father when he fires a shot into the ceiling; the lack of any comment as to why he was so upset, if this lack provoked the reader to consider the issue for himself, might well lead to some interesting reflection about so violent and aggressive a response to his daughter's pregnancy, which also would raise some of the most important issues of the story. Silences are evidently part of Kleist's strategy of drawing his reader into reacting to and thinking about what he reads. The same is true of the occasional blatant textual ambiguities; Nicolo's comment on the likeness between himself and the picture of Colino, following the comment of Xaviera's little daughter Klara, is the most obvious case.

So far, I have been discussing mainly the language of the stories, which, since all are in prose, can more easily be taken together than the plays. The language of *Penthesilea*, for example, obviously differs from that of *Der zerbrochne Krug* partly because of the difference between the convention and tone of a Greek classical tragedy on the one hand and that of a play about village characters in Holland on the other. Nevertheless, the same basic strategy can be seen in the language of the plays. One can compare with the analogous pattern in the stories, for example, the way in which the basic convention of an explicit, direct, informative style is varied or sometimes abandoned in the *Prinz von Homburg*. In that play we are given three contradictory reports of what happened to the Prince and his horse before the battle, and we have to make up our own mind what we will conclude —we are given no resolution of the inconsistencies. And we can only resolve them by interpreting the whole situation and abstracting its basic patterns; we need to see that one account minimizes the Prince's wound and one maximizes it, and we must then put this together with the reasons Hohenzollern has for the former and Truchß for the latter. Only then can we form a reasonable idea of what happened: evidently, the Prince was wounded seriously enough to be embarrassed but not enough to be incapacitated. Hohenzollern wanted to play down the first of these two facts and Truchß the second. If we think about the situation enough to find this out, we know a good deal about how the Prince's friends cover up for him and make it possible for him to avoid responsibility and to get deeper into trouble. This mental operation on the part of the spectator to the play is very like that of the reader who must put together various odd scraps of information to arrive at Elvire's age or guess what Donna Elisabeth said to Don Fernando. The conversation between Hohenzollern and the Prince after the garden scene in the first act is enigmatic, and we must pay close attention in order to form an idea of what is going on in the Prince's mind; we can, I think, discern that he has remembered at a key point in the conversation that Natalie figured in his dream, but we are not *told* that—we must guess from the external signs. Again, information is withheld, and we are made to guess at what is going on in someone's mind, just as in *Der Findling*, when we are not allowed to hear what it is that Elvire whispers. The same quality exists in the play, then, of varying an explicit, informative style with significant gaps and omissions that provoke curiosity and thought; the spectator is always being drawn into interpreting what he sees. Glaring ambiguities are found here too, and for the same purposes:

Kottwitz's "Ein Traum, was sonst" (1856) demands as much thought and interpretation as Nicolo's unfathomable reply to Klara.

Metaphor and imagery as a counterpoint to the surface outline of the plot is even more developed in the *Prinz von Homburg* than in the stories. Probably only the case of *Die Marquise von O . . .* , in which the metaphorical analogy of love and war is so important, is comparable to the *Prinz von Homburg*'s use of the images of plants and horses as a way of making us see the key relationships in a manner fundamentally different from the way we perceive their apparent shape at the surface level of the plot.

It has often been observed that Kleist's Elector is somewhat inscrutable, and that it is hard to see when he makes up his mind and why; some critics have regretted this fact about the play and thought it a blemish in the text. But this is a case in which it is very important to understand how Kleist works. It is obviously much more important to him that the reader ponder the complexity of the process, its length, and the many pressures on him which contribute to the Elector's decision than to show a definite reason and a specific point of decision; and in any case, the complexity of the situation precludes any kind of explicit statement, which would of necessity simplify it. The Prince and Natalie are not easy to comprehend either; the stage direction of line 1313 demands thought about what is going on in both their minds: "Natalie erblaßt. Pause. Der Prinz sieht sie fragend an." In this play, the reader's need to interpret and read the signs correctly is compounded, for the characters are evidently doing the same thing, without necessarily getting the right answers. Take the following, apparently trivial exchange between Hohenzollern and the Prince:

DER PRINZ VON HOMBURG.
   Sieh da! Freund Heinrich! Sei willkommen mir!
   —Nun, des Arrestes bin ich wieder los?

HOHENZOLLERN *erstaunt*.
   Gott sei Lob, in der Höh!

DER PRINZ VON HOMBURG.   Was sagst du?

HOHENZOLLERN.   Los?
   Hat er den Degen dir zurück geschickt?

DER PRINZ VON HOMBURG.
   Mir? Nein.

HOHENZOLLERN. Nicht?

DER PRINZ VON HOMBURG. Nein!

HOHENZOLLERN.   —Woher denn also los?

DER PRINZ VON HOMBURG *nach einer Pause.*
  Ich glaubte, du, du bringst es mir.—Gleichviel!

HOHENZOLLERN.
  —Ich weiß von nichts.

                                                          (791–97)

This is almost a comedy of overinterpretation; the Prince interprets
the meaning of Hohenzollern's arrival and states what he thinks it is,
then finds that Hohenzollern takes this as information that the Prince
is giving him, until they both see their mistake.

   In its movement between apparently clear, direct language on the
one hand and striking imagery or obscure and ambiguous utterances
on the other, we find in the *Prinz von Homburg* very much the same
kind of pattern that is found in the stories: a mode of exposition that
is undermined by all kinds of features that run counter to it and serve
to make us think again about the adequacy of any surface impressions
we have of what is happening.

   Even the detail of Kleist's sentence structure is best described and
understood in an interpretative framework. While earlier critics spoke
of the direct, intense forward-moving style of his narratives, Friedrich
Beißner first noticed that the structure of Kleist's sentences suggested
a modification of that view; he found "rastlose Unverzüglichkeit
des Berichts im ganzen, der im einzelnen immer wieder Umständ-
lichkeit entgegenwirkt."[14] Kayser picked up this insight to take it
further;[15] he observed not only a large number of Kleist's sentences
that were a direct series of simple past tense verbs recording a series
of actions without any interruptions but also many others in which
the same basic series of verbs was interrupted by a series of circumstantial subordinate clauses that impeded the flow of the action.
Whereas Beißner had thought of this second kind of sentence mainly
in terms of acceleration or retardation of the events of the story,
Kayser saw it as a much more meaningful part of the whole. He saw a
contrast in the typical Kleist sentence of "Geschehnisfolge" and "Um-
ständlichkeit"; the action pressed forward in the former, only to meet
a new circumstance in the latter that complicated the situation.

   Kayser's remarks fit very well the interpretative framework that I
have suggested; here is yet another aspect of that tension between
fact and interpretation, between the simple surface of the plot events
and the shaping of an attitude towards them. Events move forward
in the sequence of simple past tense verbs, but the circumstantial
details that intervene constantly suggest possible constructions that

can be placed on them or simply difficulties that must be registered and thought about. We are never really sure which is more important; the major events of the sentence may suddenly seem far less significant than the detail that is relegated to a relative clause, if, as sometimes happens, that detail links with something else to suggest a revision in the reader's understanding of what is happening. The best example of this is, once more, the introduction of Heloise late in *Michael Kohlhaas*; the grammatically major parts of the sentences concerned are far less important than the information squeezed into subordinated clauses or even more grammatically tenuous appositional elements. These overloaded sentences not only retard the action through their cumbersome grammatical structure—they return us to earlier episodes of the story to think again in the light of detail now emerging; and just as this detail complicates them grammatically in almost unbearable fashion, it complicates the whole understanding of the story even more. This kind of sentence structure, then, gives a perfect image of how a seemingly clear plot outline can be eaten away and destroyed through complicating factors that finally cause its collapse. The tension of the style per se is not the point—though it does of course strike the reader as such; the point lies in the tension within the sentence between the gross surface of events and the details that may eventually compel us to see a fundamentally different shape in those events.

One last aspect of Kleist's narrative style relevant to this view of Kleist's purposes is the question of his narrator. Kayser observed, with an accuracy and subtlety of formulation that has utterly defeated most subsequent critics who have discussed his view, that the evaluations of Kleist's narrator are "oft aus der Perspektive einer Gestalt und immer unter dem Eindruck der jeweiligen Situation. . . . Er besitzt keine Überlegenheit über die Figuren. . . . Er überschaut nicht einmal das Ganze des Geschehens; seine Voraussagen sind nur partiell, und seine Wertungen . . . gelten fast immer der jeweiligen Situation."[16] Many scholars have assumed Kayser to be saying that Kleist had no interest in evaluation, but that is of course a bad misreading, only possible because they did not see the point of Kayser's distinguishing narrator and author. My investigation of the stories confirms Kayser's observations; the narrator does indeed evaluate from the standpoint of a particular point in the narrative and often—not always—from the point of view of a given character. Most importantly, there is no sense of his being a figure who knows the *right* attitudes to the events and characters of these stories, so that his evaluations always have built into them a limited perspective. His taking Piachi's perspective in *Der Findling*, for example, must not lead us to see that as an authoritative judgment in Piachi's favor. Kayser's brief article does not go on to discuss the point of this use of the narrator; but it appears to me that by using a narrator whose understanding of the situation is limited, yet who is always raising the issue of understanding it, Kleist pushes the issue of interpreting the meaning of the events into the forefront of our attention. The narrator himself continually attempts to come to terms with the meaning of the story, in the process making mistakes and then trying again. Like the reader, the narrator learns as the story progresses, and he tells the facts of the events as if they were as inscrutable to him as to anyone else. In this tension between the narrator's desire to see coherence in the story and his wish merely to relate what actually happened, letting this speak for itself, lies the most characteristic quality of Kleist's narration. Sometimes one pole predominates, sometimes the other, and this must be why some interpreters of the stories have seen in them above all gripping realistic narratives,[17] while others have experienced them as symbolic or moral tales.

Kleist's works are about the process of trying to come to terms with the world; and in his stories his narrator is, in a sense, always the central figure, the one who tries continually to think and rethink what he sees. The situations he chooses and the people who live in them are various,[18] but what always remains, whether we are dealing with the plays or the stories, is a focus on the fact that those situations can be grasped in various competing ways, and that understanding any aspect of them can be complicated by many different levels of judgment. Time and again, what seems obvious at one level can be seen in a way that is diametrically opposite when we respond to all of the subtleties of the text.

VIII

The Character of Kleist Criticism

Criticism of Kleist is by now voluminous and increasing ever more rapidly. That being the case, it might be expected that anyone writing yet another study of Kleist would feel somewhat apologetic and even defensive about adding to this enormous amount of material. At the very least, an explanation is needed of why another study is thought to be necessary. This chapter will provide the necessary explanation, though that is not its main purpose; my intent here is to diagnose what I think to be a central weakness in virtually all studies of Kleist. To do so is not simply to carp at other critics but instead to attempt to explain how and why Kleist criticism has largely missed the essence of his work. In a sense that I shall explain shortly, Kleist's critics have fostered a view of him that stands diametrically opposed to what he tried to do in his writing. This is most obviously true, moreover, of the best-known and most influential studies of Kleist—the general books on his life and work, more prestigious and visible than the more delimited articles found in journals. This discussion is a necessary addition to that of the previous chapter, and it will provide further perspective on what I have tried to do by contrasting it with a prevailing alternative that I have sought to avoid. The distinctive character of my own view of Kleist and the reasons for it will become clearer against this background. And in the case of an author such as Kleist, who makes the process of interpretation so central to his work, there is a peculiarly instructive quality about the basic interpretative mistake that is, if I am correct, a feature of Kleist criticism generally. A last, but still very important reason for the inclusion of this discussion is that it has a strong bearing on the shape and structure of this book; the central error of Kleist criticism that I shall be discussing is, as we shall see, a likely consequence of the kind of organization that I argued against in my introductory chapter. That theoretical argument is, then, supported by the demonstration in this chapter of an important practical consequence of the more familiar kind of procedure generally used in critical studies of this and other authors. I can best begin this discussion by recapitulating a part of that theoretical argument.

I argued in my introduction that it was preferable to give close attention to a moderately small number of important works rather than to try to cover Kleist's whole output—first, because considerations of space make it impossible to discuss everything if superficiality is to be avoided; and second, because the quality of a critical discussion soon degenerates once there is a sense that everything has to be covered. If a critic begins to say things because he feels that he must say at least something about everything, rather than because he has something in each case that he wants to say, he will soon lose a sense of what is important and what is not and then begin to judge the usefulness of his statements by progressively lower standards. But the most injurious consequence of this procedure is that it results in an attempt to facilitate finding something to say about everything by adopting a theme or feature to trace through each work, pronouncing it especially Kleistian, identifying it in every text, and passing on to the next to do the same again. This procedure leads to a minimizing of any differences between individual works, and that too reinforces the superficial quality of the resulting criticism, as each work is reduced to something easily manageable. Placing a general discussion of Kleist before the discussion of individual works is similarly problematic, since it tends to limit the meaning of the individual texts to the issues set out in the general discussion. I decided to reverse the more usual order and to let my general discussion of the character of Kleist's work grow out of the results of some detailed discussions of a limited number of individual works.

This argument in its most general form is not restricted to the case of Kleist, but there are reasons to think it especially important in his case. Abstracting motifs and ideas from their context in individual works is, as we have seen, a more than usually dangerous procedure in Kleist criticism since his works demand a close attention to their twists and turns. The very notion of a context is more complicated in works that continually change direction, and in which an idea can seem to have positive value on one page but be revalued later on. It is fruitless for the critic to try to trace a motif through all Kleist's works as if the motif had a constant value, because the complete context of a whole text rarely allows the abstraction of an idea that has any unambiguous value even in one of Kleist's works.

This has, however, been the standard procedure of Kleist critics, and it is the most serious flaw in Kleist criticism. It has been common to give a fixed value throughout his work to particular notions such as trust, error, or feeling. This is not simply mistaken criticism but is in a way a recoil from Kleist's characteristic demand on his readers; for Kleist demands that the reader remain flexible and move with the texts' changes of direction, while his critics have generally responded to this disturbing openness only by taking refuge from it in fixed, rigid positions.[1] Thus Kleist's meaning is reversed. He sets his readers a challenge—to deal with a constantly developing situation—and to grasp for firm orientation points from which each text can be judged is to fail that challenge.

Here we find the reason for the sometimes extraordinary degree of disagreement among Kleist scholars as to the meaning of a particular work—especially *Prinz Friedrich von Homburg* and *Das Erdbeben in Chili*. The reduction of these complex works to the same simple messages, attitudes or ideologies, or to any other kinds of unambiguous assertions, can only be a very arbitrary procedure; one critic chooses one facet of the text as the key to interpretation while another chooses something else. Sometimes a particular reduction of the text is more tempting than others (the case, say, of the "education" theory in *Prinz Friedrich von Homburg*), and that may produce at least a majority viewpoint. In other cases, such as *Das Erdbeben in Chili*, the possibilities for reduction to a fixed viewpoint are so various that there is no majority tendency among critics. The texts clearly entertain (without finally allowing) various possible attitudes to and interpretations of them, and the great disagreement among critics on certain texts is simply due to the fact that individual critics seize on one or other possibility and on the particular limited context of the text that gives that possible interpretation its most tempting form; they then rigidify it to make of it *the* interpretation of the text. The subsequent arguments with others who have picked a different suggested interpretation always miss the point; while the critics argue over who has the better case, they do not see that the story is *about that argument*, not about the particular interpretation that they are trying to make the victor in the argument. Not all of Kleist's works have provoked this kind of controversy; *Der Findling* has not, for example. But this is because Kleist often makes one plausible explanation so explicit that it seems to offer the critic an unusually easy resting place. Here, to see only Piachi's altruism and Nicolo's depravity is an especially tempting way of avoiding the disturbing complications of the text.

So far, I have spoken in only very general terms of Kleist criticism; let me now turn to some examples to show what actually happens in typical instances. The first is a recent and relatively simple example of what I have been describing: Elmar Hoffmeister's *Täuschung und Wirklichkeit bei Heinrich von Kleist*. This title confirms a commitment to the prevailing manner of Kleist criticism, for it is clearly analogous to Friedrich Koch's *Bewußtsein und Wirklichkeit* and Walter Müller-Seidel's *Versehen und Erkennen*, to take only two examples. The double-barreled thematic title, incidentally, is a fad that seems to have originated with

Gerhard Fricke's *Gefühl und Schicksal bei Heinrich von Kleist*; it appears
to have carried over into journal articles (as in Hans-Peter Herrmann's
"Zufall und Ich") and to works in English (as in John Gearey's *Tragedy
and Anxiety*), and it is still as strong as ever—a new title is Hermann
Reske's *Traum und Wirklichkeit*.[2]

What can be seen immediately in these titles (apart from a certain
repetitiveness, for all tend to cover ground that is at least partly
covered in the others) is a prevailing habit of abstracting a motif and
tracing it throughout Kleist's work. Elmar Hoffmeister's case is typical: he goes through the texts one by one to show deception in each of
them. Piachi is deceived by Nicolo in *Der Findling*; the Prince is deceived by his own dream in the *Prinz von Homburg*; the Marquise is
deceived by events in *Die Marquise von O . . .*; and so on. His conclusion, in general terms, can only be that there is much deception in
Kleist. Two things can be said about such a book and about all the
other examples of the genre. First, the general conclusion about Kleist
is a very uninteresting one, and in that sense at least the idea of the
book is unproductive. And second, this journey through the works
with a fixed idea produces no interpretative insights into the individual texts. To take the former point first: one might look at Shakespeare's best-known plays and say that there is much deception in
them. Iago deceives Othello, Lear is deceived by his daughters, Macbeth is deceived by the witches, and so on. None of this is very
unique or interesting: there is no obvious value in taking very general
and unremarkable ideas out of context simply to list their occurrence.
There is deception in Kleist, in Shakespeare, in Goethe, and in everyday life: by itself, the notion is not startling. Some interest might be
generated if the discussion could get at a specifically Kleistian use of
the notion. But that would lead to a thorough interpretation of each
text, with attention to the place of deception within the thematic
structure of each text, and it is just such a procedure that books like
Hoffmeister's seem designed to avoid: going through all the texts
with a simple idea as an orientation point for each is not merely coincidentally a procedure that does not involve serious thought about
each text. Hoffmeister's interpretative comments—and those of all
such books—are in fact rarely new or original, and they generally
follow well-known surface readings. A good example is his view of
Der Findling. Hoffmeister simply assimilates it to his framework by
identifying Nicolo as a deceiver in a section entitled "Der Betrug des
Verführers Nicolo in der Novelle *Der Findling*";[3] that very formulation
makes it clear that the interpretation offered is the superficial one that
is well known from other general books of criticism. Evidently, this
kind of work will have no impact on our understanding of the texts.[4]

Hoffmeister's book is recent and not yet widely known. To show just how typical its failings are, I want now to turn to two cases that are superficially very different: Hans Matthias Wolff's book *Heinrich von Kleist als politischer Dichter*, and an article by Manfred Durzak, "Zur utopischen Funktion des Kindesbildes in Kleists Erzählungen."[5] Wolff's book is a well-known, somewhat older general treatment of Kleist; Durzak's is a recent article which focuses narrowly on a particular motif.

Wolff's work is dominated by a political idea: the relation of individual to state in Kleist's work. His thesis is that Kleist first felt that the individual was more important but later came to feel that the reverse was the case. Wolff goes through all the works and discusses them in this light. Just as in Hoffmeister's case, it will readily be seen that the general idea that forms the framework of the study is a fairly simple one that lacks intrinsic interest as it stands. Indeed, it is only fair to say that the idea as presented and discussed does not achieve the level of interest and complexity that one would expect from an introductory course in political science, and a reader ignorant of Kleist could surely be forgiven for concluding that Kleist was a dull and unsubtle writer if that was what his work was about. Once more, the level of interpretative comment on the individual texts which is allowed by mechanical "coverage" with the aid of such an idea is very low. In *Der zerbrochne Krug*, for example, Wolff's main idea is that Adam is "nicht allein Mensch, sondern Richter, d.h. *Beamter*, und aus dieser seiner Stellung als Beamter ergibt sich die gesamte Problematik des Werkes . . . er ist der Beamte, der seine Gewalt mißbraucht."[6] Here we can see only too clearly the way in which the pursuit of a general notion gets out of hand: that Adam is a state official—a trivial enough point—is suddenly the basis of "die gesamte Problematik des Werkes." It is easy enough to see (for example, in his very name) that Adam's being a human being is a rather larger issue than that of his being a bureaucrat. The discussion of Kohlhaas is in similar vein: according to Wolff, his troubles stem from his mistreatment by officials of the state. Together with *Der zerbrochne Krug*, then, *Michael Kohlhaas* shows how Kleist is for the individual and against the state at this stage. In *Prinz Friedrich von Homburg*, on the other hand, the Prince learns to accept the state, which means that Kleist himself now values the authority of the state over the individual. This all involves a sadly uninteresting view of all the works, and an avoidance of the really interesting issues of Kleist's texts; and in the process, no interpretative remark about the texts is made that is of any originality. Wolff's view of *Prinz Friedrich von Homburg* is simply the very familiar "education" theory; his view of *Michael Kohlhaas* is simply that there is injustice to Kohlhaas; and so on. Ironically, where *Michael Kohlhaas* questions whether it is possible to use abstractions like "the State" (a lofty abstraction that falls to pieces during the story), Wolff goes on using it regardless of what the story does to it. A determination to trace a general idea throughout all the works evidently makes this critic deaf to what any particular text is saying and to what it actually does with that idea. Wolff does not notice that one of the things that *Michael Kohlhaas* does is precisely to question the value of any analysis in the terms that he uses to examine Kleist's work; the notion of the individual versus the state evaporates in this story.

Durzak's analysis concerns the figure of the child in Kleist's work. He too traces this motif through several texts, assigning to it a fixed value—a positive one—each time it appears. This means that he motivates critical events in any story simply in terms of Kleist's belief that children represent "reine Natur" regardless of what the context of the particular work demands. So, for example, he thinks the reconciliation of the Marquise and the Count is possible because of the child, who "repräsentiert reine Natur"; that Kohlhaas's sons are knighted so that "die Katastrophe in einem utopischen Kindesbild aufgehoben wird"; and that the ending of *Das Erdbeben in Chili*, too, is optimistic because of the survival of the child.[7] None of this can be justified by the emphases of the context of the work. In each case, the critic substitutes what concerns him (the theme he is following through each text) for what concerns the work. In the *Marquise von O . . .* it is surely obvious that we must look to the whole history of what has gone on between Marquise and Count and see the ending as a result of all that; how could Kleist really motivate his story otherwise without seeming utterly arbitrary? In *Michael Kohlhaas*, the knighting of Kohlhaas's sons is surely part of the pattern contrasting the flourishing of his name and that of the house of Brandenburg with the future demise of Saxony's; there is again no trace of any emphasis on childish innocence in what happens. And in the *Erdbeben in Chili*, especially, the delicate balance of the ending is disturbed by the unambiguous assertion that the child represents a utopian solution. In this last case, to preserve his thesis, Durzak has to rewrite Kleist's crucial final sentence and see in Don Fernando's final statement "diese von Schmerz beschattete Freude." Kleist's own language is of course more guarded and much more interesting—its emphases are far removed from those of Durzak's theme. In commenting on the quality of this criticism it is not my purpose to find fault with any particular critic; my point is to stress that these are the inevitable results of a procedure in Kleist criticism that is very widespread.[8] Criticism that seizes on a general idea and sets out to use it on all the texts, whether in the form of avowedly limited articles like Durzak's, or general works that take a specific view of Kleist and his work like Hoffmeister's and Wolff's, will of necessity only produce results that reduce and distort the meaning of that work.

So far, the flaw that I have diagnosed seems simple enough, and the question may arise: if it really is that simple, why is it not more obvious, and why have not more critics seen and overcome it? The answer to this question appears to me to lie in a feature of Kleist criticism that tends to conceal the true character of the situation. As if sensing that the basic content of their arguments is excessively simple, many Kleist critics elaborate it and restate it in ever more complex terminology. Hoffmeister, again, is a representative example: "Bei den Gestalten, die in guter oder böswilliger Absicht Irrtum stifteten, wurde schon deutlich, daß sie meist in einem unzulänglichen, verfehlten Verhältnis zur Realität als gegenständlicher und gesellschaftlicher Wirklichkeit standen."[9] The impressive terminology tends to cast a spell on the reader, but it can be broken by determined reflection. Is to "stand in an insufficient relationship to reality as objective and social fact" really more than "to be in error"? Hoffmeister's verbal elaboration masks a thought so simple as to be hardly worth stating: "People spread mistakes because they themselves have made them." Hoffmeister's terminology is superficially impressive, and it may seem to lend his criticism some plausibility, but it really serves only to disguise that what he is saying is not remarkable. Another means of infusing an appearance of complexity into what is in reality very simple lies in the elaboration of distinctions that have no real point to them; for example, "Irreführung in guter Absicht" is distinguished by Hoffmeister from "Irreführung in schlechter Absicht," without his explaining why anything is gained from doing so. Categories must surely be justified as useful and pertinent ones if they are to contribute anything to an understanding of Kleist.

The technique of creating a verbal complexity in the critic's own language to compensate for a lack of substance is by no means new, nor is Hoffmeister's case an extreme one. It was already very noticeable in the work of Friedrich Braig (1925), for example. When discussing Kleist's literary works, Braig would generally give a plot summary which was interspersed with a few comments such as: "Hier kämpfte der Dichter um Sein oder Nichtsein," or "Hier hat sich Kleist bis in die letzten Tiefen der Menschenseele hinabgebohrt."[10] These remarks are virtually without content as far as interpreting or characterizing the text goes, and they represent an attempt to make the critic's statements seem interesting and impressive when he has in fact no real point to make.

Another case has already been touched upon in the preceding chapter: Herrmann's study elaborates the notion of chance events in Kleist mainly by adding linguistic complexity to an obvious thought, which is that many chance events in Kleist demand a response from those who experience them. But it is just as true of daily life anywhere, at any time, that chance events often compel a response to them; and since that is so, it cannot be very interesting to say that such is also the case in Kleist's world. Nothing is said here that is characteristic of Kleist.[11] A good test in such cases is to see whether the study concerned involves or leads to interpretative comments that differ in any way from those that are standard in other general studies of Kleist. In Herrmann's study, none such is found—linguistic complexity superimposed on the obvious is all that is there.

In some cases, the recourse to verbal complexity is recognizably a recoil from dealing with the problems of Kleist's texts. Max Kommerell's study is a case in point. Kommerell does indeed respond to the problematic nature of Kleist's texts, but he misplaces the source of this feature by locating it in the characters: "Kleists Personen sind Rätsel."[12] Since we can say equally that Hamlet, Macbeth, Othello, and most other literary figures are "Rätsel," it is clear that Kommerell has not put his finger on the specifically Kleistian problematic character of these texts. This bad start prevents further progress, and Kommerell then shifts to endless playing on the compounds of "Rätsel": "rätselhaft," "Verrätselung," "Enträtselung," without thereby adding anything to the interpretation of the texts. In *Der Findling*, for example, he finds Nicolo "ruchlos," just as most others do;[13] and his judgments are similarly unremarkable in other works. His discussion soon abandons any attempt to go beyond very well-known interpretative views to concentrate on developing its own linguistic texture per se; and a consequence of his concern with elaborating his own verbal system rather than looking at what Kleist wrote is that he begins to make serious factual errors in referring to Kleist's texts—an instructive example of where this kind of criticism is likely to lead. Let me give one example: Kommerell's discussion of *Der Findling* is essentially a plot summary using his special vocabulary ("rätselhaft," etc.), but during this he refers to Colino as the man who rescued Elvire from a fire and died of wounds received doing so "nach wenigen Tagen, während derer sie ihn nicht verließ." This is not only a bad factual error but a central one: a critic who wishes to come to terms with what is happening in this text, and what Elvire represents in it, could not possibly fail to be deeply impressed with her having spent three years (not a few days) constantly at the bedside of the dying Colino!

The examples I have discussed so far are typical of the field; quite
how typical they are can be judged from the fact that all of the fundamental criticisms I have made of them can be made with equal justice
of the work that is currently the best-known and most-quoted book
on Kleist, Walter Müller-Seidel's *Versehen und Erkennen*.[14] As his title
suggests, Müller-Seidel's work is concerned with the abstraction of a
motif from Kleist's texts: Kleist's characters first commit a "Versehen"
and then experience "Erkennen." The notion that the characters first
make mistakes and then see them is, here too, not by itself very
promising; moreover, it derives in any case from earlier writers such
as Kommerell and Koch. Elaboration is again the answer to this problem of lack of originality or inherent interest in his thesis, and Müller-
Seidel pursues it by categorizing various kinds of "Versehen" and
"Erkennen." One section of his treatise, for example, is on "Sinnengläubigkeit" as a subspecies of "Versehen," and he discusses as an
important Kleistian problem "das Vertrauen in die Verläßlichkeit der
fünf Sinne, das zur Ursache immer neuer Verkennungen wird. Es
handelt sich um eine Art von Sinnengläubigkeit, der manche Figuren
schlechterdings verfallen."[15] This is either trite, or wrong. It is trite if
it refers to people in general, wrong if it refers to Kleist's characters in
particular. It is of course not a failing of Kleist's characters but a
universal human habit to believe the evidence of the senses. No one
put in the position of the Marquise or Alkmene would be other than
baffled by what happens. The real issue is the misleading nature
of what those characters see; they do not hallucinate, they merely
draw normal conclusions from what they see, as anyone else would.
Müller-Seidel has managed to make much ado about nothing. Another example of the same procedure can be seen when he begins to
categorize and subsection the concept "Erkennen." Here there is first
a linguistically complex title: "Die Enthüllung des rätselhaft-wider-
spruchsvollen Sachverhalts und die Formen des Erkennens."[16] He
then proceeds to tell his reader that one of the forms of "das Erkennen" is "dadurch, daß die beteiligten Figuren den verrätselten Sach-
verhalt durchschauen." This could have been said more simply: one
way out of a mistake is to see one's mistake. Once the polysyllabic
terminology is cut through, only utter triviality remains. The function
of the complex terminology is surely to disguise this fact.

Interestingly, Müller-Seidel makes the same kind of factual errors
as does Kommerell when he refers to Kleist's text. For example,
Müller-Seidel refers to Colino as "den geheimen Liebhaber dieser in
einer Scheinehe lebenden Frau."[17] To be sure, the memory of Colino
is Elvire's secret obsession; but he is not and never was her secret
lover. Colino never knew Elvire until he rescued her from the fire, in

the process receiving wounds from which he died; and his death preceded her marriage. Again, this kind of example seems to confirm that criticism that strains to elaborate a simple idea, and therefore has all of its attention directed to the cultivation of its own texture, has very little time and energy left to give to what Kleist actually wrote. Müller-Seidel's interpretative judgments point to this conclusion just as surely as his inability to refer accurately to Kleist's text points to it, for those judgments are never innovative; they are in fact the reverse, always those most commonly found in previous critics. Take, for example, his view of *Prinz Friedrich von Homburg*. Müller-Seidel fits this into the general framework of his book by stressing that the Prince's seeing his mistake is the "Voraussetzung der Gnade und damit des untragischen Ausgangs."[18] Here the error motif is tacked onto a standard view of the Prince, and of the play, but in doing this Müller-Seidel simply evades all of the really important interpretative issues of the text. It was possible to raise questions here such as whether the Prince really *does* see his mistake, *how* he conceives of it, whether the ending is really positive and untragic, whether the Prince's mistake is the main issue in the play at all, and so on. This kind of criticism seems not designed to confront the complexity of Kleist's texts but instead to add linguistic complexity to rather routine views of them. To focus on the notion of error and trace it throughout Kleist's work is evidently an easy substitute for hard interpretative thought.

Because of the prestige enjoyed by Müller-Seidel's work, I have thought it worth-while to spend some time discussing his study as a representative example of Kleist criticism. I want now to turn to another very influential figure in Kleist criticism—Gerhard Fricke. Though his view of Kleist no longer enjoys the kind of universal acceptance once accorded it, Fricke did more than any other critic to create the conditions in which the criticism that I have described is able to flourish. For in Fricke's work, verbal elaboration is not simply a compensation for poverty of content, as in the case of Hoffmeister, Reusner, Müller-Seidel, and others; in his criticism the elaboration of a verbal system is an independent goal, and there is a delight in his own language that soon leaves behind any thesis about Kleist's texts. This might have made him irrelevant to Kleist criticism; instead, he was until recently the most influential of all Kleist critics, and he continues to exert influence through those who have absorbed a good deal of his manner, if not his doctrines.

The relation of Fricke's criticism and its concerns to Kleist's texts can be seen clearly enough in just one example, his discussion of *Die Marquise von O . . . .* The following quotation is long, but Fricke's characteristic quality is very much a matter of length:

Wieder ist allein die Marquise, oder besser die in der innersten und eigensten Tiefe ihres Wesens erwachende, geheimnisvolle, unendliche Kraft ihres Selbst das verborgene Ziel der Darstellung. Hier aber geht die erreichte Lösung zum ersten Male über die bisher erschienene Möglichkeit hinaus, in der die siegende, unverwirrbare Gewißheit des innersten Gefühls diesen ihren Triumph nur zu bewähren vermochte in der Preisgabe des zeitlichen Daseins, der gebrechlichen Endlichkeit, die die Herrlichkeit des vom Absoluten lebenden Ich und des unbedingten Gefühls nicht zu tragen vermochte. . . . Das Ich vermag hier kraft seiner unbegreiflichen Macht, kraft seiner Reinheit und Einheit mit sich selber und damit mit Gott,—das rätselhafte und vernichtende Schicksal zu überwinden, ohne an dem Widerspruch zwischen der Wirklichkeit und der bewahrten Reinheit des Gefühls zugrunde zu gehen. . . . Diese Kraft ist durch irgendwelche psychologische Kategorien: des Trotzes, der Selbstbehauptung—gar nicht mehr zu umschreiben. Sie ist religiösen Ursprungs. Sie stammt aus der unmittelbaren, absolut-konkreten und absolut-substantiellen Einheit des Ich mit dem ewigen Soll seiner Existenz, sie stammt aus der weltüberwindenden Kraft des Gefühls, das hier das credo quia absurdum gleichsam auf einer neuen Stufe vollbringt.[19]

This is only a sample of a lengthy discussion of the Marquise's strength of mind, in which the emphases become more and more Fricke's and less and less Kleist's. By the end, Fricke is clearly talking about what *he* thinks gives people strength of character in real life, that is, religious belief. But that is nowhere to be found in Kleist's text. The elaboration of Fricke's own text has obviously substituted for any kind of concern with what Kleist wrote; he is absorbed in the subtleties and paradoxes that he himself creates and has no wish to submit himself to the discipline of the text and to allow his train of thought to be determined by its subtleties.

All too often, then, verbal complexity compensates for a deficiency in real content in Kleist criticism; and that deficiency, in turn, has usually resulted from a desire to find a general idea with which to characterize all of his works, one by one, and from the misconceptions about the nature of his writing that must inevitably result from so reductive a procedure.

The basic ideas that have formed the framework of these studies have sometimes been derived from aspects of the texts themselves. This is the origin, for example, of "Gefühl," "Zufall," "Vertrauen," as well as the many different versions of error and illusion ("Versehen," "Täuschung," "Traum," etc.). I have argued above that Kleist's texts are badly misread if these ideas are taken as fixed and absolute ones,[20] as authors of general studies have done in order to find a theme to trace through all the texts, rather than as material that Kleist exploits at one moment and drops at the next in the interests of his larger concerns. But the basic notions of many general studies do not have even this much legitimacy; they are not the result of a misreading of the way certain motifs function in the text but instead derive from sources outside the texts. Two main kinds of source can be seen: the first consists in biographical information, the second in the ideological and critical preoccupations of the particular critic.

Kleist's biography is obviously a main source of the view that his work is above all violent and tragic, the mirror of a tormented, sick mind;[21] critics who take this view certainly have his suicide prominently in mind. But if they had looked only at the emphases of his writings, it would have been harder to reach this conclusion. *Penthesilea*, to be sure, might superficially invite such a description, but it is an exception among the major writings. If we look at *Prinz Friedrich von Homburg*, *Der zerbrochne Krug*, *Michael Kohlhaas*, *Der Zweikampf*, *Die Marquise von O . . .* , and even *Das Erdbeben in Chili*, we find ambiguous rather than solidly pessimistic works. They do not really compare in this regard to such works as *King Lear*, *Othello*, or *Hamlet*, and there is not a single scene in them that projects such deep and total despair as Faust's in "Wald und Höhle." To be sure, there are some violent and tragic elements in them, but the overall framework within which these elements occur is not of that character. One has only to compare the typically ambiguous endings of Kleist's works, hovering as they do between positive and negative attitudes to what has occurred, with the black, claustrophobic helplessness of, say, some works of Hebbel or Chekhov to see that he is indeed a serious and thoughtful writer but not an unreservedly gloomy one. Kleist's works present human life as something that must be thought and rethought, interpreted and reinterpreted; it is very much contrary to the drift of the great majority of his works to say that they present a consistently negative attitude to life.

A comparable biographically introduced notion is that Kleist's characters are extremists, "grenzenlose Menschen." In fact, there are very few of Kleist's characters who, looked at in themselves, might tempt the critic to use such a phrase. Aside from Penthesilea, Michael Kohlhaas is the only obvious other possibility, but to label him simply an extremist would be to misunderstand his position in the text, especially the way in which that position changes. Far from representing an ideal character for Kleist as an uncompromisingly self-reliant figure,[22] Michael Kohlhaas is a character whose stance is questioned by the late developments of the story. Kleist's characters are far too diverse to be reduced to a single type: Adam, the Count F., Alkmene, Prince Friedrich, Friedrich von Trota, Michael Kohlhaas, Don Fernando, Jeronimo, and Nicolo are all very different people, and their all being found in Kleist's work involves only one generalizable fact, which does not remove those differences: they are all characters who are not easy to judge, and the reader must be prepared to change his atittudes to them as new situations develop within each text.

There is one area of Kleist's biography (or what is known of it) that has at least some points of contact with the most central aspects of his work. This is the so-called Kant-crisis, which occurred when he was a student; he was severely shaken to discover in Kant's philosophy that absolute truth cannot be found. But the use of this by Kleist's critics shows only too well how even relevant biographical material can distort and limit critical understanding. For critics who proceed from the Kant-crisis and conclude from it that Kleist's works embody a despair of knowledge and truth have blinded themselves to the fact that Kleist in the next decade moved well beyond that simple beginning and added a great deal to it. His writings are not reducible simply to an expression of that early mood. Far from merely showing despair, they show a considerable fascination with how situations and people can never be judged in one authoritative way (the "truth" about them) but are instead the subject of a developing understanding that can involve several different viewpoints. This, then, is a case in which the biographical pointer does not actually lead the critic in the wrong direction; but the pointer is so rudimentary and undeveloped that for the critic simply to accept it and go no further, using it as a key to the texts and leaving them at that point, is finally just as bad as following a completely misleading biographical fact. Although that experience was obviously the earliest sign of the development of Kleist's characteristic concerns, a thorough look at the texts is necessary to see that his best work has developed so far beyond that stage that to use it as an interpretative key would restrict and limit the discussion to the point that nothing would be seen of the characteristic quality of Kleist's mature work. Despair of knowledge is a very simple and easily grasped notion with nothing distinctive or unusual in it; where Kleist went from that beginning, on the other hand, is something unique and valuable.

A practical demonstration of the value of adducing the Kant-crisis can be seen in the nature of the interpretative comments of critics who have approached the texts from this standpoint; they are rarely different from the standard judgments commonly made by critics of all persuasions.[23] At best, the Kant-crisis points to a large, vague area within which we must think about Kleist's work; it does not substitute for thinking, and the results of such thinking will look very different indeed from the mere transformation of a fact of the young Kleist's experience into an interpretative comment on his mature work. Even this, then, the most promising of biographical pointers, is eventually as misleading as it is unnecessary. A thorough look at any of the texts would lead to the more appropriate and useful notion of how a *search* for understanding is built into their structure; the primitive biographical pointer by itself has only led to still more studies of "error" and "deceit" as motifs in Kleist's work.

The other biographical pointer that is followed with regularity in Kleist criticism is the essay *Über das Marionettentheater*. Enough has been written on this essay and its relation to Kleist's work to allow a whole volume of studies to be collected and published together,[24] and at least a nod in the direction of its importance for understanding Kleist seems to be obligatory in any general study. I have no wish (and no space) to discuss the essay in detail here; and it is unnecessary to do so. Only two points need be made. First, the whole undertaking has on its face the appearance of being fundamentally another reductive search for an easy solution to the understanding of Kleist's work, yet one more way of circumventing serious thought about the texts by seizing on a simple idea to trace through them all. Any easy external key to texts as different as *Michael Kohlhaas*, *Prinz Friedrich von Homburg*, and *Das Erdbeben in Chili* is impossible to imagine, whatever its source. Second, the impact of this approach on the interpretation of the works is in practice very little. Take the example of Johannes Klein: he proclaims the importance of the *Marionettentheater* essay for an understanding of Kleist, but when it comes to a discussion of the works, he gives his readers the same view of *Der Findling*, of *Michael Kohlhaas*, of *Die Marquise von O . . .* , and so on, that can be found in the work of practically any other critic.[25]

The only other category of general ideas that has been made the basis of general studies of Kleist is that deriving not from Kleist or his work but from the ideological or critical preoccupations of the critic himself. These inevitably are very general notions that occur equally as the basis of hundreds of other studies of other authors. The real source of these ideas, then, is critical practice in general. Michael Moering, for example, writes on irony in Kleist;[26] Hans Heinz Holz, on Kleist's work as springing "aus einem sprachphilosophischen Problem";[27] Friedrich Braig introduces religious belief;[28] and so on. But the studies that are numerically most important—and most currently in vogue—are those whose framework is Marxist. That a critic determined to see definite religious viewpoints in Kleist's works will do so regardless of their meaning needs no further comment; and Moering's work and that of Holz are not sufficiently substantial to merit discussion. I shall therefore conclude this survey of the tradition of Kleist criticism by looking at the place within it of the Marxists.

Marxist criticism is currently very much in vogue. It has achieved some prominence within German literary criticism and has even gained some regard from those who are not adherents: they tend often to view it as at least the work of genuine intellectuals. But the truth appears to be, as we shall see, that it shares the worst habits of the bourgeois, old-fashioned critics on whom Marxists generally pour scorn. Moreover, since it also tends to resist whatever has been progressive in criticism over the last few decades, it is a highly conservative and even reactionary form of criticism. Let us look at some examples; it is almost obligatory to start with Georg Lukács.[29]

Lukács is concerned above all else with the political aspects of Kleist's work. He sees in *Der zerbrochne Krug* "die Mißhandlung der Bauern durch die Obrigkeit"; *Prinz Friedrich von Homburg* is about a "Konflikt zwischen Individuum und Gesellschaft"; *Michael Kohlhaas* is about the mistreatment of a normal individual by a corrupt ruling class.[30] Lukács is particularly eloquent on this last point:

Das tragische Schicksal des Kohlhaas fügt sich organisch in die Reihe der bedeutendsten Dichtungen der Neuzeit ein: in die Reihe jener Dichtungen, die die in der bürgerlichen Gesellschaft unlösbare Dialektik der Gerechtigkeit zum Vorwurf haben, in denen die unauflösbare Widersprüchlichkeit der Legalität der Klassengesellschaft gewaltig gestaltet zum Ausdruck kommt. Diese Tatsache: daß es für die Klassengesellschaft typisch ist, daß der einzelne entweder sich widerspruchslos der Ungerechtigkeit und Gesetzlosigkeit der herrschenden Klassen zu unterwerfen hat oder dazu gedrängt wird, in den Augen der Gesellschaft, ja, nach seinen eigenen moralischen Anschauungen zum Verbrecher zu werden. . . . Kleist gestaltet mit rücksichtsloser Energie die verbrecherische Roheit, die barbarisch schlaue Gaunerei der Junker dieser Zeit. Er zeigt, wie alle Behörden und Gerichte mit diesen Junkern verschwägert sind und deren Verbrechen korrupt decken und unterstützen. Der Gestalter Kleist hat sogar eine Ahnung von den Grenzen des ideologischen Anführers dieser Zeit, von den Grenzen Luthers. . . . Zu bedauern ist nur, daß dieses Meisterwerk durch einige romantisch schrullenhafte Zutaten Kleists entstellt ist.[31]

Before coming to the question of what is specifically Marxist here, we are first struck by the fact that these are the same kinds of judgments found in the writings of the stuffiest, most conservative bourgeois critics: they are almost identical with the views of Hans Matthias Wolff, for example, and exhibit all the drawbacks of this kind of criticism. Wolff too saw in *Der zerbrochne Krug* essentially no more than a corrupt state official oppressing the people, in *Prinz Friedrich von Homburg* no more than the individual versus the state, and in *Michael Kohlhaas* a struggle of an individual against corrupt state officials. Lukács even makes the same kind of comment on the allegedly unnecessary and unfortunate addition of the "romantic" ending of *Michael Kohlhaas*. The same very basic criticisms apply to both Wolff and Lukács, therefore, and the fact that they are equally valid for both shows that they need not involve any kind of hostility to Marxism as a philosophy. Wolff and Lukács both read these texts in the same superficial manner, reducing the content to an idea that obsesses them, but which is only a small part of the material of the text. Both lift elements of the text out of context and consequently destroy its thematic structure; both are deaf to anything in the text that is not connected with their very simple idea. And in both, a symptom of their reductive attitudes is the need to reject the end of the text as an unfortunate addition for which they can find no reason. Lukács's Marxist reading is in fact just like any other reductive, superficial misreading caused by the critic's obsession with a simple idea instead of trying to understand more of the text; it is no different from typical bourgeois criticism.

There are, however, further reservations that are more specifically relevant to Marxism itself. For example, Lukács clearly cannot conceive of a historical subject being used for a *thematic* purpose; his comments on Luther show that he thinks Kleist's purpose was simply to give an accurate historical portrayal. Where even Wolff thought of the text in terms of a thematic idea, however simple, Lukács thinks of *Michael Kohlhaas* in terms of its accuracy as a portrayal of the ruling class of a historical period—a reduction that goes even beyond Wolff's. And Lukács's praising this as a literary masterpiece because it is historically accurate from a Marxist viewpoint is, of course, an indicator of how very seriously he means that reduction: there is, apparently, nothing more that literature could be, or be about, than just that.

There is a great irony involved in Lukács's view of Kohlhaas, one that shows only too well its weakness. Lukács praises Kleist's portrayal of the oppression of Kohlhaas by the ruling class, but it is precisely the insufficiency of this kind of thinking that is an important theme in the story. *Michael Kohlhaas* is a story that questions whether such abstractions as "the state" or "the government" are usable; its final scenes see all political abstractions and any notion of a political "system" crumble as the reader at last recognizes that there exists only an incoherent, disorganized scene filled with individuals having no very clear ideas of what they are doing. The early part of the story seems to allow an impression of a coherent class that opposes Kohlhaas in a consistent, disciplined way to preserve its interests as a class, and that is how Lukács speaks of the whole story; but the text as a whole is partly about the fact that this is an *illusion* that the individual has. The exposure of the lack of reality in a certain kind of political thinking—such as that of Lukács—is part of the very structure of the story; no wonder Lukács could not read this text adequately!

Lukács's watchword for literary texts is "Realism," but that is highly misleading. A term as broad as "reality" must concern the whole of human life, yet for him it concerns only a narrow segment of human experience—political circumstances. To be more correct, he looks for only one aspect of that, namely, the class situation. And as a consequence of his exclusive concern with whether an author has shown the "reality" (i.e., the class situation) of any given historical moment, he cannot read anything as a thematic study dealing with human life in a way that goes beyond experience at a particular moment in history (or beyond a certain aspect of politics). *Michael Kohlhaas* is a study of how an individual is almost bound to try to think of any system that confronts him as if it were another individual with its own outlook, attitude, and personality, even though this view is pointless and conceivably disastrous. To look instead in a literary work for a realistic picture of historical circumstances is to preclude any receptivity to a thematic study that uses historical material for its own purposes; and to look only for a validation of one's political ideology in a literary work is to preclude the possibility that it has anything of its own to say.

Some more recent Marxist critics have themselves criticized Lukács, but they fail to provide any superior version of Marxist criticism that avoids his fundamental misconceptions. Manfred Lefèvre, in a recent *Forschungsbericht*, written from a Marxist point of view, concedes that some of Lukács's judgments were indeed oversimple, and he takes the view that a more advanced Marxist criticism now exists in a series of recent writers.[32] But these differences between Lukács and his successors are superficial only. What these newer Marxists quarrel with in Lukács is mainly his summary judgment that Kleist was a "bornierter preußischer Junker" into whose works reality intruded only "gegen seine Absichten," which nonetheless made him an important Realist.[33] But their concern is mainly that a somewhat more favorable judgment of Kleist be made from the same basic standpoint, not that the texts be read in a fundamentally different way. The newer writers of whom Lefèvre speaks in fact proceed much as Lukács did, and are guilty of much the same misreadings and simplifications that Lukács himself made.[34] Ernst Fischer sees Kleist's works as being about "die Wechselwirkung des Einzelnen und der Gesellschaft," with the early stories showing Kleist's negative attitude towards society but *Prinz Friedrich von Homburg* showing a final awareness of "gesellschaftliche Notwendigkeit";[35] Hans Mayer thinks Kleist's works embody Rousseauism and that *Prinz Friedrich von Homburg* is a final synthesis of "Staatsraison und Gefühlskraft";[36] Siegfried Streller too thinks the teachings of Rousseau, but also those of Adam Müller, are embodied in Kleist, and Lefèvre makes it clear when discussing Streller that he shares Streller's view: "Mit Recht wird auch darauf hingewiesen, daß die Staatsvorstellung in *Michael Kohlhaas* entscheidend von Rousseaus Naturrechtslehre bestimmt sei (S. 166 f.). . . . Kohlhaas argumentiert in seiner Debatte mit Luther vom Standpunkt Rousseaus aus."[37] Again, this is all utterly familiar: when Marxists look at the texts, they are most likely to repeat Wolff, and these are in fact all Wolff's judgments. The iconoclastic new viewpoint in practice rarely results in anything more than judgments borrowed from old-fashioned bourgeois critics. Even the elementary mistake of thinking that whatever Kohlhaas argues must be Kleist's view is Wolff's; neither Wolff nor the Marxists are able to resist taking a piece of political "Stoff" out of the work's context while ignoring its *use* in the work. But neither is this all really very far from Lukács. Lefèvre makes much of the fact that the judgments of the more recent Marxists are more sophisticated than those of Lukács. For example, where Lukács thought Kleist a "Junker" who portrayed social realism (read: the injustice of the class system) in spite of himself, Mayer sees in him a bourgeois artist who saw the limitations of bourgeois reality, and Fischer conceives of him as "vor allem ein Rebell."[38] But these differences are mostly a matter of different summary attitudes by Fischer and Mayer based on readings of the texts that in most important ways are similar: they share fully with Lukács the tendency to read the texts without much regard for their own emphases and to pursue in them a simple political idea that distorts Kleist's characteristic way of writing.

The Marxist critics I have cited make a point of saying that they read Kleist's work in the historical context of his time, which in practice means the context of political history. There are well-known arguments for and against that procedure, but they are not relevant here, for that is not what these critics really do, and it is not the source of their readings or of their misreadings of Kleist's texts. The proof of this assertion can be seen in their results, which, as readings, are no different from those of non-Marxist critics. What is really happening is that they are placing the *results* of their reading the texts in the historical context (or rather, whatever their ideological view of that context is); and everything depends on the quality of those readings, which, if inadequate, render the whole procedure useless at the outset. In fact, then, they are setting readings that are superficial and distorted into a historical context, and that can never do anything to make the readings better. There is, in a way, no test here of the usefulness of a historical approach; this is in its essence standard superficial reductive academic criticism. Marxists brandish some new terminology—but then, their bourgeois counterparts make much use of that stratagem too—and they are full of righteous fervor. But they say very much the same things about the texts that other critics have said, and to just as little purpose.[39]

All in all, then, Marxism is seen to differ only slightly (if at all) from the tradition of Kleist criticism.[40] Basic to all branches, it seems, is the practice of using a simple general idea as a key to all the texts. The unadorned results of this practice by themselves would be uninteresting indeed, and so they are usually overlaid with something that will conceal that fact, whether terminological elaboration, a political doctrine, or some other extraneous preoccupation of the actual critic. I have ended on a gloomy note, but the quality of Kleist criticism leaves no room for the enthusiasm that the quality of Kleist's extraordinarily interesting texts inspires.

                    *   *   *

The analysis of Kleist criticism that forms the main body of this chapter was written in 1976; it therefore describes the situation up to the end of 1975. As my study goes to the printer, following the usual delays of the editorial process, I can add some brief comment on significant and representative trends in work that has appeared during 1976 and 1977.

There are some hopeful signs in recent critical essays on individual works. While many such essays still tend to repeat the same interpretative views that have long predominated in Kleist criticism, a growing number of critics seem to be questioning the received opinion of the past and taking a more complex and subtle view of the texts. But as before, general studies of Kleist lag behind this interpretative progress and seem to seek only new ways of organizing familiar interpretations within a simplified and reductive thematic framework.

Die Marquise von O . . . presents a particularly striking case of improvement in recent criticism. In the first paragraphs of the interpretation of Die Marquise von O . . . included in this volume, I noted that the important and provocative scene of reconciliation between father and daughter was never mentioned in the critical literature on the story, and I argued that this was a measure of how much the traditional clichés of Kleist criticism had distracted attention from what he wrote. Since I wrote this, no fewer than four studies of the story have appeared that take this scene to be central to the interpretation of the text: Hermann F. Weiss, "Precarious Idylls: The Relationship Between Father and Daughter in Heinrich von Kleist's *Die Marquise von O . . . ,*" *Modern Language Notes*, 91 (1976), 538–42; Thomas Fries, "The Impossible Object: The Feminine, the Narrative (Laclos' *Liasons Dangereuses* and Kleist's *Marquise von O . . .*)," *Modern Language Notes*, 91 (1976), 1296–326; Heinz Politzer, "Der Fall der Frau Marquise: Beobachtungen zu Kleists *Die Marquise von O . . . ,*" *Deutsche Vierteljahrsschrift für Literaturwissenschaft und Geistesgeschichte*, 51 (1977), 98–128; Erika Swales, "The Beleaguered Citadel: A Study of Kleist's *Die Marquise von O . . . ,*" *Deutsche Vierteljahrsschrift für Literaturwissenschaft und Geistesgeschichte*, 51 (1977), 129–47. It is of course possible to have some reservations about these essays too. Mine would be, briefly, that Swales's treatment becomes rather rigidly concerned with the notion of order and Politzer's with the text's exemplifying Freudian concepts, while Weiss's short piece does little more than stress the importance of the role of the father, and Fries devotes far more time to Leclos than to Kleist in his comparative essay. None of the four quite sees how the reconciliation scene clashes with what has gone before it, stylistically and otherwise, and how it forces a rewriting of the assumptions on which the world of the Marquise and the story generally had seemed to be based. Even so, to see the importance of the reconciliation scene must and does lead to the question of the repressed emotions of the Kommandant, and to get this far is to be in an interpretative sphere well beyond that of all previous Kleist criticism. It is an odd fact that the importance of this scene is so obvious to all four of the latest critics of the story (five, including myself), for all previous critics had overlooked it in order to pursue the elaboration of concepts such as error or contradiction. This curious contrast is yet more proof of how such a style of criticism has led critics away from the problems and subtleties of Kleist's texts to ones of their own making.

Two examples of how general studies of Kleist still lag far behind critical essays on individual works are: Denys Dyer, *The Stories of Kleist: A Critical Study* (London, 1977), and Ilse Graham, *Heinrich von Kleist. Word Into Flesh: A Poet's Quest for the Symbol* (Berlin and New York, 1977). That Graham's book uses a formula all too familiar in Kleist criticsm can be seen immediately from the publicity statement in the publisher's catalogue: "She isolates a primitive model of experience as being paradigmatic of him, and traces its two principal variants through Kleist's dramatic and narrative work." As so often before, it is Kleist's essay on the *Marionettentheater* which is made to yield this key to all that he wrote. Graham's book uses the standard model that I have described: a simple idea, traced throughout the works; interpretations of the texts that agree in most important outlines with those of previous Kleist critics; and compensatory verbal elaboration—indeed this work is written in an unusually self-indulgent style.

Dyer's book certainly avoids pretentiousness, and it represents a serious attempt to introduce the general reader to the world of Kleist and Kleist criticism without striving for originality of interpretation. Unhappily, the standard views of Kleist criticism, when set out baldly and directly, look somewhat uninteresting; Dyer's book suffers as a result. The absence of any real interpretative involvement in the texts leads to inaccurate quotation, frequently in ways that are crucial to the meaning of a text. Not once, but twice (pp. 49 and 53), Dyer says that in *Der Findling*, Xaviera had been discarded by the Bishop before she seduced Nicolo; but this only happens many years later, right at the end of the story. The parallelism of both Nicolo and Xaviera being in subservient roles is lost here. The crucial phrase "zum Schauplatze seines vollen Glückes" in *Das Erdbeben in Chili* is misquoted as "ihres vollen Glückes" and, again, an enormously important interpretative point is missed (p. 22).

The magnitude of the difference in subtlety between these two general books and the best recent critical essays on individual works emerges when the judgments made by Graham and Dyer on *Die Marquise von O . . .* are contrasted with those of Fries, Weiss, Politzer and Swales. Dyer speaks obsessively of the "purity" of the Marquise (four times on p. 68 alone), and Graham in similar vein of her "serene acceptance" (p. 149). By contrast, the other four critics appear actually to be talking about human beings, not unreal black and white characters.

Two articles that have appeared recently on *Der Findling* also deserve special mention. They too point forward to better things in Kleist criticism: Erna Moore, "Heinrich von Kleists 'Findling': Psychologie des Verhängnisses," *Colloquia Germanica*, 8 (1974), 275–97; and Frank Ryder, "Kleist's *Findling*: Oedipus *Manqué*?" *Modern Language Notes*, 92 (1977), 509–24. (Moore's study, though dated 1974, actually appeared in 1976 because the journal was well behind schedule.) Both Moore and Ryder deal with the real people of Kleist's story and not with the narrator's surface judgments or the one-dimensional cliché characters of previous Kleist critics. Ryder's essay is somewhat speculative, as he himself freely admits, but whether or not his speculations are absolutely sound in each case, his results are thought-provoking and illuminating to the reader who wishes to progress beyond the superficial traditional view of the story. Moore, in the best single interpretative essay on Kleist of recent years, also goes well beyond that view. She warns that we should not allow the narrator's superficial moral judgments to deflect our attention from the actual events that he relates, following the viewpoint on this question developed in my published essay on *Der Zweikampf*, which she cites in her support. She also argues persuasively that Kleist's characters are not to be treated as pawns in a metaphysical chess-game but instead as people whose psychology and motivation are to be understood. Having begun in this way, she achieves what seems to me a far more satisfactory view of Elvire than any hitherto, and one that has many points of contact with the view I have developed in this volume. Differences between my interpretation and Moore's arise where Piachi and, to a lesser extent, Nicolo are concerned. In my view she does not go far enough in rejecting the narrator's surface judgments and looking at what the narrated events in themselves indicate. And on the more general question of the thematic basis of the story, our results are even more divergent. However, I find her essay most impressive.

If the six interpretative essays that I have discussed are an omen for the future, then Kleist criticism would seem recently to have become more promising. On the other hand, this selective discussion has dealt only with the best recent essays; there is still much evidence that unproductive criticism, of the kind discussed in the main body of this chapter, will continue to appear.

Notes

Introduction

1. Throughout the discussions of individual works in the first six chapters, numerous examples of this critical error are provided in the notes.
2. This point is elaborated in Chapter Eight, where many examples are discussed.

I. Der Findling

1. The edition used throughout this study in referring to Kleist's text is *Heinrich von Kleist: Sämtliche Werke und Briefe*, ed. Helmut Sembdner, 3rd ed., 2 vols. (Munich, 1964). The stories are all in the second volume; in my text page references to the stories are to the pagination of that volume. References to the plays, which are contained in the first volume, are by line number. Separate studies of *Der Findling* have been few: Kurt Günther, "'Der Findling'—Die frühste der Kleistschen Erzählungen," *Euphorion*, 8 (1909), Ergänzungsheft, 119–53; Albert Heubi, *Heinrich von Kleists Novelle "Der Findling*," Diss. Zurich 1948; Hans Matthias Wolff, "Heinrich von Kleists 'Findling,'" *University of California Publications in Modern Philology*, 36 (1952), 441–54; Josef Kunz, "Heinrich von Kleists Novelle 'Der Findling': Eine Interpretation," in *Festschrift für Ludwig Wolff*, ed. Werner Schröder (Neumünster, 1962), pp. 337–55; Werner Hoffmeister, "Heinrich von Kleists 'Findling,'" *Monatshefte*, 58 (1966), 49–63. See also addendum to Chapter Eight.
2. Hoffmeister's essay, the best separate study of the story to date, must be mentioned as an exception to this generalization, as can be seen from the emphasis of his comments: "Piachi ist keineswegs ein weicher und gutgläubiger Narr. Wo die Situation es verlangt, kann er unmittelbar und kraftvoll handeln" ("Kleists 'Findling,'" p. 53). Otherwise, this general view is shared both by writers of the separate studies of the story and writers of more general works, whether on Kleist or on the *Novelle*. Kunz, for example, says that even after seeing signs of trouble with Nicolo ahead, "noch ist der Alte in seiner Gutmütigkeit und Harmlosigkeit nicht genug gewarnt" (p. 337), while Johannes Klein in his *Geschichte der deutschen Novelle von Goethe bis zur Gegenwart*, 4th ed. (Wiesbaden, 1960), p. 95, and Fritz Lockemann in his *Gestalt und Wandlungen der deutschen Novelle* (Munich, 1957), p. 68, both see Nicolo as an unambiguously evil man—in Klein's words, a "Gestalt aus dem Chaos."
3. E.g., Kunz, "Kleists 'Der Findling,'" p. 347; and John Gearey, *Heinrich von Kleist: A Study in Tragedy and Anxiety* (Philadelphia, 1968), p. 78: "Although this is an interesting point to end with, what, we may ask again, has it to do with the story?"
4. E.g., Wolff, "Kleists 'Findling,'" p. 444: "Die verblüffende Aehnlichkeit Nicolos und Colinos ist ein heterogenes Element, das mit dem eigentlichen Thema der Erzählung nichts zu tun hat." Klein, *Geschichte der deutschen Novelle*, p. 95, echoes this thought and extends it to cover the general coherence of the whole story: "Die Schicksalsverknüpfungen bleiben technisch, mit dem Reiz formaler Kunst, aber ohne Geschlossenheit und Folgerichtigkeit." Hoffmeister, "Kleists 'Findling,'" pp. 49–50, argues convincingly against this kind of criticism of the story (i.e., diagnosis of inconsistencies and irrelevancies) on the part of a number of other critics.

5. Wolfgang Kayser, "Kleist als Erzähler," *German Life and Letters*, NS 8 (1954–55), 22.

6. Manfred Durzak includes some brief but relevant remarks on the relationship between husband and wife in his "Zur utopischen Funktion des Kindesbildes in Kleists Erzählungen," *Colloquia Germanica*, 3 (1969), 126–29; e.g., "Piachis Ehe mit Elvire stellt darüber hinaus die Pervertierung einer echten menschlichen Beziehung dar" (p. 127). But instead of using this insight as a starting point for a reinterpretation of *Der Findling*, he uses it only as part of an attempt to show that the child is essentially a figure of innocence in Kleist's work. I discuss this general view in Chapter Eight.

7. Most critics have accepted without question the judgment that Nicolo is a compulsive womanizer, without noting that the judgment finds no support in the evidence of the story (intense involvement with one woman for six years and an incipient equally intense involvement confined to only one other). Kunz, "Kleists 'Der Findling,'" p. 342, for example, speaks of Nicolo's "hemmungslose Triebhaftigkeit geschlechtlicher Art"; and Gearey, *Heinrich von Kleist*, p. 77, writes of Nicolo's "moral depravity," which, he thinks, clearly "causes the destruction" in this story.

8. Hoffmeister, "Kleists 'Findling,'" p. 56, notes the insufficiency of the marriage, asserting that "Elvire . . . in keiner echten und erfüllten Gemeinschaft mit Piachi lebt," and comments also on the precariousness of Elvire's psyche, in which there is "verdrängter Eros und Schuldgefühle ihrem Erretter Colino gegenüber."

9. Kunz, "Kleists 'Der Findling,'" p. 341, for example, says that the early description of Nicolo shows "Kälte und Gleichgültigkeit" and that his serious look is "fragwürdig."

10. Elmar Hoffmeister, *Täuschung und Wirklichkeit bei Heinrich von Kleist* (Bonn, 1968), p. 21, thinks that Piachi's violence at the end of the story occurs because he is "von der ansteckenden Krankheit des teuflischen Betrugs infiziert." This is a very lame explanation for an action that would be so out of character, given his general view of Piachi.

11. Werner Hoffmeister, "Kleists 'Findling,'" p. 55, noticed this quality of the narrator's evaluations of Nicolo: "Nicolos negative Eigenschaften, vom Erzähler fast formelhaft verwendet . . ." But he did not draw the conclusion from this quality that I have drawn.

II. *Die Marquise von O . . .*

1. Studies devoted specifically to *Die Marquise von O . . .* are by John C. Blankenagel, "Heinrich von Kleist's Marquise von O . . . ," *Germanic Review*, 6 (1931), 363–72; Walter Müller-Seidel, "Die Struktur des Widerspruchs in Kleists 'Marquise von O . . . ,'" *Deutsche Vierteljahrsschrift für Literaturwissenschaft und Geistesgeschichte*, 27 (1954), 497–515; Siegfried Bokelmann, "Betrachtungen zur Satzgestaltung in Kleists Novelle 'Die Marquise von O . . . ,'" *Wirkendes Wort*, 8 (1957–58), 84–89; A. Horodisch, "Eine unbekannte Quelle zu Kleists 'Die Marquise von O . . . ,'" *Philobiblon*, 7 (1963), 136–39; Michael Ossar, "Kleists's *Das Erdbeben in Chili* and *Die Marquise von O . . . ,*" *Revue des Langues Vivantes*, 34 (1968), 151–69; Donald H. Crosby, "Psychological Realism in the Works of Kleist: 'Penthesilea' and 'Die Marquise von O . . . ,'" *Literature and Psychology*, 19 (1969), 3–16; Walter H. Sokel, "Kleist's Marquise von O . . . , Kierkegaard's Abraham, and Musil's Tonka: Three Stages of the Absurd as the Touchstone of Faith," *Wisconsin Studies in Contemporary Literature*, 8 (1967), 505–16; also very recently, Dorrit Cohn, "Kleist's 'Marquise von O . . . .' : The Problem of Knowledge," *Monatshefte*, 67 (1975), 129–44; and Gerhard Dünnhaupt, "Kleist's *Marquise von O . . .* and its Literary Debt to Cervantes," *Arcadia*, 10 (1975), 147–57. See also addendum to Chapter Eight.

2. Only Cohn's "Kleist's 'Marquise von O . . . ,'" takes a more complex, because more interpreted, view of the Marquise. One aspect of her results—that the Marquise's repressed condition prior to the beginning of the story's events is an important part of its content—seems to me a valuable insight. I am more doubtful, however, about the way in which her interpretation of the story makes the problem of knowledge its most central issue. For example, Cohn argues that the Marquise's fainting is due to the fact

that "the Count elicits feelings in her, as she does in him, and that such feelings bring foreknowledge of the impending erotic happening. . . . Her flight into unconsciousness appears as an instant reaction to salvage the purity of consciousness in the moment of emerging eros" (p. 133). It does not seem to me at all plausible to suggest in this way that the Marquise faints so that the Count can rape her without her knowledge. There is simply not enough reason either to set up so elaborate a theory of why the Marquise fainted or to question the fact that a terrifying experience and an unexpected escape from it are sufficient to result in a faint. Other readings (e.g., of "unwissentliche Empfängnis" as immaculate rather than unconscious conception) also leave me unconvinced. But Cohn's essay is the best criticism of the story to date. I am inclined to think that only too determined a pursuit of a shaky thesis prevents her discussion of repression and the Marquise from getting to the fruitful ground of the scene between father and daughter, a scene to which that topic must lead, but which Cohn never mentions.

3. Ernst von Reusner, *Satz–Gestalt–Schicksal: Untersuchungen über die Struktur in der Dichtung Kleists* (Berlin, 1961). E.g., p. 100: "Und wie kann sich eine Frau einem Mann vermählen, der gegen sie handelte wie der Graf gegen die Marquise? . . . Im wirklichen Leben sind Kompromisse dieser Art nötig. . . . Aber ein Dichtwerk . . . steht unter anderen Gesetzen als die Wirklichkeit." The text obviously calls for a much greater level of imagination and insight into the complexities of a human relationship.

4. Johannes Klein, *Geschichte der deutschen Novelle von Goethe bis zur Gegenwart*, 4th ed. (Wiesbaden, 1960) pp. 86–87.

5. Müller-Seidel, "Die Struktur des Widerspruchs," p. 510.

6. Friedrich Braig, *Heinrich von Kleist* (Munich, 1925), p. 454.

7. Ossar, "Kleist's *Erdbeben*," p. 167, observes that the scene in question contains "suggestions of incest"; and Crosby notes that it "betrays what one might call a pre-Freudian realism, a flash of psychological insight which penetrates deep recesses of unconscious relationships between fathers and daughters" ("Psychological Realism in the Works of Kleist," p. 14). But in neither case does this insight affect the way in which the story is interpreted.

8. It is an unsatisfying view of the story to dwell on the misfortune of the Marquise's fate, as if she were simply the victim of bad luck, without seeing some relation between her previous overprotected state and the subsequent violence with which she is torn from it. An extreme but not entirely untypical example is Gerhard Fricke: "Das Ich vermag hier kraft seiner unbegreiflichen Macht, kraft seiner Reinheit und Einheit mit sich selber und damit mit Gott—das rätselhafte und vernichtende Schicksal zu überwinden" (*Gefühl und Schicksal bei Heinrich von Kleist* [Berlin, 1929], pp. 136–37).

9. This is essentially Müller-Seidel's view of the outcome: the Marquise accepts the Count having now experienced in his contradictory behavior "das Ineinander des Göttlichen mit dem Gebrechlichen" ("Die Struktur des Widerspruchs," p. 511).

III. *Das Erdbeben in Chili*

1. A number of studies devoted specifically to this story have appeared: John C. Blankenagel, "Heinrich von Kleist: *Das Erdbeben in Chili*," *Germanic Review*, 8 (1933), 30–39; Karl Otto Conrady, "Kleists 'Erdbeben in Chili': Ein Interpretationsversuch," *Germanisch-Romanische Monatsschrift*, NF 4 (1954), 185–95; Johannes Klein, "Kleists 'Erdbeben in Chili,' " *Der Deutschunterricht*, 8, No. 3 (1956), 5–11; Walter Silz, "Das Erdbeben in Chili," *Monatshefte*, 53 (1961), 210–38, rpt. as a chapter of his *Heinrich von Kleist: Studies in his Works and Literary Character* (Philadelphia, 1961), pp. 13–27; Benno von Wiese, "Heinrich von Kleist: Das Erdbeben in Chili," *Jahrbuch der deutschen Schiller-Gesellschaft*, 5 (1961), 102–17, rpt. as a chapter in his *Die deutsche Novelle von Goethe bis Kafka*, II (Düsseldorf, 1962), 53–70; Rodolfo E. Modern, "Sobre *El Terremoto en Chile*, de Kleist," *Torre*, 10 (1962), 39, 151–55; Walter Gausewitz, "Kleist's 'Erdbeben,' " *Monats-*

hefte, 55 (1963), 188–94; Joseph Kunz, "Die Gestaltung des tragischen Geschehens in Kleists 'Erdbeben in Chili,'" in *Gratulatio: Festschrift für Christian Wegner*, ed. Maria Honeit (Hamburg, 1963), pp. 145–70; Epifanio San Juan, Jr., "The Structure of Narrative Fiction," *Saint Louis Quarterly*, 4 (1966), 485–502; Michael Ossar, "Kleist's *Das Erdbeben in Chili* and *Die Marquise von O . . . ,*" *Revue des Langues Vivantes*, 34 (1968), 151–69; A. Owen Aldridge, "The Background of Kleist's *Das Erdbeben in Chili*," *Arcadia*, 4 (1969), 173–80; Wolfgang Wittkowski, "Skepsis, Noblesse, Ironie: Formen des Als-ob in Kleists *Erdbeben*," *Euphorion*, 63 (1969), 247–83; R. S. Lucas, "Studies in Kleist: II. 'Das Erdbeben in Chili,'" *Deutsche Vierteljahrsschrift für Literaturwissenschaft und Geistesgeschichte*, 44 (1970), 145–70; Richard L. Johnson, "Kleist's *Erdbeben in Chili*," *Seminar: A Journal of Germanic Studies*, 11 (1975), 33–45; Peter Horn, "Anarchie und Mobherrschaft in Kleists 'Erdbeben in Chili,'" *Acta Germanica*, 7 (1972), 77–96. The interpretation offered in this chapter has its origin in a paper read before the English Goethe Society in May, 1963, and published in the *Publications of the English Goethe Society*, NS 33 (1963), 10–55. Of interpretations that have appeared since that time, only those by Wittkowski and Johnson have commented on my own, but neither has provided any compelling reason to rethink its basic position. Wittkowski so misconceived and misstated my position that it is unnecessary to discuss his comments here. Moreover, both he and Johnson took a disappointingly shallow and moralistic view of the story.

2. Raymond Bonafous, *Henri de Kleist* (Paris, 1894), p. 383; Wilhelm Herzog, *Heinrich von Kleist*, 2nd ed. (Munich, 1914), p. 350; Hermann August Korff, *Geist der Goethezeit*, IV (Leipzig, 1953), 86.

3. Friedrich Gundolf, *Heinrich von Kleist* (Berlin, 1922), p. 165; Bonafous, *Henri de Kleist*, p. 380.

4. Herzog, *Heinrich von Kleist*, p. 352, speaks of the story's "pessimistische Erkenntnis" of the "gebrechliche Einrichtung der Welt"; Philipp Witkop, *Heinrich von Kleist* (Leipzig, 1922), pp. 181–82, writes of the story's fatalism on the question of the inherent evil of human nature; Hans Matthias Wolff, *Heinrich von Kleist: Die Geschichte seines Schaffens* (Berkeley and Los Angeles, 1954), pp. 42–46, stresses social corruption; Silz, *Heinrich von Kleist*, pp. 23–24, is impressed by the fortuitousness of both life and death in the face of the earthquake.

5. Hermann Pongs, *Das Bild in der Dichtung*, II (Marburg, 1939), 152 f. and 292 f., sees the child as a symbol of divine redemption through the power of love; Gunter Blöcker, *Heinrich von Kleist oder Das Absolute Ich* (Berlin, 1960), p. 137, sees the earthquake as an influence that makes man stronger; Otto Brahm, *Heinrich von Kleist* (Berlin, 1884), p. 172, thinks that Kleist shows "wie unter dem Eindruck des Zusammensturzes alles Bestehenden eine neue, bessere Ordnung der Dinge sich vorbereiten will"; Bonafous, *Henri de Kleist*, pp. 380–81, believes that it shows divine benevolence.

6. Wolff, *Heinrich von Kleist*, p. 42; Blöcker, *Heinrich von Kleist*, p. 137; Bonafous, *Henri de Kleist*, p. 380; E. K. Bennett, *A History of the German "Novelle,"* 2nd ed., rev. and cont. by H. M. Waidson (Cambridge, 1961), p. 45; Conrady, "Kleists 'Erdbeben,'" p. 186; Klein, "Kleists 'Erdbeben,'" p. 11; Emil Staiger, "Heinrich von Kleist," in *Heinrich von Kleist: Vier Reden zu seinem Gedächtnis*, ed. Walter Müller-Seidel (Berlin, 1962), p. 55.

7. Herzog, *Heinrich von Kleist*, p. 332; and Klein, "Kleists 'Erdbeben,'" p. 10.

8. For a good account of the currents of thought, the "earthquake theology," surrounding the Lisbon earthquake, see Thomas Downing Kendrick, *The Lisbon Earthquake* (London, 1956).

9. The concentration on the episode as an experience of Jeronimo, his "Glück," and words like "Schauplatz" all project the event as one that he has engineered for his own satisfaction, rather than as part of a relationship with devotion on both sides. The story's critics have missed this and other innuendoes that show the narrator's uncertainty about the guilt or innocence of the lovers and assume that the narrator is unambiguously on their side: e.g., Blankenagel, "Heinrich von Kleist: *Das Erdbeben in Chili*," pp. 34–35, gives a list of the means by which Kleist arouses sympathy for the

lovers and leaves the matter there. The list is a good one, but another list pointing in the other direction could be made. Wittkowski's view of this episode as a "Triumph des Natürlichen" and "'Provokation' des Christentums" does not take account of the crucial emphasis given to the masculine triumph ("Skepsis, Noblesse, Ironie," p. 258).

10. Throughout the story the very large number of references to chance as an explanation of an event in itself throws doubt on this kind of explanation. By his frequent use of the concept, the narrator clearly invites us to think again; this is another device through which the narrator tries to stick to his facts and avoid interpretation but in so doing impresses us all the more with the need for some interpretation. Cf. Walter Müller-Seidel, *Versehen und Erkennen* (Cologne, 1961), p. 86: "Hinter dem vermeintlichen Zufall ahnen wir den Plan dessen, der ihn schickt." Silz, *Heinrich von Kleist*, p. 20, points to the unlikeliness, even unreality, of these chances but notes their enormous scope to produce great consequences.

11. Silz, *Heinrich von Kleist*, p. 14, notes the paradox of Jeronimo "clinging for safety to the very pillar on which he was minded to die."

12. Both Silz, *Heinrich von Kleist*, p. 20, and Müller-Seidel, *Versehen und Erkennen*, pp. 138–40, stress the use of "as if" in the story. But Müller-Seidel restricts the idea to the middle section ("Die Struktur Als-ob bestimmt in *Erdbeben in Chili* den Mittelteil der Erzählung"); in my view it is equally relevant to all sections of the text. And while he correctly notes, "Fast durchweg sind religiöse Momente das eigentliche Charakteristikum dieser Sphäre des Als-ob," Müller-Seidel then draws from this the strange conclusion, "Im sprachlichen Ausdruck wird faßbar, wie Göttliches ins irdische Dasein hineinwirkt," mistaking the narrator's provisional constructions as interpretative facts. He finally arrives at the view that God works for the good in the story, while man and his institutions are the source of evil.

13. Lucas, "Studies in Kleist," pp. 147–48, here seems remote from the tone and setting of the story: "So many reversals may easily become comic; and yet, though one may smile at the naivety . . . each moment in itself has a natural justification that draws one's sympathy. . . . It is unlikely to have occurred in anyone but Jeronimo to see the hand of God in what happened."

14. Silz, *Heinrich von Kleist*, p. 15.

15. Von Wiese, *Die deutsche Novelle*, II, 60, sees this sign pointing in what seems at the time to be the wrong direction, but he overlooks its function of helping to break down one concept of the story and produce another.

16. I refer here to the three sections into which Kleist divided his story in the *Erzählungen* of 1810. Sembdner, *Heinrich von Kleist: Sämtliche Werke und Briefe*, 3rd ed. (Munich, 1964), II, 902, regrettably reintroduces the much larger number of paragraphs used in the first printed version of the September, 1807, *Morgenblatt für gebildete Stände*, on the grounds that only lack of space caused the reduction to three. The three sections do, however, have structural importance.

17. Wolfgang Kayser, "Kleist als Erzähler," *German Life and Letters*, NS 8 (1954–55), 28. Von Wiese, *Die deutsche Novelle*, II, 63, and, following him, Lucas, "Studies in Kleist," p. 160, both misunderstand Kayser here and take his remark to be an adverse criticism of the *Erdbeben*. Conrady, "Kleists 'Erdbeben,'" p. 189, rightly describes this passage as "märchenhaft," though his metaphysical treatment of this is not convincing; the point is that fairy stories are unreal.

18. Wittkowski, "Skepsis, Noblesse, Ironie," p. 251, misses the text's implied reservation about the couple's mood being unchanged by the misery they see and therefore thinks of even this self-centeredness as displaying their nobility: "Die Liebenden schleichen nicht beiseite, *obwohl* die Armen jammern, sondern *weil* sie jammern, weil sie diese nicht mit ihrem Glück 'betrüben' wollen. Sie nehmen mitleidsvoll Rücksicht, und zwar mit feinem Taktgefühl."

19. Lucas, "Studies in Kleist," p. 152, misconstrues this passage: "Josephe feels that the disproportion of suffering is an argument against the happiness that is now hers,

and has to overcome this feeling before she can gratefully acknowledge the blessings of the day." The text puts the "overcoming" of feelings very differently. Wittkowski, "Skepsis, Noblesse, Ironie," p. 251, calls this kind of gratitude "ein nobles Zuviel," but mention of "nobility" seems out of place here.

20. See especially Friedrich Koch, *Heinrich von Kleist* (Stuttgart, 1958). Koch thinks that their "naive Deutung der Welt und Menschen" (p. 84) is what leads to their downfall and their foolish belief that "der Kosmos sei in Einklang mit ihrem Schicksal" (p. 77); see also Lucas, "Studies in Kleist," p. 156.

21. This sinister picture also points forward to the death of the child Juan, who is dashed against one of these same "Pfeiler." This is one more relation that the reader is invited to ponder. A similar example of irony is Josephe's wish to lay her face "in den Staub" (154) before her creator; this is what she will do but in a different way than she had imagined.

22. Wittkowski, "Skepsis, Noblesse, Ironie," p. 249, makes the sentence a flat assertion: "Trotz der schrecklichen Erfahrungen meldet sich die Freude." He justifies this simplification with a strange argument (p. 266): "Wieder macht solch kritisch-redliche Reserve das Ergebnis, statt es zu beeinträchtigen, nur um so glaubwürdiger." Avoidance of the complexity of this last sentence is a common critical failing; see Lucas, "Studies in Kleist," p. 164.

23. E.g., Pongs, *Das Bild in der Dichtung*, II, 153; Klein, "Kleists 'Erdbeben,'" p. 10; Conrady, "Kleists 'Erdbeben,'" p. 194 (the child is for him the "geheime Mitte der Novelle"); and von Wiese, *Die deutsche Novelle*, II, 69, who follows Pongs and calls the child a "Symbol für die ganze Erzählung. . . . Es steht in seiner Unschuld stellvertretend für jeden dem Menschen neu geschenkten Anfang." Silz, *Heinrich von Kleist*, p. 24, gives the corrective to this view when he says that the child "is an example of the fortuitousness of existence in an incomprehensible world," though this is also an incomplete because too definite view of the situation; Pongs is a corrective to Silz too.

24. Wittkowski, "Skepsis, Noblesse, Ironie," by contrast, treats Don Fernando, Jeronimo, and Josephe as comparable in character (see, e.g., pp. 264 and 272).

25. Blöcker, *Heinrich von Kleist*, pp. 134–35. It is worth noting here that Kleist honors Don Fernando with quotation marks for his direct speech. Most editions unfortunately treat this as a mistake, and restore a consistency to the text that Kleist evidently did not want. Cf. Sembdner, *Heinrich von Kleist: Sämtliche Werke und Briefe*, II, 903: "Kleist setzt jeweils nur die Worte seines Helden Fernando in Anführungsstriche."

26. See Lucas, "Studies in Kleist," p. 161: "Don Fernando, though less far-seeing, even to the extent of irritation at her warning . . ." The irritation is, however, not to do with his judgment but with the challenge to his code of behavior. See also Wittkowski, "Skepsis, Noblesse, Ironie," p. 264: "Fernando und das Paar machen also sicher einen Erkenntnisfehler."

IV. *Der Zweikampf*

1. Separate studies of *Der Zweikampf* have been few: Heinrich Meyer, "Kleists Novelle 'Der Zweikampf,'" *Jahrbuch der Kleist-Gesellschaft*, 17 (1933–37), 136–69; Horst Oppel, "Kleists Novelle 'Der Zweikampf,'" *Deutsche Vierteljahrsschrift für Literaturwissenschaft und Geistesgeschichte*, 22 (1944), 92–105; Karl Otto Conrady, "Der Zweikampf: Zur Aussageweise Heinrichs von Kleist," *Der Deutschunterricht*, 3, No. 6 (1951), 85–96; Donald H. Crosby, "Heinrich von Kleist's 'Der Zweikampf,'" *Monatshefte*, 56 (1964), 191–201; Joachim Müller, *Literarische Analogien in Heinrich von Kleists Novelle "Der Zweikampf,"* (Berlin, 1969); Wolfgang Wittkowski, "Die heilige Cäcilie und *Der Zweikampf*: Kleists Legenden und die romantische Ironie," *Colloquia Germanica*, 6 (1972), 17–58; Katharina Mommsen, "Kleist's Duel Story as 'Erlebnisdichtung,'" *Carleton Germanic Papers*, 2 (1974), 49–66.

2. Meyer, "Kleists Novelle 'Der Zweikampf,'" p. 147.

3. Conrady misses the crucial factor of the narrator's telling the story in the light of a stereotype that will not fit the events that he describes: "Der Dichter ist ein objektiv Berichtender, der das tatsächlich sich Ereignende wie aus einer Chronik zu erzählen scheint" ("Der Zweikampf," p. 85).

4. It is very interesting to note that Martin Greenberg, in his *Heinrich von Kleist: The Marquise von O— and Other Stories* (New York, 1960), completely changes the impression of the original in his translation of this passage. His version asserts that Friedrich "once during a hunt had courageously snatched her from the path of a wounded boar" (p. 293). Greenberg obviously cannot believe the German here and so translates what in a sense ought to be there but is not: the text says nothing about courage, nor does it present the vivid image of Friedrich's snatching Littegarde from the boar's path.

5. It is a remarkable fact that the critics of this story have persistently praised Friedrich as a wholly positive character: Crosby terms him "the idealized knight and ardent apostle of *Vertrauen*" in *Heinrich von Kleist: Das Bettelweib von Locarno, Der Zweikampf*, ed. Donald H. Crosby (Waltham, Mass., 1968), p. xiii; he also calls him "the masculine pole of the new romantic attraction added by Kleist" ("Kleist's 'Der Zweikampf,' " p. 196); Oppel summarizes the view common to three well-known Kleist critics (Pongs, Fricke, Lugowski) that the story presents "ein Musterbild herrlichster Bewährung der unendlich vertrauenden Liebe" ("Kleists Novelle 'Der Zweikampf,' " p. 96); and even Klaus Müller-Salget, who writes on "Das Prinzip der Doppeldeutigkeit in Kleists Erzählungen," *Zeitschrift für deutsche Philologie*, 92 (1973), senses no ambiguity here, only "das unbedingte Vertrauen und die völlige Hingabe an den geliebten Menschen" (p. 201). All of its critics not only accept but even glorify and exaggerate further a stereotype that is questioned within the story itself.

6. For a contrary view of the scene as one that "supplies one of the most moving tableaus in Kleist's entire Novellistik," see Crosby, "Kleist's 'Der Zweikampf,' " p. 197. Wittkowski is more extreme: "Als Trota im Gefängnis Littegarde überrascht, da stilisiert Kleist Wort und Gebärde nach dem Vorbild Christi und der Sünderin zu religiöser Form und Inbrunst. Das ist die Vergöttlichung des Menschen, die sich bei Kleist allenthalben findet. Ihr Grundzug ist die Noblesse" ("*Die Heilige Cäcilie* und *Der Zweikampf*," p. 52). This loss of contact with the very different emphases of Kleist's story is the result of Wittkowski's general belief that "Noblesse" and "Vergöttlichung des Menschen" are basic, unambiguous values in Kleist.

7. *H. v. Kleists Werke*, ed. Erich Schmidt, Georg Minde-Pouet and Reinhold Steig (Leipzig, 1904–05), III, 132.

8. Crosby, "Kleist's 'Der Zweikampf,' " p. 193.

9. The idea that everything preceding the duel is only an introduction without any thematic significance occurs throughout Meyer's "Kleists Novelle 'Der Zweikampf' "; e.g., on p. 149 it has "kein selbständiges Interesse, hat lediglich einleitenden Charakter, dient der Hauptgeschichte zum Sprungbrett"; on p. 157 it is "nur ein dienendes Hilfsorgan, ein vorgesetztes Portal, ein Einführungsstück ohne selbständiges Interesse"; and on p. 167 the story is stated to be a "Zusammensetzung aus zwei Geschichten ganz verschiedenen Inhalts." One then puzzles over his conclusion that the story is "ein Werk aus einem Gusse und ein Werk reifer Kunst" (p. 169).

10. As Meyer puts it in "Kleists Novelle 'Der Zweikampf,' " p. 150, the story's "Luft ist nicht die der Aufklärung, sondern die des naiven Wunderglaubens." Crosby, "Kleist's 'Der Zweikampf,' " pp. 199–200, thinks differently: "The author obviously does not insist that *we* believe that the delayed revelation of the true victor of the trial by combat is a manifestation, say, of God's mills grinding slowly but exceedingly fine. . . . That it is sheer presumption to expect God to adjudicate human quarrels, 'unmittelbar' or any other way, does not and cannot occur to the Emperor, who unlike Trota is every inch a man of his time." The author cannot, of course, dictate his reader's real-life beliefs, but the narrative convention can and does ask that God's adjudication of human quarrels in the duel be considered part of the story. Far from being ahead of his

time, Trota more than anyone else clings to the convention of simple faith while the Emperor, seeing its weakness, introduces a change in the statutes that embody it.

11. Conrady's view of the ending is speculation: "Nicht immer und zu jeder willkürlichen Anrufung spricht dieser Gott, sondern, wie es die Schlußworte sagen: *Wenn es Gottes Wille ist.* Das aber heißt, so will uns nun scheinen: es muß etwas in den Herzen der Menschen sich ereignen, und dann fällt, wenn zwei Menschen in Vertrauen und Liebe gegen die verwirrende und täuschende Umgebung der gebrechlichen Welt durchhalten, auf sie durch alles Dunkel hindurch ein Strahl jenes Gottes, und eine heile Welt wird sichtbar" ("Der Zweikampf," p. 96). What was being explained and dealt with by the change in wording was not (as Conrady implies) the fact that the duel sometimes, in meritorious cases, reveals the truth, but that it sometimes appears *not* to do so, *even* in meritorious cases.

V. *Michael Kohlhaas*

1. A complete list of nearly forty separate studies concerned specifically with *Michael Kohlhaas* is given in the bibliography.

2. Karl Schultze-Jahde, "Kohlhaas und die Zigeunerin," *Jahrbuch der Kleist-Gesellschaft*, 17 (1933–37), 108–35. Schultze-Jahde emphasized the consistency of Kohlhaas's thought, which formed "ein klares System" (p. 109).

3. Gerhard Fricke, "Kleists 'Michael Kohlhaas,'" *Der Deutschunterricht*, 5, No. 1 (1953), 21 and 25.

4. Richard Matthias Müller, "Kleists 'Michael Kohlhaas,'" *Deutsche Vierteljahrsschrift für Literaturwissenschaft und Geistesgeschichte*, 44 (1970), 107.

5. R. S. Lucas, "Studies in Kleist: I. Problems in 'Michael Kohlhaas,'" *Deutsche Vierteljahrsschrift für Literaturwissenschaft und Geistesgeschichte*, 44 (1970), 124, 128, 132, 133, and 136.

6. Lucas, "Studies in Kleist," pp. 133–34.

7. Lucas's smug, schoolmasterly reproof of Kohlhaas is probably the key to those misreadings: "We may sympathize deeply with the passionate resentment of these words. . . . Nobody who has gone through such experiences as Kohlhaas could banish such feelings utterly, but we are not all capable of adhering to them for long" ("Studies in Kleist," p. 131). This is academic criticism at its most remote from life outside the professorial study.

8. Fricke, "Kleists 'Michael Kohlhaas,'" p. 18, (essentially followed by Gunter Blöcker, *Heinrich von Kleist oder Das Absolute Ich* [Berlin, 1960], p. 213, and Müller, "Kleists 'Michael Kohlhaas,'" p. 108) argued that the "Chronist" was the maker of the overt judgments in the story, not Kleist, and in so doing he set up an adequate framework for investigating the relation of the narrator to his story—though for the wrong reason, since the same holds in a narrative not prefaced by "Aus einer alten Chronik." But he used this insight in order to undercut (and even to disregard and discard from the text) only the *negative* judgments on Kohlhaas.

9. Ludwig Büttner, "Michael Kohlhaas—eine paranoische oder heroische Gestalt?" *Seminar: A Journal of Germanic Studies*, 4 (1968), 41.

10. Clifford Bernd has given a clear and succinct account (which my own partly follows) of how this apparent inconsistency in the text has been treated by its critics in his "On the Two Divergent Parts of Kleist's Michael Kohlhaas," in *New York University Department of German Studies in Germanic Languages and Literature*, ed. Robert A. Fowkes and Volkmar Sander (Reutlingen, 1967), pp. 47–56.

11. Heinrich Meyer-Benfey, "Die innere Geschichte des 'Michael Kohlhaas,'" *Euphorion*, 15 (1908), 103; Karl Otto Conrady, *Die Erzählweise Heinrichs von Kleist: Untersuchungen und Interpretationen*, Diss. Münster 1953, p. 193. Lionel Thomas in "Heinrich von Kleist and his Stories," *Proceedings of the Leeds Philosophical and Literary Society*, 10 (1962), 84, went so far as to praise the action of an editor who removed the whole episode as

"improving the tale." This kind of response is still common: e.g., T. J. Reed, in his very recent essay "The 'Goethezeit' and its Aftermath," in the important compendium *Germany: A Companion to German Studies*, ed. Malcolm Pasley (London, 1972), calls the episode "a jarring aberration into a supernatural sub-plot at the eleventh hour" (p. 527).

12. The readings of the gypsy by Benno von Wiese, "Heinrich von Kleist: Michael Kohlhaas," in his *Die deutsche Novelle von Goethe bis Kafka*, I (Düsseldorf, 1956), 47–63, and by P. Horwath, "The 'Nicht-um-die-Welt' Theme: A Clue to the Ultimate Meaning of Kleist's *Michael Kohlhaas*," *Studia Neophilologica*, 39 (1967), 261–69, are both recognizably of the same general kind as that of Schultze-Jahde and subject to the same criticisms, even though neither mentions him. Bernd, "On the Two Divergent Parts," in rounding off his account of previous attempts to deal with the gypsy episode, gives his own general interpretation, which is that it functions to cause confusion in the story. Here, he is absolutely correct, and it would have been intriguing to see Bernd pursue the point in more detail in a longer article: e.g., what issues become confused and why? Müller's view, in his "Kleists 'Michael Kohlhaas,'" is that the Elector of Saxony deserved to be deposed in a revolution, and that since historical fact did not permit this, Kleist was compelled to find a form of punishment that would substitute for a social upheaval and thus decided on the gypsy. What makes this suggestion implausible is that the gypsy is surely a very poor substitute for a revolution. In any case, the Marxist reading of the story that is behind it is inconsistent with the text. Nowhere in *Michael Kohlhaas* is there any stress on class war, and the story cannot be seen as critical of the nobility in general, since the Elector of Brandenburg is granted a long and glorious reign, and Kohlhaas's sons are knighted.

13. Fricke, "Kleists 'Michael Kohlhaas,'" p. 38.

14. Otto F. Best makes the point that one should not speak of the romantic "Schluß-teile" of the story since, while the passages in question occur towards the end of the text, they fill gaps in our knowledge of chronologically much earlier events; the story covers pp. 9–103, the gypsy is first mentioned on p. 82, but the events described at that point relate back to the time reached chronologically on p. 31 ("Schuld und Vergebung: Zur Rolle von Wahrsagerin und 'Amulett' in Kleists 'Michael Kohlhaas,'" *Germanisch-Romanische Monatsschrift*, NF 20 [1970], 180–89).

15. Lucas says that Wenk's answer is only due to his irritation over the presence of the Nagelschmidt band, and that "Kohlhaas' conclusion that only flight remains is the wrong one" ("Studies in Kleist," p. 135). This argument ignores the change in the sentry arrangements that Wenk had ordered, his reconfirming those arrangements before his answer to Kohlhaas, and the fact that, whatever the *cause* of Wenk's very emphatic "Ja! ja! ja!" its *effect* is to make Kohlhaas a prisoner and break the amnesty.

16. John R. Cary, by contrast, says that the Elector of Saxony "is nowhere shown to be acting in anything but good faith," is "fallible but well-intentioned," is only "inadvertently guilty," and is "civilized, not unappealing" ("A Reading of Kleist's *Michael Kohlhaas*," *PMLA*, 85 [1970], 215–16). These judgments seem to me astonishing.

17. See my analysis of all the odd effects of the weather in the story in "Der Herr läßt regnen über Gerechte und Ungerechte: Kleist's 'Michael Kohlhaas,'" *Monatshefte*, 59 (1967), 35–40.

18. Müller, "Kleists 'Michael Kohlhaas,'" p. 117, regards Kohlhaas's final behavior toward the Elector of Saxony as a continuation of his "Aufstand gegen die ungerechte Obrigkeit"; while Lucas, "Studies in Kleist," p. 125, thinks Kohlhaas's earlier actions are a search for revenge rather than justice. One makes the end like the beginning, the other the beginning like the end, but both try to remove the difference between them.

19. The gypsy herself introduces the notion of reducing the impossibly grandiose scale of Kohlhaas's concerns when, after he has retorted "Nicht um die Welt!" to her suggestion that he use the capsule to buy his freedom, she replies: "'Nicht um die Welt, Kohlhaas, der Roßhändler; aber um diesen hübschen, kleinen, blonden Jungen!'" (97). Horwath takes the phrase "Nicht um die Welt" to stress temporal as opposed to

higher concerns in his "The 'Nicht-um-die-Welt' Theme," but that reverses the direction of the contrast; the gypsy's point is to direct Kohlhaas's attention to the concrete, immediate, real things that he can see (this particular little boy) rather than to more cosmic, but less immediately real, concerns.

20. Lucas, "Studies in Kleist," pp. 133–34; and Cary, "A Reading of Kleist's *Michael Kohlhaas*," pp. 215–16. Lucas praises the "feeling for justice shown in the Elector's adherence to the views of Count Wrede," as if the text did not make it obvious that his motives are entirely different from Wrede's.

21. Contrast Cary, "A Reading of Kleist's *Michael Kohlhaas*," p. 217: "It remains unclear why he [the Elector of Brandenburg] is spared a fate similar to that of the Elector of Saxony." See also Lucas, "Studies in Kleist," p. 134, who sees in the courts of Saxony and Brandenburg "the mixture of good and bad men in each place." Both critics seem extraordinarily unreceptive to the ways in which the text contrasts the two Electors.

22. Clifford A. Bernd, "Der Lutherbrief in Kleists 'Michael Kohlhaas,'" *Zeitschrift für deutsche Philologie*, 86 (1967), 627–33.

23. Walter Silz sees "the older man unable or unwilling to recognize his younger self in the man he faces" and the link between them in Luther's "equally obstinate pursuit of what seemed to many a small matter but to him was a sacred principle" ("Three Themes in *Michael Kohlhaas*," in his *Heinrich von Kleist: Studies in his Works and Literary Character* [Philadelphia, 1961], pp. 191–92). Silz saw here the most fundamental point of Luther's thematic place in the story, an important critical achievement.

24. See, for example, Deuteronomy 9:13–14: "Der Herr sprach zu mir: Ich sehe, daß dies Volk ein halsstarriges Volk ist. Laß ab von mir, da mit ich sie vertilge und ihren Namen austilge unter dem Himmel: aber aus dir will ich ein stärkeres und größeres Volk machen"; Job 18: 16–17; and Proverbs 10:7: "Das Andenken des Gerechten bleibt im Segen; aber der Name des Gottlosen wird verwesen." I am much indebted to the learning of my colleague Joseph H. Silverman for these references. My earlier article "Der Herr läßt regnen über Gerechte und Ungerechte: Kleist's 'Michael Kohlhaas'" showed another way in which biblical material relating to the notion of justice enters into the story. Henrik Lange, in his "Säkularisierte Bibelreminiszenzen in Kleists 'Michael Kohlhaas,'" *Kopenhagener Germanistische Studien*, 1 (1969), 213–26, points to other biblical material in the story but makes little interpretative use of it.

VI. *Prinz Friedrich von Homburg*

1. The critical literature on *Prinz Friedrich von Homburg* is enormous. A full bibliography to 1963 is given in *Heinrich von Kleist: "Prinz Friedrich von Homburg. Ein Schauspiel*," nach der Heidelberger Handschrift herausgegeben von Richard Samuel, unter Mitwirkung von Dorothea Coverlid (Berlin, 1964); this is supplemented to 1968 by the bibliography of my *Kleist's "Prinz Friedrich von Homburg": A Critical Study* (Berkeley and Los Angeles, 1970). That very much fuller study of the play contains detailed comment on the critical literature, and I have therefore largely avoided duplicating such comment in the present volume. On the other hand, the present bibliography brings the earlier one up to date.

2. See Gerhard Fricke, "Kleists 'Prinz Friedrich von Homburg,'" in his *Studien und Interpretationen* (Frankfurt a.M., 1956), pp. 239–63.

3. Hellmuth Kaiser, "Kleists 'Prinz Friedrich von Homburg,'" *Imago*, 17 (1930), 119–37.

4. Donald H. Crosby thinks rather that the Elector leads only a "diversionary flank attack" (in his review of my *Kleist's "Prinz Friedrich von Homburg*," *German Quarterly* [AATG *Membership Directory*], 46 [Sept. 1973], 149), but that is a misreading of the text. Dörfling's reading of the battle plan makes quite clear that Hennings commands the right wing and Truchß the main center; the Elector is with Truchß's contingent during

the battle. Richard Samuel's accurate diagram of the battle shows the positions of all participants clearly, and it assumes, correctly, that the major confrontation is between the Swedes under Wrangel and the Brandenburg center under the Elector and Truchß (*Heinrich von Kleist: "Prinz Friedrich von Homburg,"* p. 206). This view is obviously confirmed by the fact that, when Wrangel's position is seen to be broken and he retreats, all present cry, "Triumph! Triumph! Triumph! Der Sieg ist unser!" (467). They could not make this claim if they did not all assume that the main part of the battle is decided in their favor already; i.e., they all know that this is *not* a diversionary flank attack, and that the battle is essentially won before the Prince's entry, as it was meant to be.

5. Two reviewers of my *Kleist's "Prinz Friedrich von Homburg"* misconceived this point; Charles E. Passage, *Journal of English and Germanic Philology*, 70 (1971), 120–23, spoke of the Elector's being shown as "sly, cunning, cruel"; and Crosby, pp. 148–50, spoke of "malice" and "imputation of ad hominem motives." In using this language of consciously evil intent both of course missed the whole point of my argument about the different levels of understanding involved in the relationship of the two main characters.

6. J. M. Benson, "Kleist's *Prinz Friedrich von Homburg,*" *Modern Languages*, 46 (1965), 98–103, is an example.

VII. The Character of Kleist's Literary Work

1. Fritz Martini, *Deutsche Literaturgeschichte von den Anfängen bis zur Gegenwart*, 7th ed. (Stuttgart, 1956), p. 293.

2. Not surprisingly, some critics have simply concluded that the stories are inconsistent. The most thoroughgoing version of this attitude is that of Hans Matthias Wolff in his *Heinrich von Kleist: Die Geschichte seines Schaffens* (Berkeley and Los Angeles, 1954). Wolff was convinced that each of the stories must have originally existed in what would have been from his point of view a clear, consistent version without any problematic later episodes, and that those episodes were added only much later when Kleist's interests had changed; Wolff even printed his reconstructed original material (e.g., of *Der Findling*) in an appendix to his book. Typical, then, of his judgments of the stories is that on *Der Findling*, which "leidet an einer sonderbaren Verworrenheit. . . . Dieser klare Handlungsablauf ist durch ein heterogenes Thema kompliziert" (p. 53). As for the *Zweikampf*, he thought that it contained "zwei verschiedene Handlungen" that were "so oberflächlich miteinander verknüpft, daß von einer Einheit keine Rede sein kann" (p. 194).

3. Helmut Koopmann, "Das 'rätselhafte Faktum' und seine Vorgeschichte: Zum analytischen Charakter der Novellen Heinrich von Kleists," *Zeitschrift für deutsche Philologie*, 84 (1965), 508–50. Koopmann is simply critical of Kleist here: "Zu oft biegt Kleist vom direkten Weg ab . . . er greift zu oft zu weit zurück und motiviert sogar übergenau" (p. 509). He calls this a "Pedanterie der Genauigkeit." Eberhard Lämmert's attitude to Kleist's sudden introduction of striking new material from the past is similarly unimaginative, and he too deals with it only as low-level technique, e.g., as "Der abschweifende Rückschritt," as "Retardation," or as "Pause in der Haupthandlung" (*Bauformen des Erzählens* [Stuttgart, 1955], p. 116).

4. Max Kommerell, "Die Sprache und das Unaussprechliche: Eine Betrachtung über Heinrich von Kleist," in his *Geist und Buchstabe der Dichtung* (Frankfurt a.M., 1944), pp. 243–317. In this article originated the phrase "das rätselhafte Faktum," since much used in criticism of Kleist. Kommerell's arbitrariness in designating this or that event a "rätselhaftes Faktum" has much to do with his thinking in terms of orthodox *Novelle* theory, which requires an equally arbitrary designation of an event that is "unerhört."

5. This is also the kind of approach taken by Hans-Peter Herrmann, "Zufall und Ich: Zum Begriff der Situation in den Novellen Heinrich von Kleists," *Germanisch-*

Romanische Monatsschrift, NF 11 (1961), 69–99. Herrmann looks to the upheavals in the lives of the characters, rather than in the text as a whole; e.g., "ein unerwartetes Ereignis tritt in ihr Leben . . . nun bedingt es ihr Handeln und gestaltet ihr Schicksal" (p. 70). This is neither especially characteristic of Kleist nor very interesting; all forms of literature deal with events that are not entirely commonplace.

6. In my "Kleist's *Das Erdbeben in Chili*," *Publications of the English Goethe Society*, NS 33 (1963), 54. Koopmann refers to the fact that Kleist's stories have qualities of the "Kriminalgeschichte" ("Das 'rätselhafte Faktum,'" p. 513), but only in the much more superficial sense that they sometimes are about the solution of a real crime mystery, e.g., who killed the Duke in *Der Zweikampf*, or who raped the Marquise in *Die Marquise von O . . . .*

7. See, for example, Klaus Müller-Salget, "Das Prinzip der Doppeldeutigkeit in Kleists Erzählungen," *Zeitschrift für deutsche Philologie*, 92 (1973), 185–211. Here the postulation of a double meaning is a restriction on the meaning of the stories, which move among several different possibilities rather than between just two. K. H. Lepper, "Zur Polarität der Weltsicht in Kleists Novellen," *Trivium*, 2 (1967), 95–119, is similar in this respect. Müller-Salget's argument sometimes appears closer to my own; he refers to and correctly sums up the point of my interpretation of *Das Erdbeben in Chili* ("Überzeugend weist [Ellis] nach, daß hier die Problematik der Interpretation selbst zum Thema geworden ist," p. 192) and for a time appears to have almost completely adopted the view of Kleist's prose narrative that I had set forward. Compare, for example, my pp. 14–15 with his view that in *Die Heilige Cäcilie* the focus of attention is shifted "vom Geschehen selbst auf die *Deutung* des Geschehens" (p. 196); or my pp. 39–40 and 53 with his comment on *Michael Kohlhaas*: "Der Interpret verfehlt den Sinn dieser wie der übrigen Erzählungen Kleists, wenn er versucht, eine gewaltsame Eindeutigkeit herzustellen" (p. 191). Müller-Salget also adopts my procedure (p. 14) of learning something about *Michael Kohlhaas* from the persistence of contradictory critical opinions on the story. Yet he makes little progress beyond this point, largely because he allows the notion that the stories are "doppeldeutig" to be the conclusion that he reaches, not an indispensable framework and beginning for a thematic investigation of the texts. Consequently, he easily reverts to familiar static attitudes to Kleist's stories, rather than the tentative and flexible ones that are required by the view that a continual process of interpretation goes on in them. It is, for example, quite inconsistent with the framework he has adopted to say that there is strong "Gesellschaftskritik" in *Das Erdbeben* (p. 207); or to say that there remains in *Der Zweikampf* the certain (therefore unambiguous) value of "das unbedingte Vertrauen und die völlige Hingabe an den geliebten Menschen" (p. 201); or that in *Der Findling*, Nicolo is a "verwilderter Bösewicht" and that at the end of the story there is "kein Zweifel daran, wem die Sympathien des Erzählers gelten," i.e., Piachi (p. 203).

8. References to these critics are given in Chapter Eight.

9. The outstanding example is Gerhard Fricke, *Gefühl und Schicksal bei Heinrich von Kleist: Studien über den inneren Vorgang im Leben und Schaffen des Dichters* (Berlin, 1929).

10. Hans-Peter Herrmann, for example, thinks Kleist's world one "in der der Zufall vorherrscht" ("Zufall und Ich," p. 73). He develops this idea by saying that Kleist's stories, though different in many ways, all have a basic schema, which is characterized by "die Zufälligkeit, mit der einzelne Ereignisse in das Leben eines (oder mehrerer) Menschen einfallen," by "die herausfordernde Kraft" of the events for the people concerned, and by the fact that "Zufall und reagierender Mensch im Raum eines einzigen sprachlichen Gebildes vorgestellt werden" (p. 71). But these circumlocutions only show how uninteresting it is to focus on the simple idea that there are chance events in Kleist, unless one sees this within a wider framework. All that Herrmann does with the idea is to elaborate it verbally, but that adds nothing of substance to the bare fact that unexpected events do occur, and that people have to deal with them—as happens in the writings of many other authors.

11. Koopmann again reduces this to something that is of little consequence: "Kleist ist ein pedantischer Erzähler. Wo immer er nur geht, motiviert er, begründet er und macht es verständlich, warum sich dieses oder jenes ereignet hat. Auf nichts kommt es ihm so sehr an wie gerade darauf, und manchmal ruft er sogar den Zufall zu Hilfe, wenn sich ein Zusammenhang anders nicht mehr erklären lassen will" ("Das rätselhafte Faktum,'" p. 508).

12. For example: Hans Heinz Holz, *Macht und Ohnmacht der Sprache: Untersuchungen zum Sprachverständnis und Stil Heinrich von Kleists* (Frankfurt, 1962), p. 134, speaks of Kleist's "nüchterne Faktizität des Erzählstils," which "auf alle schmückenden Zutaten der Subjektivität verzichtet" (p. 141) and is even "karg" and "sehr auf das Notwendigste beschränkt" (p. 143). Or Karl Otto Conrady, "Das Moralische in Kleists Erzählungen: Ein Kapitel vom Dichter ohne Gesellschaft," in *Heinrich von Kleist: Aufsätze und Essays*, ed. Walter Müller-Seidel (Darmstadt, 1967): "Nur die Fakten des Geschehens werden erzählt, sachlich, nüchtern, ohne Kommentar des Erzählers" (p. 725). This view of Kleist's style is virtually universal.

13. It may even be the case that excessive and *really* irrelevant detail is on occasion part of this strategy; see, for example, the description of the crabs sold by the fake intermediary between Kohlhaas and Nagelschmidt, as discussed by Wolfgang Kayser, "Kleist als Erzähler," *German Life and Letters*, NS 8 (1954–55), 26–27.

14. Friedrich Beißner, "Unvorgreifliche Gedanken über den Sprachrhythmus," in *Festschrift Paul Kluckhohn und Hermann Schneider gewidmet zu ihrem 60. Geburtstag*, hrsg. von ihren Tübinger Schülern (Tübingen, 1948), p. 442.

15. Kayser, "Kleist als Erzähler," p. 26. Müller-Salget also addresses himself to the question of Kleist's "eigenwilligen Satzbau" (pp. 208 ff.) but, strangely, restricts himself to a tiny fraction of cases by writing only of those few where a real or implied dialogue takes place. His conclusion is that these sentences "demonstrieren, in wie hohem Maße der einzelne auf Grund der täuschenden Beschaffenheit der Welt angewiesen ist auf die Wahrhaftigkeit des anderen, darauf, daß der andere die Frage nicht mit einer Lüge beantwortet." But these sentences are far from representative of Kleist's "Satzbau," the conclusion drawn from them is unnecessary (one person is always at the mercy of the truthfulness of the person telling him things, regardless of sentence structure), and the conclusion that "Vertrauen" is an unambiguous value in Kleist is equally unnecessary and unjustified.

16. Kayser, "Kleist als Erzähler," pp. 22–24. Critics who have found fault with these perceptive remarks have generally only succeeded in showing how they have misunderstood them. When discussing the *Erdbeben*, for example, Wolfgang Wittkowski, Benno von Wiese, and R. S. Lucas all state what they *think* Kayser has said, and the results are revealing. Wittkowski thinks that Kayser "für die Sinnlosigkeit der Ereignisse plädiert," and that Kayser believes "durchweg werte Kleist nur momentan und überblicke nicht das Ganze" ("Skepsis, Noblesse, Ironie: Formen des Als-ob in Kleists *Erdbeben*," *Euphorion*, 63 [1969], 249). Wittkowski evidently did not follow Kayser's distinction between narrator and author. The narrator's limitations are not Kleist's; Kayser of course knew that *Kleist* had a view of the whole, and that otherwise the story would be meaningless. Von Wiese makes a similar error when he offers what he thinks is a corrective to Kayser by saying that Kleist is indeed concerned with the "Wirklichkeit des Geschehens" ("Heinrich von Kleist: Das Erdbeben in Chili," in his *Die deutsche Novelle von Goethe bis Kafka*, II [Düsseldorf, 1962], 57). Actually, nothing Kayser says would imply that that was not true of *both* narrator and author. Misquotation is often a key to misunderstanding, as is the case when von Wiese wrongly states Kayser's view to be that the narrator evaluates "vom jeweiligen Standort der Gestalten aus" (p. 54). Lucas perhaps reads von Wiese's misquotation rather than Kayser himself when attempting to correct Kayser by saying that "the narrator does not always abstain from all comment, submerging his mentality in that of the characters" ("Studies in Kleist," *Deutsche Vierteljahrsschrift für Literaturwissenschaft und Geistesgeschichte*, 44 [1970], 149).

Neither of these critics of Kayser has correctly observed the positions of the words "Gestalt," "Situation," "oft," and "fast immer" in his very careful formulation.

17. Though Conrady missed the sense of Kleist's narration bursting out of a realistic mode (see above), he understood that realism is not the point: "Realistisch ist Kleist im einzelnen Detail, legt aber im ganzen auf Realismus keinen Wert" ("Das Moralische in Kleists Erzählungen," p. 727). Unlike most critics, Conrady also saw the force and meaning of Kayser's insights; and starting out from them, he made some interesting remarks on the character of Kleist's narration, which also have some points of contact with those made in my interpretation of the *Erdbeben*. Coincidentally, both studies appeared in the same year (1963). For example: "Der Dichter ohne Gesellschaft bleibt selbst Fragender, ist suchender Erzähler. . . . Das Moralische der Kleistschen Erzählungen ist jenes Suchen selbst. . . . Es ist identisch mit der Art des Erzählens, das den Leser zum fragenden Partner des suchenden Dichters werden läßt" (pp. 733–35). On closer inspection, however, Conrady's view of Kleist's narration, and of the stories, is very far removed from that which I have presented. For example, he sees the process of searching as returning to two absolute values, which are "das Zusichselbstfinden" and "das Vertrauen zum Du," and calls them "diese unableitbaren Festpunkte letzter Wahrheit"; these rigid judgments are not at all in tune with the spirit of a narrative in which *everything* is tentative and part of a search for orientation points. As a consequence, his interpretations of the stories are just as hampered by rigidity as those of other critics. Conrady's use of a potentially more flexible framework is evidently limited by two factors: first, he confuses narrator and author, and second, he concentrates on "das Moralische." The two factors are linked: the equation of the narrator with Kleist, the "Dichter ohne Gesellschaft," leads to the limiting moral emphasis. The issues with which Kleist's narrator grapples, in the process making the reader also grapple with them, are much more diverse than this framework allows. But though Conrady's actual readings of the texts are as a result not nearly flexible enough—in fact are barely different from very familiar traditional readings—it remains true that with his notion of a "suchender Dichter" who made the reader his partner in the search, he got much nearer to an adequate view of Kleist's narrator than any other German critic of Kleist.

18. Attempts to characterize them as specifically Kleistian types have been unsuccessful; I pursue this point in the next chapter.

VIII. The Character of Kleist Criticism

1. An interesting indication of the strength and persistency of this desire on the part of many Kleist critics to abstract specific and definite authorial viewpoints is provided by some responses to my previously published essays. Other critics have often read them as advocating a specific authorial viewpoint that happened not to be the one that they prefer, instead of a different attitude to authorial viewpoint in Kleist's work. What seems to be involved here is a refusal to see that one might not want to simplify the text in the way that these critics want, to obtain a clear message from it. See, for example, in the case of the *Prinz von Homburg*, the instances cited at the end of Chapter Six, and in the case of the *Erdbeben in Chili*, Wolfgang Wittkowski's "Skepsis, Noblesse, Ironie: Formen des Als-ob in Kleists *Erdbeben*," *Euphorion*, 63 (1969), 247–83. Wittkowski reads my demonstration of the way in which the text at one point questions Don Fernando's role as an unambiguous assertion that Fernando is viewed negatively in the story (p. 272); and he makes my discussion of the attitude to the Viceroy that the text at one point seems to allow into an assertion that the Viceroy is definitely to be seen as the symbolic representative of the corrupt society in this story (p. 262).

2. Full references to titles mentioned in this paragraph are: Elmar Hoffmeister, *Täuschung und Wirklichkeit bei Heinrich von Kleist* (Bonn, 1968); Friedrich Koch, *Heinrich von Kleist: Bewußtsein und Wirklichkeit* (Stuttgart, 1958); Walter Müller-Seidel, *Versehen und Erkennen: Eine Studie über Heinrich von Kleist* (Cologne, 1961); Gerhard Fricke, *Gefühl*

und Schicksal bei Heinrich von Kleist: Studien über den inneren Vorgang im Leben und Schaffen des Dichters (Berlin, 1929); Hans-Peter Herrmann, "Zufall und Ich: Zum Begriff der Situation in den Novellen Heinrich von Kleists," *Germanisch-Romanische Monatsschrift*, NF 11 (1961), 69–99; John Gearey, *Heinrich von Kleist: A Study in Tragedy and Anxiety* (Philadelphia, 1968); Hermann Reske, *Traum und Wirklichkeit im Werk Heinrich von Kleists* (Stuttgart, 1969).

3. Hoffmeister, *Täuschung und Wirklichkeit*, p. 20.

4. Cf. my *Kleist's "Prinz Friedrich von Homburg": A Critical Study* (Berkeley and Los Angeles, 1970), p. 106; here I noted that general books on Kleist all tended to repeat one view of this play—the simplest possible.

5. Hans Matthias Wolff, *Heinrich von Kleist als politischer Dichter* (Berkeley and Los Angeles, 1947); an essentially similar position is taken in his later *Heinrich von Kleist: Die Geschichte seines Schaffens* (Berkeley and Los Angeles, 1954). Though in the earlier work Wolff acknowledged that he was seizing on one strand in Kleist (see the "Einleitung"), the interpretative comments in his later study make it clear that he sees this as the most important way to look at Kleist, since the comments of the 1947 volume are in substance repeated. Durzak's "Zur utopischen Funktion des Kindesbildes in Kleists Erzählungen" is from *Colloquia Germanica*, 3 (1969), 111–29.

6. Wolff, *Heinrich von Kleist als politischer Dichter*, p. 396.

7. Durzak, "Zur utopischen Funktion des Kindesbildes," pp. 121–26. *Der Findling* is evidently a real stumbling block for Durzak, and so he says that "Kleist im *Findling* die Problematik seiner eigenen utopischen Lösung reflektiert" (p. 129), since an innocent child like Nicolo has to grow up and lose his innocence. Here we see another case of the issues of a text being forgotten and replaced with issues that originate in the critic's attempt to preserve the consistency of his own view; there is neither any trace of a utopian solution *nor* any issue of its not being present in *Der Findling*.

8. A random example of an article essentially like Durzak's is Joseph W. Dyck's "Heinrich von Kleist: Ehre und Ehrgeiz als Ursache der Schuld," in *Husbanding the Golden Grain: Studies in Honor of Henry W. Nordmeyer*, ed. Luanne T. Frank and Emery E. George (Ann Arbor, 1973), 64–74.

9. Hoffmeister, *Täuschung und Wirklichkeit*, p. 52.

10. Friedrich Braig, *Heinrich von Kleist* (Munich, 1925), pp. 450–51.

11. See above, p. 131. See also the further case shown in Chapter Two, p. 21, of Müller-Seidel's article on *Die Marquise von O . . .* , which restates an obvious fact of the story (the Marquise's sense of being pregnant conflicts with her awareness of having done nothing that could have led to this result) in complex critical terminology that adds nothing of substance to it; again, the interpretation of the story is substantially that found elsewhere, so that nothing is added to the discussion of this text by the verbal elaboration.

12. Max Kommerell, "Die Sprache und das Unaussprechliche: Eine Betrachtung über Heinrich von Kleist," in his *Geist und Buchstabe der Dichtung* (Frankfurt a.M., 1944), p. 245. Kommerell's enormously influential article initiated the line of thought that is the essential basis for much later work, e.g., Walter Müller-Seidel's *Versehen und Erkennen*, Hermann Reske's *Traum und Wirklichkeit im Werk Heinrich von Kleists*, and Helmut Koopmann's "Das 'rätselhafte Faktum' und seine Vorgeschichte: Zum analytischen Charakter der Novellen Heinrich von Kleists," *Zeitschrift für deutsche Philologie*, 84 (1965), 508–50.

13. Kommerell, "Die Sprache und das Unaussprechliche," p. 257.

14. Friedrich Koch is another much quoted writer who belongs to the genre of Kleist criticism discussed in the text. Koch elaborates the same fact of the Marquise's experience that Müller-Seidel chose to elaborate, but in different terms: "Zwischen der Welt des Bewußtseins und der Wirklichkeit besteht grundsätzlich eine Differenz" (*Heinrich von Kleist*, p. 43). Just as in Müller-Seidel's case, nothing is added to the obvious facts of the story but a new terminology, the elaboration of which substitutes for and pre-

vents a good look at the text and its problems. Ernst von Reusner's *Satz–Gestalt–Schicksal: Untersuchungen über die Struktur in der Dichtung Kleists* (Berlin, 1961), represents something of a caricature of the tradition. Much of this work descends to an extreme of triviality: e.g., "Jeder Satz ist wie ein Blick auf etwas, das ist" (p. 17).

15. Müller-Seidel, *Versehen und Erkennen*, p. 54.

16. Müller-Seidel, *Versehen und Erkennen*, pp. 172–73.

17. Müller-Seidel, *Versehen und Erkennen*, p. 73. His misreading (p. 205) of the Elector's remark on Hohenzollern in line 1720 of *Prinz Friedrich von Homburg* is another failure to grasp the literal sense of Kleist's text; here he takes the Elector's "Die delphsche Weisheit meiner Offiziere" to be a straightforward *positive* evaluation of Hohenzollern in spite of the obvious scorn of the context ("Tor, der du bist, Blödsinniger!").

18. Müller-Seidel, *Versehen und Erkennen*, p. 175.

19. Fricke, *Gefühl und Schicksal*, pp. 136–39. And on *Michael Kohlhaas*, we have the following: "Das Ich des Kohlhaas selber als die heilige und letzte, sinngebende und sinntragende Wirklichkeit inmitten der endlichen Welt ist der Held der Dichtung" (p. 124). Again, the interpretative problems of the text are by-passed.

20. Chapter Seven, pp. 130–31.

21. The emphasis, for example, of Friedrich Braig, *Heinrich von Kleist*; John Gearey, *Heinrich von Kleist*; Friedrich Gundolf, *Heinrich von Kleist* (Berlin, 1922); and Michael Hamburger, "Heinrich von Kleist," in his *Reason and Energy: Studies in German Literature* (London, 1957), pp. 107–44 (this essay is obviously the source of the unsigned article "Heinrich von Kleist" in the *Times Literary Supplement*, 21 August 1953, pp. 529–30).

22. E.g., Gunter Blöcker, *Heinrich von Kleist oder Das Absolute Ich* (Berlin, 1960), p. 16: "Der grenzenlose Mensch, geschüttelt von den Schauern der Existenz, befeuert vom Willen zum Absoluten, umstrahlt von der Glorie der Selbstverantwortung, ist Kleists Held."

23. See, e.g., Raimund Belgardt's working his way through the Kant-crisis to a laboriously deduced interpretation of *Prinz Friedrich*, which turns out to be identical with that found in at least a hundred other critics, in his "Kleists Weg zur Wahrheit: Irrtum und Wahrheit als Denkformen und Strukturmöglichkeit," *Zeitschrift für deutsche Philologie*, 92 (1973), 161–84.

24. *Kleists Aufsatz "Über das Marionettentheater": Studien und Interpretationen*, ed. Helmut Sembdner (Berlin, 1967).

25. Johannes Klein, "Heinrich von Kleist," in his *Geschichte der deutschen Novelle von Goethe bis zur Gegenwart*, 4th ed. (Wiesbaden, 1960), pp. 77–98.

26. Michael Moering, *Witz und Ironie in der Prosa Heinrich von Kleists* (Munich, 1972). Somewhat predictably, Moering sees as much comedy and irony in the stories as he can, which is a good deal more than is there, but does little else.

27. Hans Heinz Holz, *Macht und Ohnmacht der Sprache: Untersuchungen zum Sprachverständnis und Stil Heinrich von Kleists* (Frankfurt, 1962), p. 161. Generally speaking, this work is devoted to an elaboration of what had already been a familiar critical cliché in many previous writers, that Kleist was trying to express "das Unaussprechliche," as in Kommerell, "Die Sprache und das Unaussprechliche," or felt the "Not der Sprache," as in Paul Böckmann, "Heinrich von Kleist," in *Heinrich von Kleist: Aufsätze und Essays*, ed. Walter Müller-Seidel (Darmstadt, 1967), pp. 296–316. But as is so frequently the case in such works, Holz pushes his point so far that it becomes meaningless. To claim that "die Sprache selbst das dramatische Urmotiv Kleistscher Dichtung ist" (p. 91) does not sound at all plausible, and a sample of the evidence offered to support this conclusion confirms that the necessary careful distinction between linguistic and other issues eludes Holz. E.g.: "Kleists Mißtrauen gegen alle Zeugniskraft des bloßen Wortes war so stark, daß er nicht Rosaliens Vernehmung allein, die die Täuschung eingestand, sondern nur in Verbindung mit einem sicheren dinglichen Zeichen, dem Ring Jakobs, als Entlastung gelten lassen wollte" (*Macht und Ohnmacht der Sprache*, p. 102).

The ring is of course an old and popular motif in such circumstances, and it is extremely fanciful to see a linguistic issue in it.

28. Fricke and Reusner are in varying degrees also in this category.

29. Georg Lukács, "Die Tragödie Heinrich von Kleists," in his *Deutsche Realisten des 19. Jahrhunderts* (Berlin, 1951), pp. 19–48.

30. Lukács, "Die Tragödie Heinrich von Kleists," pp. 42, 35, and 40.

31. Lukács, "Die Tragödie Heinrich von Kleists," pp. 40–41.

32. Manfred Lefèvre, "Kleist-Forschung 1961–1967," *Colloquia Germanica*, 3 (1969), e.g., pp. 22 and 38.

33. Lukács, "Die Tragödie Heinrich von Kleists," p. 48.

34. E.g., Ernst Fischer, "Heinrich von Kleist," *Sinn und Form*, 13 (1961), 759–844; Hans Mayer, *Heinrich von Kleist: Der geschichtliche Augenblick* (Pfullingen, 1962); and Siegfried Streller, *Das dramatische Werk Heinrich von Kleists* (Berlin, 1966).

35. Fischer, "Heinrich von Kleist," pp. 826 and 833.

36. Mayer, *Heinrich von Kleist*, p. 50.

37. Lefèvre, "Kleist-Forschung 1961–1967," p. 36.

38. Lefèvre, "Kleist-Forschung 1961–1967," pp. 22 and 31.

39. Some things are indeed said by Marxists that are not found elsewhere—but they are scarcely to the credit of this genre of criticism. See, for example, Werner Preuß's view in his *Heinrich von Kleist und die Nationale Frage*, Diss. Potsdam 1962, that the real point of the introduction of the Elector of Brandenburg in *Michael Kohlhaas* is to make it possible for Kleist to avoid, "daß die feudalistische Gesellschaftsordnung selbst in Frage gestellt wird" (cited by Lefèvre, "Kleist-Forschung 1961–1967, p. 43). That is an original Marxist view and surely implausible. Or take Streller, who pronounces *Prinz Friedrich von Homburg* an "Apologie" for the feudal regime, even though he also says this was not Kleist's intent (*Das dramatische Werk Heinrich von Kleists*, p. 222). Again, this is original only at the cost of being plainly erroneous; since *all* of the characters are from the ruling class, it is impossible to see any interclass issue here.

40. Siegfried Mews, in his "Brechts 'dialektisches Verhältnis zur Tradition': Die Bearbeitung des *Michael Kohlhaas*," *Brecht-Jahrbuch* (1975), 63–78, makes the further point that Brecht's Marxist interpretation of Michael Kohlhaas was in important respects shared in the 1930s even by fascists! For the Nazis, too, Kleist was a "Volksführer" (p. 75).

Bibliography

The time is long since past when it was possible to append even a reasonably complete bibliography of writings on Kleist to a volume of criticism such as this. The general section of this bibliography is therefore restricted to those items that are cited during the course of the book. The sections on the five stories to which I have devoted individual chapters, on the other hand, list titles devoted specifically to those works that are complete up to the end of 1975. Complete bibliographies of work appearing in 1975 are not themselves published until late 1976 or early 1977; this study was completed in 1976. As my study goes to press, however, I have included, in an addendum to Chapter Eight, discussion of some significant findings and trends in selected items that appeared in 1976 and 1977; these are included in the bibliography. The scope of what has been written on *Prinz Friedrich von Homburg* again makes completeness something that only a specialized bibliography could or should aspire to; in that section of the bibliography, I have primarily sought to bring up to date the two special bibliographies that I mention there, although all works cited in the chapter are included. The most valuable Kleist bibliography to have appeared so far is that by Eva Rothe: "Kleist-Bibliographie 1945–1960," *Jahrbuch der deutschen Schiller-Gesellschaft*, 5 (1961), 414–547. Rothe gives references to the Kleist bibliography of Georg Minde-Pouet, which covers the years from 1914 to 1937 and is printed in installments in the *Jahrbuch der Kleist-Gesellschaft* from 1921 to 1937. Readers who wish to read further in Kelist criticism of the last fifteen years have at the moment no better resource than the Kleist bibliographies published each year as part of the *Year's Work in Modern Language Studies* and of the *Annual Bibliography* in the *PMLA*. Other bibliographical resources are the periodical *Germanistik* and the biannual *Bibliographie der deutschen Literaturwissenschaft*, ed. H. W. Eppelsheimer and C. Köttelwesch (Frankfurt, 1957 ff.).

There are many editions of Kleist's works, but only two of them are used by scholars on a regular basis: *Heinrich von Kleist: Sämtliche Werke und Briefe*, auf Grund der Erstdrucke und Handschriften herausgegeben von Helmut Sembdner, 2 vols. (Munich, 2nd ed., 1961; 3rd ed., 1964; 4th ed., 1965); and *H. v. Kleists Werke*, im Verein mit Georg Minde-Pouet und Reinhold Steig herausgegeben von Erich Schmidt, 5 vols. (Leipzig, 1904–05; 2nd ed. rev. by Georg Minde-Pouet, 7 vols., 1936–38). I have used Sembdner's third edition. An historical-critical edition is planned by the Carl Hanser Verlag; the editorial principles that it will follow are discussed by Klaus Kanzog, *Prolegomena zu einer historisch-kritischen Ausgabe der Werke Heinrich von Kleists: Theorie und Praxis einer modernen Klassiker-Edition* (Munich, 1970). See also Hans-Joachim

Kreutzer, *Überlieferung und Edition: Textkritische und editorische Probleme, dargestellt am Beispiel einer historisch-kritischen Kleist-Ausgabe*, mit einem Beitrag von Klaus Kanzog, Beiheft zum *Euphorion*, Heft 7 (1976).

GENERAL

Anon. "Heinrich von Kleist." *The Times Literary Supplement*, 21 August 1953, pp. 529–30. [See also Hamburger, Michael.]

Beißner, Friedrich. "Unvorgreifliche Gedanken über den Sprachrhythmus." In *Festschrift Paul Kluckhohn und Hermann Schneider gewidmet zu ihrem 60. Geburtstag*. Herausgegeben von ihren Tübinger Schülern. Tübingen, 1948, pp. 427–44.

Belgardt, Raimund. "Kleists Weg zur Wahrheit: Irrtum und Wahrheit als Denkformen und Strukturmöglichkeit." *Zeitschrift für deutsche Philologie*, 92 (1973), 161–84.

Bennett, E. K. "The Metaphysical Novelle—Kleist." In his *A History of the German "Novelle."* 2nd ed. Rev. and cont. by H. M. Waidson. Cambridge, 1961, pp. 37–46.

Blöcker, Gunter. *Heinrich von Kleist oder Das Absolute Ich*. Berlin, 1960.

Böckmann, Paul. "Heinrich von Kleist." In *Heinrich von Kleist: Aufsätze und Essays*. Ed. Walter Müller-Seidel. Darmstadt, 1967, pp. 296–316. First published as "Heinrich von Kleist 1777–1811." In *Die großen Deutschen: Deutsche Biographie*. Ed. Hermann Heimpel, Theodor Heuß, and Benno Reifenberg. Vol. II. Berlin, 1956, 362–77.

Bonafous, Raymond. *Henri de Kleist: Sa vie et ses oeuvres*. Paris, 1894.

Brahm, Otto. *Heinrich von Kleist*. Berlin, 1884.

Braig, Friedrich. *Heinrich von Kleist*. Munich, 1925.

Conrady, Karl Otto. *Die Erzählweise Heinrichs von Kleist: Untersuchungen und Interpretationen*. Diss. Munster 1953.

————. "Das Moralische in Kleists Erzählungen: Ein Kapitel vom Dichter ohne Gesellschaft." In *Heinrich von Kleist: Aufsätze und Essays*. Ed. Walter Müller-Seidel. Darmstadt, 1967, pp. 707–35. First published in *Literatur und Gesellschaft vom neunzehnten ins zwanzigste Jahrhundert: Festgabe für Benno von Wiese zu seinem 60. Geburtstag am 25. September 1963*. Ed. Hans Joachim Schrimpf. Bonn, 1963, pp. 56–82.

Durzak, Manfred. "Zur utopischen Funktion des Kindesbildes in Kleists Erzählungen." *Colloquia Germanica*, 3 (1969), 111–29.

Dyck, Joseph W. "Heinrich von Kleist: Ehre und Ehrgeiz als Ursache der Schuld." In *Husbanding the Golden Grain: Studies in Honor of Henry W. Nordmeyer*. Ed. Luanne T. Frank and Emery E. George. Ann Arbor, 1973, pp. 64–74.

Dyer, Denys. *The Stories of Kleist: A Critical Study*. London, 1977.

Fischer, Ernst. "Heinrich von Kleist." *Sinn und Form*, 13 (1961), 759–844.

Fricke, Gerhard. *Gefühl und Schicksal bei Heinrich von Kleist: Studien über den inneren Vorgang im Leben und Schaffen des Dichters*. Berlin, 1929.

Gearey, John. *Heinrich von Kleist: A Study in Tragedy and Anxiety*. Philadelphia, 1968.

Graham, Ilse. *Heinrich von Kleist. Word Into Flesh: A Poet's Quest for the Symbol*. Berlin and New York, 1977.

Greenberg, Martin, trans. and introd. *Heinrich von Kleist: The Marquise von O— and Other Stories*. Preface by Thomas Mann. New York, 1960. [See also Mann, Thomas.]

Gundolf, Friedrich. *Heinrich von Kleist*. Berlin, 1922.

Hamburger, Michael. "Heinrich von Kleist." In his *Reason and Energy: Studies in German Literature*. London, 1957, pp. 107–44.

Herrmann, Hans-Peter. "Zufall und Ich: Zum Begriff der Situation in den Novellen Heinrich von Kleists." *Germanisch-Romanische Monatsschrift*, NF 11 (1961), 69–99.

Herzog, Wilhelm. *Heinrich von Kleist: Sein Leben und sein Werk*. 2nd ed. Munich, 1914.

Hoffmeister, Elmar. *Täuschung und Wirklichkeit bei Heinrich von Kleist*. Bonn, 1968.

Holz, Hans Heinz. *Macht und Ohnmacht der Sprache: Untersuchungen zum Sprachverständnis und Stil Heinrich von Kleists*. Frankfurt, 1962.

Kayser, Wolfgang. "Kleist als Erzähler." *German Life and Letters*, NS 8 (1954–55), 19–29.

Klein, Johannes. "Heinrich von Kleist." In his *Geschichte der deutschen Novelle von Goethe bis zur Gegenwart*. 4th ed. Wiesbaden, 1960, pp. 77–98.

Koch, Friedrich. *Heinrich von Kleist: Bewußtsein und Wirklichkeit*. Stuttgart, 1958.

Kommerell, Max. "Die Sprache und das Unaussprechliche: Eine Betrachtung über Heinrich von Kleist." In his *Geist und Buchstabe der Dichtung*. Frankfurt a.M., 1944, pp. 243–317.

Koopmann, Helmut. "Das 'rätselhafte Faktum' und seine Vorgeschichte: Zum analytischen Charakter der Novellen Heinrich von Kleists." *Zeitschrift für deutsche Philologie*, 84 (1965), 508–50.

Korff, Hermann August. *Geist der Goethezeit*. 4 vols. Leipzig, 1953.

Lämmert, Eberhard. *Bauformen des Erzählens*. Stuttgart, 1955.

Lefèvre, Manfred. "Kleist-Forschung 1961–1967." *Colloquia Germanica*, 3 (1969), 1–86.

Lepper, K. H. "Zur Polarität der Weltsicht in Kleists Novellen." *Trivium*, 2 (1967), 95–119.

Lockemann, Fritz. "Heinrich von Kleist." In his *Gestalt und Wandlungen der deutschen Novelle*. Munich, 1957, pp. 64–77.

Lukács, Georg. "Die Tragödie Heinrich von Kleists." In his *Deutsche Realisten des 19. Jahrhunderts*. Berlin, 1951, pp. 19–48.

Mann, Thomas. "Kleist and his Stories." In Martin Greenberg, trans. and introd. *Heinrich von Kleist: Die Marquise von O— and Other Stories*. New York, 1960, pp. 5–23. First published as "The Genius of Kleist." In *The American Scholar*, 24 (1955), 187–94.

Martini, Fritz. *Deutsche Literaturgeschichte von den Anfängen bis zur Gegenwart*. 7th ed. Stuttgart, 1955.

Mayer, Hans. *Heinrich von Kleist: Der geschichtliche Augenblick.* Pfullingen, 1962.

Moering, Michael. *Witz und Ironie in der Prosa Heinrich von Kleists.* Munich, 1972.

Müller-Salget, Klaus. "Das Prinzip der Doppeldeutigkeit in Kleists Erzählungen." *Zeitschrift fur deutsche Philologie*, 92 (1973), 185–211.

Müller-Seidel, Walter. *Versehen und Erkennen: Eine Studie über Heinrich von Kleist.* Cologne, 1961.

Pongs, Hermann. *Das Bild in der Dichtung.* Vol. II. Marburg, 1939.

Preuß, Werner. *Heinrich von Kleist und die Nationale Frage.* Diss. Potsdam 1962.

Reed, T. J. "The 'Goethezeit' and its Aftermath." In *Germany: A Companion to German Studies.* Ed. Malcolm Pasley. London, 1972, pp. 493–553.

Reske, Hermann. *Traum und Wirklichkeit im Werk Heinrich von Kleists.* Stuttgart, 1969.

Reusner, Ernst von. *Satz–Gestalt–Schicksal: Untersuchungen über die Struktur in der Dichtung Kleists.* Berlin, 1961.

Sembdner, Helmut, ed. *Kleists Aufsatz "Über das Marionettentheater": Studien und Interpretationen.* Berlin, 1967.

Silz, Walter. *Heinrich von Kleist: Studies in his Works and Literary Character.* Philadelphia, 1961.

Staiger, Emil. "Heinrich von Kleist." In *Heinrich von Kleist: Vier Reden zu seinem Gedächtnis.* Ed. Walter Müller-Seidel. Berlin, 1962, pp. 63–74.

Streller, Siegfried. *Das dramatische Werk Heinrich von Kleists.* Berlin, 1966.

Thomas, Lionel. "Heinrich von Kleist and his Stories." *Proceedings of the Leeds Philosophical and Literary Society*, 10 (1962), 77–91.

Witkop, Philipp. *Heinrich von Kleist.* Leipzig, 1922.

Wolff, Hans Matthias. *Heinrich von Kleist als politischer Dichter.* Berkeley and Los Angeles, 1947.

——. *Heinrich von Kleist: Die Geschichte seines Schaffens.* Berkeley and Los Angeles, 1954.

INDIVIDUAL WORKS (Chapters I–VI)

Der Findling

Günther, Kurt. " 'Der Findling'—Die frühste der Kleistschen Erzählungen." *Euphorion*, 8 (1909), Ergänzungsheft, 119–53.

Heubi, Albert. *H. von Kleists Novelle "Der Findling."* Diss. Zurich 1948.

Hoffmeister, Werner. "Heinrich von Kleists 'Findling.' " *Monatshefte*, 58 (1966), 49–63.

Kunz, Josef. "Heinrich von Kleists Novelle 'Der Findling': Eine Interpretation." In *Festschrift für Ludwig Wolff.* Ed. Werner Schröder. Neumünster, 1962, pp. 337–55.

Moore, Erna. "Heinrich von Kleists 'Findling': Psychologie des Verhängnisses". *Colloquia Germanica*, 8 (1974), 275–97.

(see below)

Ryder, Frank. "Kleist's *Findling*: Oedipus Manqué?" *Modern Language Notes*, 92 (1977), 509–24.

Wolff, Hans Matthias. "Heinrich von Kleists 'Findling.'" *University of California Publications in Modern Philology*, 36 (1952), 441–54.

Die Marquise von O . . .

Blankenagel, John C. "Heinrich von Kleist's Marquise von O . . . ." *Germanic Review*, 6 (1931), 363–72.

Bokelmann, Siegfried. "Betrachtungen zur Satzgestaltung in Kleists Novelle 'Die Marquise von O . . . .'" *Wirkendes Wort*, 8 (1957–58), 84–89.

Cohn, Dorrit. "Kleist's 'Marquise von O . . .' : The Problem of Knowledge." *Monatshefte*, 67 (1975), 129–44.

Crosby, Donald H. "Psychological Realism in the Works of Kleist: 'Penthesilea' and 'Die Marquise von O . . . .'" *Literature and Psychology*, 19 (1969), 3–16.

Dünnhaupt, Gerhard. "Kleist's *Marquise von O . . .* and its Literary Debt to Cervantes." *Arcadia*, 10 (1975), 147–57.

Fries, Thomas. "The Impossible Object: The Feminine, the Narrative (Laclos' *Liasons Dangereuses* and Kleist's *Marquise von O . . .*)." *Modern Language Notes*, 91 (1976), 1296–326.

Horodisch, A. "Eine unbekannte Quelle zu Kleists 'Die Marquise von O . . . .'" *Philobiblon*, 7 (1963), 136–39.

Müller-Seidel, Walter. "Die Struktur des Widerspruchs in Kleists 'Marquise von O . . . .'" *Deutsche Vierteljahrsschrift für Literaturwissenschaft und Geistesgeschichte*, 27 (1954), 497–515.

Ossar, Michael. "Kleist's *Erdbeben in Chili* and *Die Marquise von O . . . .*" *Revue des Langues Vivantes*, 34 (1968), 151–69.

Politzer, Heinz. "Der Fall der Frau Marquise: Beobachtungen zu Kleists *Die Marquise von O . . . .*" *Deutsche Vierteljahrsschrift für Literaturwissenschaft und Geistesgeschichte*, 51 (1977), 98–128.

Sokel, Walter H. "Kleist's Marquise von O . . . , Kierkegaard's Abraham, and Musil's Tonka: Three Stages of the Absurd as the Touchstone of Faith." *Wisconsin Studies in Contemporary Literature*, 8 (1967), 505–16.

Swales, Erika. "The Beleaguered Citadel: A Study of Kleist's *Die Marquise von O . . . .*" *Deutsche Vierteljahrsschrift für Literaturwissenschaft und Geistesgeschichte*, 51 (1977), 129–47.

Weiss, Hermann F. "Precarious Idylls: The Relationship Between Father and Daughter In Heinrich von Kleist's *Die Marquise von O . . . .*" *Modern Language Notes*, 91 (1976), 538–42.

Das Erdbeben in Chili

Aldridge, Alfred Owen. "The Background of Kleist's *Das Erdbeben in Chili*." *Arcadia*, 4 (1969), 173–80.

Blankenagel, John C. "Heinrich von Kleist: *Das Erdbeben in Chili*." *Germanic Review*, 8 (1933), 30–39.

Conrady, Karl Otto. "Kleists 'Erdbeben in Chili': Ein Interpretationsversuch."
   Germanisch-Romanische Monatsschrift, NF 4 (1954), 185–95.
Ellis, John M. "Kleist's Das Erdbeben in Chili." Publications of the English Goethe
   Society, NS 33 (1963), 10–55.
Gausewitz, Walter. "Kleist's 'Erdbeben.'" Monatshefte, 55 (1963), 188–94.
Horn, Peter. "Anarchie und Mobherrschaft in Kleists 'Erdbeben in Chili.'"
   Acta Germanica, 7 (1972), 77–96.
Johnson, Richard L. "Kleist's Erdbeben in Chili." Seminar: A Journal of Germanic
   Studies, 11 (1975), 33–45.
Klein, Johannes. "Kleists 'Erdbeben in Chili.'" Der Deutschunterricht, 8, No. 3
   (1956), 5–11.
Kunz, Joseph. "Die Gestaltung des tragischen Geschehens in Kleists 'Erdbe-
   ben in Chili.'" In Gratulatio: Festschrift für Christian Wegner zum 70. Geburts-
   tag am 9. September 1963. Ed. Maria Honeit and Matthias Wegner. Hamburg,
   1963, pp. 145–69.
Lucas, R. S. "Studies in Kleist: I. Problems in 'Michael Kohlhaas.' II. 'Das
   Erdbeben in Chili.'" Deutsche Vierteljahrsschrift für Literaturwissenschaft und
   Geistesgeschichte, 44 (1970), 120–70.
Modern, Rodolfo E. "Sobre El Terremoto en Chile, de Kleist." Torre, 10 (1962),
   39, 151–55.
Ossar, Michael. "Kleist's Das Erdbeben in Chili and Die Marquise von O . . . ."
   Revue des Langues Vivantes, 34 (1968), 151–69.
San Juan, Epifanio, Jr. "The Structure of Narrative Fiction." Saint Louis Quar-
   terly, 4 (1966), 485–502.
Silz, Walter. "Das Erdbeben in Chili." Monatshefte, 53 (1961), 210–38.
Wiese, Benno von. "Heinrich von Kleist: Das Erdbeben in Chili." In his Die
   deutsche Novelle von Goethe bis Kafka: Interpretationen. Vol. II. Düsseldorf,
   1962, 53–70.
Wittkowski, Wolfgang. "Skepsis, Noblesse, Ironie: Formen des Als-ob in
   Kleists Erdbeben." Euphorion, 63 (1969), 247–83.

Der Zweikampf

Conrady, Karl Otto. "Der Zweikampf: Zur Aussageweise Heinrichs von
   Kleist." Der Deutschunterricht, 3, No. 6 (1951), 85–96.
Crosby, Donald H., ed. Heinrich von Kleist: Das Bettelweib von Locarno, Der
   Zweikampf. Waltham, Mass., 1968.
———. "Heinrich von Kleist's 'Der Zweikampf.'" Monatshefte, 56 (1964),
   191–201.
Ellis, John M. "Kleist's 'Der Zweikampf.'" Monatshefte, 65 (1973), 48–60.
Meyer, Heinrich. "Kleists Novelle 'Der Zweikampf.'" Jahrbuch der Kleist-
   Gesellschaft, 17 (1933–37), 136–69.
Mommsen, Katharina. "Kleist's Duel Story as 'Erlebnisdichtung.'" Carleton
   Germanic Papers, 2 (1974), 49–66.
Müller, Joachim. Literarische Analogien in Heinrich von Kleists Novelle "Der
   Zweikampf." Berlin, 1969.
Oppel, Horst. "Kleists Novelle 'Der Zweikampf.'" Deutsche Vierteljahrsschrift

für Literaturwissenschaft und Geistesgeschichte, 22 (1944), 92–105.

Wittkowski, Wolfgang. *"Die Heilige Cäcilie* und *Der Zweikampf*: Kleists Legenden und die romantische Ironie." *Colloquia Germanica*, 6 (1972), 17–58.

Michael Kohlhaas

Anstett, Jean-Jacques. "A propos de *Michael Kohlhaas.*" *Études Germaniques*, 14 (1959), 150–56.

Aragon, Louis. "Le 'Michael Kohlhaas' d'Heinrich von Kleist." In his *La Lumière de Stendhal*. Paris, 1954, pp. 199–214.

Bernd, Clifford A. "The 'Abdeckerszene' in Kleist's *Michael Kohlhaas.*" *Studia Neophilologica*, 39 (1967), 270–80.

————. "Der Lutherbrief in Kleists 'Michael Kohlhaas.'" *Zeitschrift für deutsche Philologie*, 86 (1967), 627–33.

————. "On the Two Divergent Parts of Kleist's Michael Kohlhaas." In *New York University Department of German Studies in Germanic Languages and Literature*. Ed. Robert A. Fowkes and Volkmar Sander. Reutlingen, 1967, pp. 47–56.

Best, Otto F. "Schuld und Vergebung: Zur Rolle von Wahrsagerin und 'Amulett' in Kleists 'Michael Kohlhaas.'" *Germanisch-Romanische Monatsschrift*, NF 20 (1970), 180–89.

Büttner, Ludwig. "Michael Kohlhaas—eine paranoische oder heroische Gestalt?" *Seminar: A Journal of Germanic Studies*, 4 (1968), 26–41.

Cary, John R. "A Reading of Kleist's *Michael Kohlhaas.*" *PMLA*, 85 (1970), 212–18.

Dechert, Hans-Wilhelm. *"Indem er ans Fenster trat* . . . : Zur Funktion einer Gebärde in Kleists *Michael Kohlhaas.*" *Euphorion*, 62 (1968), 77–84.

Dyer, Denys. "Junker Wenzel von Tronka." *German Life and Letters*, NS 18 (1965), 252–57.

Ellis, John M. "Der Herr läßt regnen über Gerechte und Ungerechte: Kleist's 'Michael Kohlhaas.'" *Monatshefte*, 59 (1967), 35–40.

Fricke, Gerhard. "Kleists 'Michael Kohlhaas.'" *Der Deutschunterricht*, 5, No. 1 (1953), 17–39.

Gemkow, Heinrich. "Heinrich von Kleist: 'Michael Kohlhaas.' Zur Behandlung im 10. Schuljahr." *Deutschunterricht*, 5 (1952), 311–16.

Goheen, Jutta. "Der lange Satz als Kennzeichen der Erzählweise im 'Michael Kohlhaas.'" *Wirkendes Wort*, 17 (1967), 239–46.

Heber, Fritz. " 'Michael Kohlhaas': Versuch einer neuen Textinterpretation." *Wirkendes Wort*, 1 (1950–51), 98–102.

Hertling, Gunter H. "Kleists *Michael Kohlhaas* und Fontanes *Grete Minde*: Freiheit und Fügung." *German Quarterly*, 40 (1967), 24–40.

Hofacker, Erich. "Bergengruen's 'Das Feuerzeichen' and Kleist's 'Michael Kohlhaas.'" *Monatshefte*, 47 (1955), 349–57.

Horwath, Peter. "The 'Nicht-um-die-Welt' Theme: A Clue to the Ultimate Meaning of Kleist's *Michael Kohlhaas.*" *Studia Neophilologica*, 39 (1967), 261–69.

————. "Auf den Spuren Teniers, Vouets und Raphaels in Kleists *Michael Kohlhaas.*" *Seminar: A Journal of Germanic Studies*, 5 (1969), 102–13.

———. "Michael Kohlhaas. Kleists Absicht in der Überarbeitung des Phöbus-Fragments: Versuch einer Interpretation." *Monatshefte*, 57 (1965), 49–59.

———. "Gerechtigkeit und Gnade in Kleists *Michael Kohlhaas*: Über die Substanzkraft traditionell-religiöser Elemente." In *Husbanding the Golden Grain: Studies in Honor of Henry W. Nordmeyer*. Ed. Luanne T. Frank and Emery E. George. Ann Arbor, 1973, pp. 151–68.

King, Rolf. "The Figure of Luther in Kleist's *Michael Kohlhaas*." *Germanic Review*, 9 (1934), 18–25.

Körner, Josef. *Recht und Pflicht: Eine Studie über Kleists "Mich. Kohlhaas" und "Prinz Friedrich von Homburg*." Berlin, 1926.

Lange, Henrik. "Säkularisierte Bibelreminiszenzen in Kleists 'Michael Kohlhaas.'" *Kopenhagener Germanistische Studien*, 1 (1969), 213–26.

Lindsay, J. M. "Kohlhaas and K.: Two Men in Search of Justice." *German Life and Letters*, NS 13 (1960), 190–94.

Linnartz-Kaiser, Franz. "Das Problem des Michael Kohlhaas: Eine Ehrenrettung." *Denkendes Volk*, 2 (1948), 6–11.

Lucas, R. S. "Studies in Kleist: I. Problems in 'Michael Kohlhaas.' II. 'Das Erdbeben in Chili.'" *Deutsche Vierteljahrsschrift für Literaturwissenschaft und Geistesgeschichte*, 44 (1970), 120–70.

Marson, Eric. "Justice and the Obsessed Character in 'Michael Kohlhaas,' 'Der Prozess' and 'L'Étranger.'" *Seminar: A Journal of Germanic Studies*, 2 (1966), 21–33.

Mews, Siegfried. "Brechts 'dialektisches Verhältnis zur Tradition': Die Bearbeitung des *Michael Kohlhaas*." *Brecht-Jahrbuch* (1975), 63–78.

Meyer-Benfey, Heinrich. "Die innere Geschichte des 'Michael Kohlhaas.'" *Euphorion*, 15 (1908), 99–140.

Müller, Richard Matthias. "Kleists 'Michael Kohlhaas.'" *Deutsche Vierteljahrsschrift für Literaturwissenschaft und Geistesgeschichte*, 44 (1970), 101–19.

Passage, Charles E. "*Michael Kohlhaas*: Form Analysis." *Germanic Review*, 30 (1955), 181–97.

Rodrigues, Wilma. "Michael Kohlhaas oder Die verbrecherische Einrichtung der Welt." *Revista de Letras de Faculdade de Filosofia, Ciências e Letras de Assis*, 10 (1967), 179–90.

Schlütter, Hans-Jürgen. "Kohlhaas, Ide und die Welt." *Zeitschrift für deutsche Philologie*, 86 (1967), 634.

Schultze-Jahde, Karl. "Kohlhaas und die Zigeunerin." *Jahrbuch der Kleist-Gesellschaft*, 17 (1933–37), 108–35.

Silz, Walter. "Three Themes in *Michael Kohlhaas*." In his *Heinrich von Kleist: Studies in His Works and Literary Character*. Philadelphia, 1961, pp. 173–98.

Tellenbach, Hubert. "Die Aporie der wahnhaften Querulanz: Das Verfallen an die Pflicht zur Durchsetzung des Rechts in H.v. Kleists 'Michael Kohlhaas.'" *Colloquia Germanica*, 7 (1973), 1–8.

Wächter, Karl. *Kleists Michael Kohlhaas: Ein Beitrag zu seiner Entstehungsgeschichte*. Weimar, 1918.

Wiese, Benno von. "Heinrich von Kleist: Michael Kohlhaas." In his *Die deutsche Novelle von Goethe bis Kafka: Interpretationen*. Vol. I. Düsseldorf, 1956, 47–63.

Prinz Friedrich von Homburg

An enormous bibliography up to 1963 on this, Kleist's most read and discussed work, is contained in Richard Samuel's edition of the only surviving manuscript of the play: *Heinrich von Kleist: "Prinz Friedrich von Homburg. Ein Schauspiel,"* nach der Heidelberger Handschrift herausgegeben von Richard Samuel, unter Mitwirkung von Dorothea Coverlid (Berlin, 1964). Samuel's list contains 300 titles. I published a supplement to this list, including titles that appeared after Samuel's edition had been published, as well as some that his list had missed, in my *Kleist's "Prinz Friedrich von Homburg": A Critical Study* (Berkeley and Los Angeles, 1970). My list closed in 1968 and contained a further 60 items. The following list is intended mainly to bring the two that I have noted up to date: it lists all that has appeared since my supplement closed, as well as those previous works that I have mentioned in the present chapter on the play.

Atkins, Stuart. "Taught by Success: Kleist's Prince of Homburg." *German Quarterly*, 50 (1977), 1–9.

Benson, J. M. "Kleist's *Prinz Friedrich von Homburg.*" *Modern Languages*, 46 (1965), 98–103.

Burkholz, Gerhard. "Bertolt Brecht: Über Kleists Stück *Der Prinz von Homburg*. Eine Interpretation." *Der Deutschunterricht*, 25, No. 2 (1973), 31–33.

Crosby, Donald H. "Kleist's Prinz von Homburg—An Intensified Egmont?" *German Life and Letters*, NS 23 (1970), 315–22.

———. Rev. of *Kleist's "Prinz Friedrich von Homburg": A Critical Study*, by John M. Ellis. *German Quarterly* (AATG *Membership Directory*), 46 (Sept. 1973), 148–50.

Fricke, Gerhard. "Kleists 'Prinz Friedrich von Homburg.'" In his *Studien und Interpretationen*. Frankfurt a.M., 1956, pp. 239–63.

Garland, Mary. *Kleist's "Prinz Friedrich von Homburg": An Interpretation through Word Pattern*. The Hague, 1968.

Hackert, Fritz. "Kleists 'Prinz Friedrich von Homburg' in der Nachkriegs-Interpretation 1947–1972: Ein Literaturbericht." *Zeitschrift für Literaturwissenschaft und Linguistik*, 3 (1973), 53–80.

Kaiser, Hellmuth "Kleists 'Prinz Friedrich von Homburg.'" *Imago*, 17 (1930), 119–37.

Kanzog, Klaus. "Rudolf Köpkes handschriftliche Aufzeichnungen der Kleist-Bemerkungen Tiecks: Zugleich ein Schlußwort zur Manuskript-Lage des *Prinz von Homburg*." *Euphorion*, 62 (1968), 160–68.

Leeuwe, Hans de. "Brechts Sonett über Kleists *Prinz von Homburg* oder: Ein Dichter als Leser." In *Dichter und Leser: Studien zur Literatur*. Ed. Ferdinand van Ingen, Elrud Kunne-Ibsch, Hans de Leeuwe, and Frank C. Maatje. Groningen, 1972, pp. 261–75.

Linn, Rolf N. "Die prästabilierte Harmonie in Heinrich von Kleists *Prinz von Homburg*." *Modern Language Notes*, 88 (1973), 1029–34.

Nehring, Wolfgang. "Kleists *Prinz von Homburg*: Die Marionette auf dem Weg zum Gott." *German Quarterly*, 44 (1971), 172–84.

192 Bibliography

Passage, Charles E. Rev. of *Kleist's "Prinz Friedrich von Homburg": A Critical Study*, by John M. Ellis. *Journal of English and Germanic Philology*, 70 (1971), 120–23.

Politzer, Heinz. "Kleists Trauerspiel vom Traum: *Prinz Friedrich von Homburg*." *Euphorion*, 64 (1970), 200–20.

Scholl, Margaret A. "German 'Bildungsdrama': Schiller's *Don Carlos*, Goethe's *Torquato Tasso*, and Kleist's *Prinz Friedrich von Homburg*." *Dissertation Abstracts International*, 34 (1973), 1934A (Washington Univ.).

Tatar, Maria M. "Psychology and Poetics: J. C. Reil and Kleist's *Prinz Friedrich von Homburg*." *Germanic Review*, 48 (1973), 21–34.

For other volumes in the "Studies" see page ii and following page.

Send orders to: (U.S. and Canada)
The University of North Carolina Press, P. O. Box 2288
Chapel Hill, N.C. 27514
(All other countries) Feffer and Simons, Inc., 31 Union Square, New York, N.Y. 10003

UNIVERSITY OF NORTH CAROLINA
STUDIES IN THE GERMANIC LANGUAGES
AND LITERATURES

For other volumes in the "Studies" see preceding page and p. ii.

Send orders to: (U.S. and Canada)
The University of North Carolina Press, P. O. Box 2288
Chapel Hill, N.C. 27514
(All other countries) Feffer and Simons, Inc., 31 Union Square, New York, N.Y. 10003

Volumes 1–44 and 46–49 of the "Studies" have been reprinted.
They may be ordered from:
AMS Press, Inc., 56 E. 13th Street, New York, N.Y. 10003
For a complete list of reprinted titles write to:
Editor, UNCSGL&L, 442 Dey Hall, 014A, UNC, Chapel Hill, N.C. 27514